mm

D1095688

Margel:
Have a lovely Happy Time!
Harold

7/30/63

UNDER A COLORED CAP

By the same Author

Autobiographies

I KNOCK AT THE DOOR
PICTURES IN THE HALLWAY
DRUMS UNDER THE WINDOWS
INISHFALLEN, FARE THEE WELL
ROSE AND CROWN
SUNSET AND EVENING STAR

Plays

JUNO AND THE PAYCOCK
THE SHADOW OF A GUNMAN
THE PLOUGH AND THE STARS
THE END OF THE BEGINNING
A POUND ON DEMAND
THE SILVER TASSIE
WITHIN THE GATES
THE STAR TURNS RED
PURPLE DUST
RED ROSES FOR ME
HALL OF HEALING
OAK LEAVES AND LAVENDER
COCK-A-DOODLE DANDY
BEDTIME STORY
TIME TO GO
THE BISHOP'S BONFIRE
THE DRUMS OF FATHER NED
BEHIND THE GREEN CURTAINS
FIGURO IN THE NIGHT
THE MOON SHINES ON KYLENAMOE

An Anthology

FEATHERS FROM THE GREEN CROW

UNDER
A COLORED CAP

Articles Merry and Mournful
with Comments and a Song

BY

SEAN O'CASEY
(The Green Crow)

'Tell me to whom you are addressing
yourself when you say that.'
'I am addressing myself — I am
addressing myself to my cap.'
Molière

NEW YORK
ST MARTIN'S PRESS INC
1963

MACMILLAN AND COMPANY LIMITED
St Martin's Street London WC 2
also Bombay Calcutta Madras Melbourne

THE MACMILLAN COMPANY OF CANADA LIMITED
Toronto

ST MARTIN'S PRESS INC
New York

PRINTED IN GREAT BRITAIN

For

LITTLE ALISON AND LITTLER OONA

To be read when the sturdier airs of womanhood
flow around them—
should they then desire to do so

PUBLISHERS' NOTE

SEAN O'CASEY'S collection of colored caps (he prefers the American spelling) has come to him from friends and admirers in many different countries, and has given him a symbol for the gay, free, intrepid life and outlook which he defends in several of the papers included in this volume. He has little sympathy with those modern writers who are shut away by their own grudges and grievances from the brightness and variety of the real world and the courage and humor of its ordinary people. Anyone who knows Mr. O'Casey's work will be well aware that this is not because he has never seen the darker side of things. Indeed, the book begins with a tragic memory of a dying boy in Dublin who could never join his friends in their street games but kept their 'army' richly supplied with badges and adornments in colored paper. Later years, too, have brought him his share of losses and sorrows — there is a profoundly moving record here of the keenest of these, the death from leukaemia of a well-loved son whose life was just opening out before him.

Among the other longer papers are some typically combative discussions of orthodox beliefs and the myths and mysteries behind them, while contemporary 'Culture, Inc.' and criticisms of a recent production of *Purple Dust* come in for some very candid and pungent comments. Altogether, with a sprightly song and a few verses for good measure, the reader is assured of some rewarding hours in the company of 'The Green Crow', a pen-name which the author adds to his title-page because it is so well known in the United States.

CONTENTS

		PAGE
1.	UNDER A COLORED CAP, PART ONE	1
2.	UNDER A COLORED CAP, PART TWO	29
3.	THE GREEN BUSHES: A SONG	56
4.	THE GREEN CROW CAWS	58
5.	UNDER A GREENWOOD TREE HE DIED	100
6.	THE LARK IN THE CLEAR AIR STILL SINGS	134
7.	IMMANUEL	142
8.	MERRICAL OF MIRACLES	202
9.	THE PEOPLE AND THE THEATRE	213
10.	CULTURE, INC.	224
11.	OUT, DAMNED SPOT	254
12.	PURPLE DUST IN THEIR EYES	261

UNDER A COLORED CAP, PART ONE
AN ARMY WITH BANNERS

I'm sittin' all alone in th' gloamin',
It mighta been but yestherday.

JOHNNIE heard his mother liltin' *Bantry Bay* while
she was washin' their few things, an' a lot belongin' to
others, plungin' her able arms into a tunful of soapy
water, an' he listenin' to her with half an ear, thinkin'
at th' same time, an' he sittin' beside the little window,
under the shade of his mother's scarlet-runner and
fuchsia. Johnnie, having finished the last folding of a
newspaper cocked-hat, stretched the work out, held it
a little way from him, and thought it good; dowdy,
though, for it was colorless, and it looked sad; not
sprightly, not cocky, as a cocked-hat should look; no
darin' in it. He had made eight altogether, two big
ones for him an' Warren, th'other six for th' kids
who'd folly them. But would th' kids folly? Newspaper hats didn make Warren nor him feel like
officers, nor t'other kids feel like soldiers; they were
too common-lookin'. What good's newspaper hats?
t'others would say, gigglin' as they put them on, didn
care whether they tore them or no; an' if there was a
row, they'd fling them on the ground, an' yell Who
wants your oul' hats? Wouldn wear a one if yeh paid
me. Even if Warren an' him led, th'others follyin',
it 'ud be no good, for they couldn feel like soldiers, an'
couldn shape before th' chisulers o' th' better streets
when they marched through them. In old newspaper-
hats them kids 'ud feel no envy; just jeer an' cock

I

their snouts if they even stopped to look. In these oul'
hats, they'd have to keep away from the better streets.
Better not to march anywhere really in these oul' hats,
for instead o' lookin' grand, these hats looked funny,
an' people laughed, an' called out with a jeer, Look,
here come th' gallant soldiers!

If they could only get, or feck, colored paper, it
would be different. Even if the colored paper wasn
big enough to make whole hats aself, they could em-
broider the newspaper with strips an' stars of red,
green, yella, or black; then th' cocky kids of th' better
streets couldn jeer or laugh; only stare with their big
mouths watherin'. Long time since they collared even
a strip of colored paper. The few grocers here put
out boxes of paper an' wrappins only occasional, an'
then it was a chance only that there was any colored
paper in them; besides, they had to watch for a time
the grocer wasn't near, for he didn like his paper to
be messed about, and threatened the polis on any kid
caught fingerin' them, even though it was only rubbish waitin' to be took away.

Once, when little Kit Curran was caught be th'
grocer, he was hauled inta th' shop an' shook an'
threatened, an' packed in among th' bags 'n' bins an'
called you sneakin' little ragamuffin, you quick-
fingered little dirty gutthersnipe, you mischeevous
little robber, what 'r your oul fella an' oul wan doing
lettin' you run wild? D'ye know your catechism, d'ye,
d'ye know your duty to your neighbour d'ye to keep
your hands fr'm pickin' an' stealin pickin' an' stealin
d'ye with a kid bawlin' fr'm the door, That's not his
catechism, he's not a Protestan' he's a Catholic kid,
while horse-thrams rattled by up Dorset Street an'
lorries an' dhrays passed with drivers' cries of yep yep

up there to th' horses an' some windas in houses opposite twinkled, tickled into thinkin' itself to be th' shining sun, an' th' little kid screamin' let me go, sir, lemme go I wont do it again no more never sir cross me heart never no more, sir, an' th' grocer catchin' a holt of th' kid's hand liftin' it high an' bringin' the little knuckles down thump on th' counther an' he shoutin' Keep your hands from pickin an' stealin', yeh pillagin' monkey, and your hands behind your back passin' me shop, he pushed th' kid fr'm him and gave him a flyin' kick in th' little arse as he went tumblin' out through the gauntlet o' kids at the door makin' for home bent in two fr'm the kick he'd got that if he'd ha' been near enough to get th' full force would have near desthroyed him while the kids be th' door yelled inta th' shop before they scooted off, Yeh mangy-kiss-ered bastard of a Swadler. The grocer wasn a Swadler, but th' kids thought, maybe, only a Swadler would kick a Catholic kid's arse, an' bruise his knuckles again' a counther.

It was th' oney way we kids could handle a bit o' color. There was none at home, in th' street, or at school — oney in th' boxes left out be th' grocers. At Christmas color come inta the shops, but it was at too far a distance for us to handle; all we got was a passin' look at them, longin' an' hopeless. A mother got by a toy-filled shop soon as she could, for she didn like lookin', or lettin' her chiselur look either, at gay things she couldn hope to get for him or for herself. Th' kids often hoped, as they were hurried along past a gay shop, that Santy Claus would come to lay beside them somethin' bright an' glittery so's they could have a happy Christmas that everyone gossiped an' blathered about; but the red-robed bastard, Santy Claus, always passed by th' littler streets an' paraded through th' wider ones, winda be winda, chimney be chimney, never leavin' a glossy-doored house out, but gev a dip, an' a good one, f'r every one o' them. Afther an empty Christmas, th' kids marched through th' streets singin' to th' air o' Glory, Glory, Hallelujah, a song made up be a kid who was paralysed in his legs, an' could never get outa bed,

> Oh Santa Claus he doesnt care as he goes throttin' by,
> He doesnt even leave behind a twinkle fr'm his eye,
> We'll hang him from a lamp-post, an' we'll leave him
>   there to die,
> As we go marchin' on!

It always made him an' Warren mad when at Sunday school th' teacher tole them th' meanin' of envy, th' word in the catechism, they mustnt think they should have what another boy had, a nicer suit or a nicer toy at Christmas, with Warren sayin' we never have no toys at Christmas, an' th' teacher takin' no notice, goin' on sayin' you mustnt dislike a boy who has somethin' youse havent got, or wish he'd lose it or break it; even when a boy friend shows off with it before youse, youse must remember your duty towards your neighbour, and feel no anger or envy, with Johnnie tryin' not to hear Warren whisperin' I'd break his snot so I would. If any of them come shapin' in front o' me, he said when he came outa school, he'll get a wallop on th' conk that'll keep him cryin' out f'r a week, forgettin' all he got a' Christmas, an' he was right, for when Rocky struck you'd think lightnin' had hit th' thing he hot.

When it was found out th' paralysed kidger could make poethry, we made our place for pow-wows in

4

th' little room where he lay in bed, an' made him th' officer commandin' when he tole us that th' bed wasnt a bed really, but a stretcher he had to lie on afther havin' his legs massacreed be a burst of grape-shot. We found too that he was a right dandy at decoratin' hats, cuttin' out stars an' all figaries betthern we could. Once, when we groused that he was puttin' too much decoration on the orinary hats, he said No, for high-up officers often put less on them than lower ones, too much to think on, see, an' besides, plenty of it on th' little hats'll please th' others, an' make them more ready to folly Rocky an' you. A right cute kid. Rocky an' him had often watched the long waxy fingers moiderin' paper inta folds an' then whippin' up scissors to cut here an' snip there, turning out wonderful stars an' harps an' things to go on to th' common paper hats transfigurin' them inta a glow an' color any kid 'uld be proud to fix on his napper. Now th' kid was waitin' sittin' up in bed, scissors, paste his mother made, twine an' thread, a packet o' needles, big an' small, on a wide thray in front o' him; waitin' there ready for any call that might come fr'm us to start work again to brighten out a little army he could see goin' up an' down, wearin' th' gorgeous hats his white waxy fingers had made for them. Cute an' clever kid he was.

Two weeks now Rocky an' him had prowled about, day after day, watchin' f'r a chance of pryin', but the grocers seemed always on the key veev, so boxes of papers came out an' went away without a single prod from a probin' hand. Once Johnnie had tried th' polite way, goin' inta th' shop an' sayin' Please, Mister, may I have a decko through th' papers?—; but before he could get goin' th' bastard was shouting at

him Get ta hell outa this, getta hell, an' mind yeh, if
I ketch yeh divin' among th' papers, it'll be th' polis,
th' polis, mind yeh, an' no blundherin' this time, mind
yeh, yeh little thievin' get! So Rocky an' Johnnie
went on prowlin' whenever they could, an' the waxy-
faced kid in th' bed went on waitin'. Johnnie was
handicapped in his searchin', for with a bandage round
an eye, he couldnt well search a box with one eye while
watchin' out for the grocer with another, seein' that it
was hidin' in the darkness because it couldnt stick th'
light. So he waited in the shadda of the fuchsia an'
th' scarlet-runner, th' purple bells with their white
waxy lappin', just like the white waxy fingers of the
kid waitin' in his bed f'r Johnnie an' Rocky to enther
bearin' gifts of gold 'n frankincense of colored papers
f'r his delicate waxy fingers to fondle.

Th' kid's Da was a porther in a railway goods
depot, an' never came inta th' room unless he had
something to give the kid, a colored pencil, some
sweets, a book o' transfers, or something. Though
the kid stared straight at him, the Da always looked
askew whenever he handed him anything, mutterin'
about him feeling bether later on, an' advisin' th' kid
to have a good time as he edged an' inched himself
outa th' room; but his Ma didnt mind lookin' at th'
kid at all, sthrokin' his hair, settlin' th' bed-clothes,
an' tellin' him th' sun would soon be sthronger so's
he could sit out at th' door an' watch, or talk with,
t'other kids o' th' sthreet: just like as if th' kid was
gettin' outa th' measles or something like that; but
th' Da seemed to know there was something bigger
wrong with him. The neighbours round all said
among themselves that th' dawny kid would never
last through th' comin' winther, for there was oney a

few ripples o' life left in him; and Rocky an' him was bothered, for if th' remainin' ripples left him went, th' ripples in his thin waxy fingers would go too; an' then for want of them to color their caps properly they'd be nicely banjaxed. Little J. J. Milod fingers on th' move was th' one hope they had of keepin' things goin'. It would be terrible one day to look down on them white waxy fingers knowin' there'd never be a stir outa them again for ever an' ever, an' ever, an'—

Didn you hear th' knock? He heard his Ma's voice buttin' inta his thinkin'; Rocky Warren's at th' door wantin' you.

When Johnnie got to the door, Rocky caught his arm, and began pullin' him down th' narrow street.

—Come on, he said, shrill excitement on his voice; come on — Kearney in his yard of th' corner grocer shop's killin' a pig!

—Aw, I dont care, said Johnnie, tryin' to get his arm free; I heard a pig in its killin' squealin' before, an' I dont want to hear it again.

—Nor me, nor me, said Rocky. Mitched school today, for when I was on me way, I seen them pilin' papers in boxes to be thrown away, an' I seen blue ones, whole sheets, an' red, an' yella; yis, an' a green one too; so there! Th' two of them'll be in th' yard, an' while the pig's squealin' we'll know we're safe, an' can dive to th' bottoms — come on!

They started to trot, Rocky speaking breathlessly the whole way down: Never seen such colored papers before; stuffed in, crumpled 'n' twisted, terrible, th' bastards 'ive no regard for anythin'; wish we had a bag, you'll smooth them out someway quick as yeh can an' I'll do th' divin'. Like lightnin' we'll go,

7

gettin' all an' skeetin' off before th' pig stops squealin';
and they broke into a swift gallop when halfway down
the little street.

When they got to the gate, they heard a rushing
of feet in the yard within, and in the rushing sudden
and sharp sounds, of frightened squeals, followed by
gruff grunts, a patter of feet and more of the sharp
anguished squeals.

—He's dodgin' them, thryin' to, said Rocky;
curious how they know what theyre in for, more'n we
do often; wouldn think a pig 'ud mind one way or
th' other. Looka, Johnnie — a whole square o' glossy
yella; I told yeh, didn I? Two black an' a red an'
now a yella, never seen so many before 'n all me whole
puff. Jasus, hear that! Both were startled for a
moment by shrill squeals, one after another, short,
rapid, piercing.

—Theyve got him now, went on Rocky, hear? as
a squeal shriller than all the others halted them again;
must a got th' knife that time. Whatja got now?
Another red, another yella, two green, an' here's a
blue like I told yeh. Whisht! faint squealing came
from the yard, a kind of a squealing sigh, fading off
into silence as the two lads listened at the gateway.

—Snuffed it, said Rocky; gone to kingdom come.

—Funny, said Johnny, how they squeal with their
throats sliced.

—Begod, I'd squeal if me throat was bein' sliced!
said Rocky emphatically.

—I know, said Johnnie; me, too; but afther
a while theyre goin', goin' on squealin' fainter an'
fainter; funny.

—They havta dhrain th' blood outa them, havent
they? While it's dhrainin', dhrainin', th' squealin'

8

goes on, an' when th' dhrainin' goes slower, th' squeals grow lower till they give out altogether. See? Like ourselves, 'suppose, when we're dyin', dyin', dyin', like th' pig.

—Aw, pigs is different, Rocky, a lot. We die different.

—I dunno 'bout that, Johnnie. Didn you see your oul' fella dyin'?

—Nix; me Ma wouldn let me in where he was.

—Well, we betther shift, or they might be on top of us. So come on.

They left the gateway and strolled off towards where the kidger in bed lived, Johnnie with a great pack of thick colored sheets of paper under an arm; Rocky with a package of smaller bits, of differing colors from those of the sheets. They were happy, triumphant.

—Yeh see, Johnnie, I seen me brother passin' through his last few minutes, with me Ma's head close to his, an' he talkin' th' way you couldn make head or tail of anythin', an' Ma listenin' betthern than if it was a priest in a pulpit, an' poor Paddy's voice goin' lower an' lower, breathin' goin' fainter an' fainter, till you could only see his lips movin' slowlike, an' his Ma puttin' an ear to his mouth to hear what he was sayin'; you see, dhrainin' away, dhrainin' outa th' world just like a pig — see?

—Aw, no, Rocky, not like a pig; we're different, all of us, see? different.

—Not th' way we die, I'm tellin' you. Maybe in a bed, yes; but from a hurt in battle it 'ud be the same. Supposin' a soldier on th' field o' battle got a one that dropped him; supposin' an assegai flyin' fast dived into his chest, see? Or a bullet fr'm one o' them crooked Indian guns, y'know? An' supposin' th' soldier was me, or you, maybe, lyin' still, blood dhrainin' outa th' place where th'assegai stuck, an' me or you callin' to comrades f'r help, frightened, an' then startin' a squeal-call, chancin' a loud one with no one listenin', while th' blood gives a spurt out with th' force o' th' shout, an' goes on dhrainin' an' dhrainin', an' th' call-squeals gettin' fainter an' fainter, till th' lips move like me brother Paddy's, without soundin' a word, till they stopped movin' too, an' he snuffed it. You see, Johnnie, th' soldier bled like a pig an' died like one. There's no differ, he died jus' like th' pig we heard givin' his last faint squeaks in Kearney's yard, jus' like a pig.

—Yeh, murmured Johnnie; jus' like a pig.

—Yeh, added Rocky; No differ at all; you've only got ta think; jus' like a pig.

They hurried along, turned into the narrow street where their paralysed friend lived. The kid's mother was at the door staring down the street, and when she caught sight of them, she waved her hand for them to hurry, and they came to her at a run.

—Thank God, you're here, she said. He's beside himself waitin' for yous, wondherin' if yous got anythin' or was nabbed be the grocer; once he fainted he was so pent-up, an' I had to borra a shillin' to get a sup of whiskey for him. He had me plagued watchin' out for yous.

In they went, coming close to the bed of the boy, and Johnnie noticed how red his bony face was, and how the waxy fingers twitched and the thin hands shook, all with just excitement, said his mother.

They had spread the colored wonders on the floor of the room, sheets of royal blue, emerald green, scarlet as shiny as the Sunday tunic of a colonel in the Guards, rich deep yella sheets, next to the color of gold, and two sheets of black, glossy an' gleamin' as the wing of a raven; and the sick boy's Ma hurried out and hurried in with a glass of yella-tinted water, making the sick boy sip up a few mouthfuls when she saw him getting pale, then flushed, with the sight of so much gorgeousness on the floor beside him.

—It's tainted with whiskey, the Ma said to the other boys; bending down to whisper to Johnnie, slippin' off he'd be without th' help of it.

—Black hat for th' officers, I think, said the sick boy, because all army high-ups wears ones less braided than them under them.

—Chiefs didn, said Rocky; they wore golden ones, so I want a yella hat.

—Looka, said Johnnie, breakin' through a silence; looka; you John Joe, bein' the head one, th' chief commander, should wear a black one; Rocky here, bein' next, a yella one, an' me, third, could wear a blue one, see? Th' biggest lot of sheets we have is red, so th' hats for the soldiers should be red ones.

So it was; and the magic waxy fingers set to work, making fourteen hats, with cunnin' colored ornaments on the officers' hats, and braided lines round the hats of the soldiers. For some weeks, the sick boy worked under such excitement that his Ma let him do only in short spurts, not moren an hour a day done in patches of a quarter of an hour each time, very trying work on the other boys; but they took it gamely because they knew there was none other could do it the way Joe of the waxy fingers did and the way he lay back in bed staring upwards and he thinking out the titivation and figaries he'd put on a hat he'd just made, putting on his own black one a circle going round a shamrock, its three leaves like triangles instead of being curved, and a moon as a crescent, made of silver paper, above to one side, and half a shamrock in a bottom corner, the other half cut off by a golden circle. It looked grand on the black, standing out as if saying Look at this now. All the same we said it didn look like a real shamrock, not the real McCoy. After waiting to get his breath back that had suddenly left him, he said, 'Tisnt a real shamrock anyway. Means the Trinity. Th' three straight sides joined together meaning the Trinity, each of them one person, and the three together springin' from one stem windin' you into rememberin' th' thruth that the blessed Trinity is three in one.

—He's a little saint, so he is, said his Ma, once, as they were goin' to let little waxy fingers sleep; a little saint. Do a body good to hear him prayin'. Knows near all of them, prayers, catechism, an' all; a body 'ud think he was growin' up to be a priest. I thought he looked a teeny weeny bit better today. With th' help o' God, he may get over it yet.

—Dunno what th' oul' wan meant, d'ye, Johnnie? Rocky asked when they had got clear of th' house. What kinda little saint?

—Oh, you know—one o' them that get a high place in heaven; dressed-up chaps, y'know; like us officers, only different.

—What? If y'ask me, he'd rather be runnin' 'bout with us than he to be th' sorrowful way he is. J'ever see his legs? Got a decko at them once an' his oul' wan straightenin' th' bed — like match-sticks, they were; no stiffness in them; just danglin': shockin'!

I'll bet he'd give up his prayers for to have legs like ours. You ask his oul' wan.

—No, no; we darent ask her.

—Well, ask himself then, cant you?

—No, nor him either. He likes bein' a little saint. You heard th' way when he sinks back half faintin', how he mutters, Welcome be th' will o' God. Doesn that go to show you?

—Balls! bawled Rocky. It shows me nothin'. What's any chiselur want to be a saint for? Prayers and such things is for oul' wans an' oul' fellas, if y'ask me. You an' me's made go to Sunday school, but arent we bulgin' to get it over an' get out always?

—Yis, I know, agreed Johnnie.

—Thinka what it 'ud be if he could run round like us; it 'ud be wonnerful with no more on him than a patch o' prayer at night slidin' inta bed, an' a patch at mornin' slidin' outa it. Makin' him commander-in-chief when he has to stick in bed with his legs gone, is oney a kinda sharin' in what th' rest of us do.

—I know, I know, again agreed Johnnie, but he'll always dangle an' dhroop, for th' doctor gave up comin' long ago, an' oney th' priest comes now.

—What would he do if he hadn us? said Rocky, stoppin' to make his remark emphatic. We feck th' colored paper for him, dont we? Risk gettin' copped be Kearney, an' sent, maybe, to some industhrial school f'r years an' years an' years.

—Yis, agreed Johnnie, an' we'll never get th' army goin' properly if she goes on th' way she's goin'. It's hard lines on us.

—'Course it's hard lines on us, said Rocky, angrily. Them oul' fellas an' oul' wans get in th' way of every-thin'. Banjax all we chaps are doin'. While we're

13

there, she keeps poppin' in to see he's not tired, an'
gawkin' in whenever she's passin' th' door; an' th'
minute she sees him breathin' quick, she whips th'
rosary fr'm undher his pillow an' fixes them between
his waxy fingers, then she goes bobbin' up an' down
before the light in th' red bowl an' th' statue of the
Virgin behind it, before she hunts us outa th' room,
to bloody-well wait again, sittin' on a winda-sill or a
kerb, idle, an' nothin' to say, except to wait an' wait
till th' statue likes to give th' kid another spell of bein'
useful, an' th' oul' wan waitin' till she's sure th' statue
has done th' job proper an' th' rosary's back again
undher th' pilla.

—I wouldnt go on about th' statue, said Johnnie,
a note of anxiety in his voice. Y'never know, an' walls
has ears.

—I dunno th' hell how he gets tired an' his breath
goes, seein' he's always in bed sthretchin' himself,
movin' nothin' but his waxy fingers, th' way you'd
think he'd never get tired, said Rocky resentfully.
Coolin' our arses here on the stones till th' oul' wan
lets us in again.

—It's agrifyin', right enough, murmured Johnnie.

—Aw, I'm sick of th' statue, the light, th' oul'
wan's bobbin', an' him fallin' back in a faint, an' all
afther th' risks we've took to bring him th' colored
papers. Makes me near spew.

So for weeks they had waited, in and out of the
sick kid's room, handing him paste, scissors, and strips
of colored paper as he had wanted them; through
patches of time, at times, an hour in a day, at times,
but for a quarter of the hour; at times not at all,
according to the way the thin face had flushed or
grown pale; or when the breath had come too fast;

14

again, when it came too slow; the oul' wan always on the watch, always ready to whoosh them out to sit on the pavement, impatient and sulky; wondering if the hats would ever be finished, waiting till the dusk fell before going home; for when the dusk fell, they knew that what they had done earlier — an' that was damned little, growled Rocky — would be all for the live-long day; and they must wait for another morning to begin another day; wondering how long would the lightning stay in the waxy fingers tomorrow, dreading that they should see again, as they so often had, the fingers going slower, the breath faster, till the thin hands fell away from their work; a calling out for his mammy as he lay back on the pillows; then the cough would come, hard and brassy, bringing his Ma in with a rush, and sending Rocky and Johnnie hurrying away to get outside of the sound of th' raspin' barks of the boy.

—Like a bitthern boomin' through th' gob of a corncrake, said a country kid to Johnnie once, an' he cockin' an ear listening to the bitter grinding cough coming from the kid in the bedroom within. Thrumps turned up at last; the bony body and the waxy fingers kept goin' till the hats were made and decorated. The army assembled in the tiny bedroom, twelve all told, some of them flowing out into the tiny hall; the General from his bed speakin' to th' throops:

—At ease, lads, stan' at ease, murmured the General, with a gentle gesture of the waxy hand, stan' at ease, and Stan' at ease! said the Brigadier, and the men stood easy leanin' again' th' rail o' th' bed or again' th' wall.

—Men, he went on, I look to yous to uphold the honor of our fightin', never to give in, to die where yous stand an' fall sooner 'n' surrendher. There is big bouts o' battles facin' yous, an' lots of yous'll never come back to where yous live any more; but that wont bother yous, for yous are soldiers, scornin' wounds an' scornin' death, proud to die on th' field o' battle. I'm not able to lead yous this time, because of me legs bein' raked to flitthers be grape-shot, an' I've to stay stuck here, prayin' for yous durin' your campaignin'; but yous have two officers, Brigadier Warren an' Colonel Casside to take me place, an' better'n them isnt in any army of th' worrld.

He put out his waxy fingers, like long chips of ivory, an' grapped holt of papers lyin' beside him on th' bed, havin' a plan of th' whole places round about, marked down in blue, red, an' green pencil — a wunnerful bitta work.

—Th' plan o' campaign, he said. Mountjoy Jail, the big fort o' th' counthry, he went on, is th' bugger of all we have to take. Before it can be done, all other forts and enthrenchments'll have to fall. Derrynane Parade, Killarney, an' Glengarriff Parades, forts on the left side—

—Flank, whispered Rocky, left flank.

—Left flank — went on the kid, forts on the left flank will be attacked first, one at a time, see? But we'll have to keep nix that a sortie fr'm th' main fort of Mountjoy doesnt catch us arse-way on—

—Catch us in th' rear, whispered Warren.

—Get us in th' rear, for then we'd be, we'd be— and he stuttered over a proper word.

—We'd be balls'd, said a voice from the listening soldiers.

—Yis, said the chief, we'd be balls'd; so yous'll have to make sure we arent. Youve reconnoitred th' fort, Brigadier, he said to Rocky, so what would you do?

—Lemme see the map, said the Brigadier, an' he took th' plan fr'm th' bed, an' looked at it, dottin' it here and there with a pencil. We'll set two men an' a corporal undher Colonel Casside to march up Inisfallen Parade to th' waste ground frontin' Mountjoy; they'll enthrench there to hold back any sally fr'm th' fort; if theyre hard-pressed, Corporal Dempsey to blow three blasts on th' whistle he has.

—Oh, said th' kid in th' bed, will yous be able to hear them?

—Easily, said Dempsey, salutin', it's a referee whistle, an' lets outa frightenin' blast.

—Where th' hell didya get that? asked the kid in wondher.

—Me uncle was a referee once, said Dempsey, an' gev it to me.

—You'll have to be more'n a corporal with that, said th' chief; I promote you to be a sargeant-major. Come over here till I fix yeh up.

Dempsey came up to th' bed, an' saluted. Th' chief made a badge with three lines in red on it — like what a real sargeant wears, an' he fixed a yella shamrock over them, an' all with a strong kinda paste, on th' right breast o' Dempsey's coat. Dempsey saluted again, an' went back to his place.

—When we hear three blasts, went on th' Brigadier, then I'll let go of half me regiment, and hurry them to reinforce Colonel Casside; the other half'll hold what theyve taken till th' sally's beaten back.

So us the captains, Rocky an' me, an' our men fought many fights, retreatin' and advancin', capture an' loss, but, in the end, always gaining a fort, a town, a country for the Shamrock Legions; till one day, after a stiff time, flushed with a victory of takin' St.

Ignatius' Road, that flanked the Fort of Mountjoy, Rocky an' me hurried a chiselur who could run like a hare to tell the chief of the good news, while we with our army waited for the chiselur's return; all of us squattin' down on the kerb of the road; them on this side, Rocky and me on the opposite side.

We hadnt to wait long. He come tearin' round the corner towards them, shoutin' as he panted along, He's gone! He's snuffed it! Waxy!

—What d'ye mean — snuffed it? asked Rocky, when the chiselur came up to them. Rocky, Johnnie, an' all were frightened be what th' news might mean, an' they all crowded in on the chiselur.

—Snuffed it? asked Rocky again. How d'ja know? Did his oul' wan tell you?

—No one, no one, panted out the chiselur. I seen it, seen it writ up, plain as plain.

—How writ up? Where's it writ up? Jasus, man, speak proper!

—On his door, his own door, Waxy's; writ in ink on a card, black-edged, folded about with crépe, an' a bow of white ribbons; an' below writ Sweet Jesus, have mercy on his soul.

—Betther make sure, muttered Rocky, and he set off slowly, Johnnie one side, the sargeant bugler on the other, the rest followin' spread out any way they chose; along a bit of Drumcondra Road, turning into Inisfallen Parade, where I, Rocky, Waxy, and some of the others lived; turning by Father Gaffney's School, a big bright-red new brick building, just on the corner facing the road, and Kearney's bacon and provision shop on th'other corner, facing the road, too, but winding round into the narrow Parade where the big gate was hiding the place where the pigs were killed.

Gone was the glow now from all the gay hats, gone the stiff backs, the steady march, left right, left right; the proud looks: the happy and thrilling past was goin' away from them within the thinned-out body, and tangled up among the stretched-out bones of Waxy, covered with a skin that was like the yellowing white top of a toy drumhead stuck in a corner of the room where the kid who had owned it had played. Sadly and slow they came to number fifteen of the Parade, going slower and slower as they came close, afraid to see what was before them, knowing they must face it whether they liked it or no; came up to the door and looked up at the sad little banner of death hanging from the knocker — a thick flowing bunch of crêpe, tied with narrow white satin ribbon, enclosing a black-edged envelope carrying the words John Joseph Milod, aged 10 years, beloved and only child of Mary and James Milod. Sweet Jesus Have Mercy on his Soul.

—It's him, said Rocky; Waxy's a gonner right enough.

—Musta been sudden, murmured Johnnie.

—Them kind go off sudden, said Rocky; like the snuff of a candle.

—It means th' army's banjaxed, said the sargeant.

—Aw, shut your big gob! said Rocky angrily to the sargeant. Th'army's not banjaxed. Waxy snuffin' it is a bit of a buggerin' drawback, that's all; you'll see. But there was doubt in his voice, and it went deep into Johnnie's heart.

Colonel Warren stood before the door for more than a minute, as if he was counting the naked spots on it, caused by the paint blistering and many busy hands of kids using finger-nails to pick them to pieces, so that the door was pockmarked by many reddish-brown spots reaching as high up as any kid's scratching nail could stretch. Then he knocked at it. It opened to show Mrs. Milod all in black from chin to toe, lookin' like a nun gone thin whose face was wizening; while Mr. Milod gaped along from the end of a hall, narrow near as the dead boy's windpipe. He was dressed as per usual, but wore a thick and wide band of crêpe around a coat-arm.

—Oh, it's yous, she said. Comin' to see th' last of him. Come in, but go very quiet, and first leave them glory-hats of yours in the kitchen — they arent fit things for the holiness of th' room where our poor dead boy's lyin'.

They handed over their colored hats to Mr. Milod who saluted each soldier before he took the hat from him, which was a mannerly thing for him to do, and suitable to the solemn occasion, bein' an old swaddy himself. Then they tiptoed into the still room, Mrs. Milod gently closing the door behind them. Before Rocky or me had time to take a decko at the dead image, the rest of the army had gone down on their knees round the bed, making him and me feel awkward till both of us sank down on our adorers too. Neither Rocky nor me could make head or tail of the low mumblin' that went on, and we were still listenin' when a tap on the shoulder from one of them showed us the army was on its two feet again; so we got up, too, and looked around.

There he was sthretched out in a snow-white bed. The little head, with its dark hair sprinklin' the white pilla, the closed eyes so shrunk you could see only dark hollas, the yellowin' waxy skin covered nothing but bone, and the bluish lips had thinned so much that Johnnie had to bend low to see the sign of a mouth; a fussy frill half hid the neck, thin as a pipe-stem; his arms encased in flouncy white material, sthretched down over the white quilt, meeting in a handclasp, the long, thin, waxy fingers enchained together be a set of black rosary beads; at either side of the head of th' bed two thick lighted candles were stuck in tall brass candlesticks, resting on stands, giving a curious flickering light to the darkened room; over the bed's head, on a bracket, stood the red bowl with its rosy light, throwing a timid gleam on to the little china statue of the Blessed Virgin above it; and on the side wall, towards the bed's centre, hung a black crucifix, the yellowing figure bending downwards, as if it longed to be within the cool comfort of the snow-white bed, and lie in quietness and peace beside the worn-out Waxy.

The General was dead, right enough. No sign now of the colored papers, the scissors and paste, the cut-out decorations, the colored pencils — all were gone, and there was nothing here save the dead figure in the bed, the dead yella figure on the black cross, the tall candlesticks, the flickering light, with the odd sparkle of the crimson bowl carryin' the timid floating rosy flame. So in this spotless room, with everything in a motionless alignment, the army stood, headed be their officers, staring at their dead General, Waxy, who had bucked them up, told them what to do an' not to do; an' clothed them in purple an' fine linen.

—The lot that was in th' little of him's fluthered off for ever, said Rocky.

—He should be right get a soldier's funeral, said Johnnie.

—Aw, what's th' use o' talkin'? said Rocky crossly;

we cant give him one; even our sargeant's whistle couldnt pipe even a bar of the Last Post.

After a last look, the army filed out of the room, the house, and scattered to their different homes. The others, after another look, a longing, woeful look at Waxy, left the room, too, and waited in the hall to tell Mrs. Milod how sorry they were, but they were pushed aside by the arrival of the coffin, carried by a car like a long black casket on wheels, drawn by one horse, attended by a young man and an elderly one wearing half-tall hats and long dark-blue coats reaching to their ankles, a fixed doleful look enthroned on each of their ugly mugs. They opened the back of the car and drew out the golden-brown box that was to encase the bones and skin of Waxy, carried it in slowly, laying it down between two chairs Mrs. Milod had hurriedly brought into the room, an end resting on either chair; then they stripped the quilt from the bed, one getting Waxy by the heels, the other getting a holt of his shoulders, and swung him swiftly into the coffin; Johnnie peeping in at the room door, an' wonderin' how stiff Waxy had become, for all th' world like a plasther figure; then they lifted the coffin on to the bed, and after muttering to the mother that they were sorry for her throuble, and she had murmured It is th' will o' God, they lowered a glass of malt into their bellies, then hurried off, sayin' they had a lot to do, for there was a deal of deaths about the neighborhood; more'n usual, but nothin' alarmin'.

Him and Rocky sat gloomily down on the kerb a little way from the house of the dead boy, hardly venturing to think of what their army might do now. Waxy was gone now, the one chiselur about the whole place who could give them gorgeous things to wear and grand things to do. Tomorrow mornin' what was of him here would go, too, an' they'd never be in the house again, never see the quick fingers workin', an' there'd be no spell in colored paper ever again.

—We should do somethin' to honor th' poor little bugger while he's still with us — but what? asked Rocky, suddenly breaking up Johnnie's brooding. That's the rub — what?

—That's th' rub—what? echoed Johnnie.

—Wish we could give Waxy th' burial th' great Sir John Moore got, said Rocky, like he was in a dhream, ye know? Remember?

—Yis, said Johnnie, I know, but cant remember; for he had never heard of Moore.

—Th' oul' poem, ye know? One I learned at school; th' bit that goes

> We buried him darkly at dead o' night,
> Th' sods with our bay'nets turnin',
> Be th' sthrugglin' moonbeam's misty light
> An' our lantherns dimly burnin'.

Ye know? That's th' kinda buryin' really we should give to Waxy.

—Aw, if we oney could, echoed Johnnie sorrowfully.

Him an' me were silent again, glancing aimlessly at a few sparrows pecking up bits from the roadway, or resentfully down at a group of the army men, now noisily playing at Ball in the Decker a little way down the narrow street.

—Little gets! ejaculated Rocky; already not botherin' about Waxy; dont care a damn about anything. Little gets! Didn deserve ever to have th' geenus of little Waxy.

—I'll tell you what — couldnt we put Waxy's

general's hat on Waxy's coffin, soon as they screw him down? ventured Johnnie.

—Jasus — that's a spiffin' idea! said Rocky enthusiastically. We could do that as a last honor. Come on, we'll ask his oul' wan to let us.

They scrambled up from their cramped sitting on the kerb, and hurried to the house where Waxy was being waked. They knocked, and th' oul' fella came to the door.

—Like to see Mrs. Milod for a minute, said Rocky.

—Yes? What for, me lads?

—'Bout puttin' his general's hat on top of his coffin.

—General's hat? He thought for a while, then added, Betther see th' missis 'bout that, boys. Come on in.

They went into the little hall, and the oul' fella called his missis. She came, and the lads could see she had been cryin' over somethin'. She looked at them, and said Well?

—Me an' Johnnie, here, 'ould like to lay his general's hat on John Jo's coffin afther he's screwed down, said Rocky, showin' respect an' how we liked him, ma'am. John Jo 'ud like to see we were sorryin' for him.

—Aw no, said Mrs. Milod, John Jo wouldnt like it at all. John Jo's now where he isnt botherin' about yous an' your military get-up. He wouldnt like it at all.

—How d'ye know, ma'am? asked Johnnie foolishly.

—I know because he's with God up in heaven, that's why. Yous mean well, but John Jo wouldnt like it.

—Th' general's hat 'ud look Ay 1 on th' coffin, said Johnnie.

24

—Ay 1 or ay 2, it's not goin' on John Jo's coffin, she said sharply. I never liked this soldier-nonsense of yours. Betther if John Jo had spent th' time prayin' to our Holy Mother or th' Blessed Saints. John Jo's up now where there's nothin' but oney love an' peace. No wars in heaven, lads, never was either.

—Once there was, said Johnnie quickly; th' time a crowd o' angry angels, crowin' disobedience, thried to down God!

—Angry angels! Down God! ejaculated th' oul' wan, horrified. In God's name, what terrible things are you thryin' to say, son!

—I heard me Da tellin' me Ma once that years an' years ago, a lotta bad angels, led be a powerful one, rose up in heaven to down God, an' it took St. Michael all his time to get an army of other angels to keep things goin' right up there.

—'deed, ma'a'm, said Rocky in a loud murmur, you'll find bowsies an' goughers everywhere!

—Begod, youre right there, son! said a sudden voice behind them, and there was lanky Da Milod standing be th' kitchen door, armed with a cocked ear an' open gob; bowsies an' goughers fittin' themselves in anywhere a flea can land!

Ma stood for near a minute like a stuffed stork, shocked be the sudden slap o' talk from Da Milod; then her fat hand shot across, an' up an' down, her bosom in th' sign of the cross, givin' her relief of a safe feelin', as she turned towards the sudden remark from th' sudden voice: I never thought to live an' hear th' Da of our little John Jo holdin' that goughers an' fleas could get a foot in heaven!

—I didn say they did; I oney said that a gougher

c   25

could fit in anywhere a flea could land; goughers is penethratin' mortals.

—They are that, said Rocky, braver now that he felt Da Milod was behind him; an' it 'ud be no great wondher if a few of them got into where they couldnt go.

—Yis, said Johnnie, braver now, too, for there musta been some of them hidden undher th' wings of th' angels they led asthray.

—You see, Da Milod, what your dangerous blather is leadin' to? said Ma Milod angrily, again shieldin' her bosom with th' furious-made sign of the cross. She turned again fiercely on the two boys. This comes o' your military coddin' that wasted so much of me poor little John Jo's time, with God only knows what kinda talk goin' the while th' two of yous were with him, with the Blessed Mother o' God forced to listen to your nonsense, which God grant was only nonsense, an' not somethin' far worse, such as rowdies an' goughers sthruttin' th' sthreets o' heaven, with big fleas an' little fleas hoppin' afther them, maybe.

—Well, anyway, said Da Milod from the kitchen doorway, his chums gave our poor John Jo a bitta innocent fun.

—God grant it was only innocent fun, said Ma Milod doubtfully. She turned towards the two boys; if it wasnt, she went on, seein' yous are Protestants, it wouldnt be right to blame yous; but yous meant well, an' he liked th' pair of yous, so yous may be sure he'll not forget yous in his prayers up where he is now close to our Blessed Mother; an' neither will I, she added, gently nudging them towards the open door, an' I hope when yous grow up into more sense, that th' pair of yous'll come to see the full light. Goodbye, now, an' God bless yous. She watched them go a

little way down the Parade, then she softly closed the
door, an' sight an' sound of Waxy was gone for ever
fr'm them.

The two of them strolled silent up the Parade to
th' waste ground surroundin' a side of Mountjoy Jail,
aboundin' with dandelion, thistle, scutch grass, big
moon-faced daisies, an', here an' there, small clumps
of scarlet poppies; an' they sat down undher th' oul'
thorn-three where they'd often sat before, staring
gloomily at the powerful wall and windows of the
Mountjoy Jail.

—If oney th' poor little bugger had managed to
hold out for another day or two, we could ha' finished
th' campaign with a bang, said Rocky at last.

—Aw, if oney, echoed Johnnie.

—One enthrenchment, one was all we had to over-
come, an' th' fort was in our hands. One more day
was all we wanted, if he had oney held out; if oney
he hadda.

—If oney he hadda, echoed Johnnie again.

—We can do what we like with them now, said
Rockey, pointing to th' two colored hats they had laid
beside them on th' grass. Throw them in th' ashpit,
I would.

—I'll keep mine, said Johnnie, for y' never know
— th' army might hold together.

—Aw, for God's sake! Rocky said with venom.
Yeh saw th' way they scuttled off into their game o'
Ball in th' Decker. Didn even wait for th' ordher o'
Dismiss. Couldn see their arses for dust. No dis-
cipline. Dont give a damn for little Waxy.

—Suppose we go for a sthroll 'long th' canal, an'
thry to forget all about Waxy? said Johnnie.

No, said Rocky; let's sit here for a while an' think.

—It's a shockin' thing, said Rocky, bitther an' gloomy afther a long silence, it's a shockin' thing that little Waxy'll be carted to th' boneyard without a sign showin' what he meant to all us Inisfalliners while he was here among us.

UNDER A COLORED CAP, PART TWO

Must be seventy-five years or more since Waxy
kissed or cursed the world goodbye; that long, too,
since Rocky and he had strutted the narrow streets
under the colored caps of authority, commanding
troops that didn't care a button if the odds were on
the foe. The troops had done a good job — exactly
what officers said nowadays, officers who had come
safe from where maybe a thousand younger men had
been hidden away after a battle; they did a good job
would be said of the thousand now sealed down in the
everlasting cellarage of death; good wine for the vin-
tage of the judgement day. Many years, many, many
years ago, he had removed the epaulette from his
shoulder, making a tidy and secure place for Picasso's
Dove of Peace when it came first to perch there, but
he hadn't fallen out with a colored cap, but his first
colored cap spoke of war, while the one he wore now
chanted of peace. He hadn't meant it to be any kind
of a symbol, nor did he start to wear one to set himself off from others: its adoption was purely accidental.
The school our boy, Niall, went to, organised a Jazz
Band in which he played a trombone. Playing for a
Christmas party, the Band decided to wear long dark
gowns, topped off by a skull-cap of black and crimson.
I stuck one on my head when the party had ended,
and found it warm, comfortable, and colorful: I liked
it. Some time after, our daughter, Shivaun, presented
me with two gayly-colored ones; so the wearing of
them became a habit, and a colored cap gradually

became a part of me. The wearing of one came naturally to me during the family-film made by the N.B.C. of the United States, headed by Robert Graff. So tens of thousands of Americans saw O'Casey's colored cap, and from the cornucopia of American generosity came a stream of colored caps to Torquay; caps from Austria, Switzerland, Uzbekistan, the last gift a beautiful crimson one, white-embroidered, a cord from its centre trickling over the side, to dangle a long, lovely silky tassel; a gift from Robert Graff and his wife, Marjorie, the young American who had made the first film, and who saw me wearing the first of the colored caps.

So this colored cap has brought back the colored cap of younger years, and in an occasional reverie Rocky and he prowled round the streets searching for colored treasures, while little Waxy toiled to dress an army, from his sweated bed sending toy gunpeal and slogan cry echoing through the narrow dusty streets from Synott's Row to Binn's Bridge spanning the Royal Canal, beyond which the grandiloquent Drumcondra Road began; the colored memories darkened by the echo of the agonised squeal the unseen pig gave when the knife began to slice its throat. Ireland now has many little industries, a gorgeous airport, a gigantic Shannon Scheme, bursting with electrical energy; but Binn's Bridge still spans the silent canal, and a young American friend recently told me that Inisfallen Parade is still there, and Number Nine is standing where it stood when I roamed the streets with Rocky; where I saw the golden coffin boxing me Da coming slowly out on bent shoulders; where he had listened to the cab-drivers' gossip, and had watched their stampede to their cabs to hold the doors open for mourners and neighbours who came forward half-running to their several cabs, as soon as the tip of the coffin was seen coming out of the house, carrying its head away from home and life for ever. The cabs! The whole little street had been full of them, for all the neighbours took a cab, if they could get one, thinking it more decent and fitting to attend a funeral boxed up than to go bare and exposed to the world on the side-seat of a jaunting car. Dublin has few cabs now, and these have been adopted by friends trying to preserve some signs of Dublin's Georgian past, and today the Dublin cab that George Moore's uplifted stick so often stopped that it might carry him to some pleasant meeting of friends, has gone, leaving a few bedizened vehicles, looking like old-time whores, scented and painted, out for a last look at each other, till the best of them find a bed for the dying in some innocent museum anxious to fill a corner standing empty for too long a time.

It was odd and a little frightening to think that among all these simple nostalgic memories of things past lurked the power that would make past, present, and future disappear, a power that could sweep away past memories, present activities, and future hopes, quicker than a sun can brush away a morning dew. All places full of sweet noises will fall silent; silent for ever will be our song and music heritage from Haydn to Sibelius, and beyond; gone the fair and majestic pictorial art of church, hall, and home, from Giotto to John, and beyond; and no one will be left standing to send a sigh after them. Opera singer and jazz crooner will mingle their dust, if any dust be left. All Rachel's children will be snapped out of life, and no Rachel will be left to mourn them. Niobe, too, will lose her children, and never live to know it. The Earth will become a wanderer indeed: the Lone Ranger.

Odd to have to think of a hydrogen-bomb within the arms of a green garden, when life is tending to become a 'green thought in a green shade', but the damned thing hangs high and hangs low everywhere. Ever since I had come to England, I had never been without a tiny garden, except once — when we lived in Battersea, and then the great garden of Battersea Park was just across the road, with the lordly Thames bordering the other side of it. By the waters of England's Thames, I sat me down and sang, for I had just come back from the United States with enough dollars to keep us going for another year. There was something more here than the Liffey, even when Gogarty's swans floated by on its clogging waters. Here was opulence, confidence in width and power. A full tide lifted the massive waters to the parapet's protesting brim, so that the surface was much higher than the path where I stood to watch while barge and tug went steadily on the ample breast of the famous river whose swelling pomp made the Liffey in memory a tiny push-and-pull stream, and its bridges, compared with the thrust and sweep of those over the Thames, are like unto goosey-gander gantries. The Shannon is Ireland's river; but bar the hydro-electric construction and her grand airport, nothing is done with it; no traffic disturbs it, no pleasure gives it a thrill; it idly comes and it idly goes: God has given it to the wrong countrie.

Sitting in the morning sun, or sitting all alone in the gloaming, is forced by no natural inclination within me; I have been shoved down into a chair by the push-push of many years, though each day I walk, and walk rapidly, thro' the streets and roads of Marychurch. St. Marychurch is three hundred feet above sea-level, and the O'Caseys' flat rises thirty feet or so higher, looking over the top of many trees. Twenty-two concrete steps lead to the front door, before which stretches a concrete balcony where I sit for many hours when the weather is good. Looking straight before me, I can see the green cliffs of Babbacombe guarding Babbacombe Bay; to the left, the north, on the Barton Heights, sits the village of Barton, rising in stages along the hill so that when night comes the lights of street lamps and in the homes of the people shine out tier upon tier, reminding me whenever I glance at them of the lights of New York, making me a little sad thinking of a city I love, and shall never see again. There is a tiny garden down below, but the balcony gives a wide view, and I choose it usually, unless the sun is so strong that it becomes an oven. On this balcony I sit in the midst of a tinier garden than the tiny one below; a great and flaming red hydrangea, flanked by a voluptuous clump of purple and crimson petunias, shedding a gentle tobacco-like scent in the evening, blending with the fragrant tea-like smell of a big bunchy heliotrope, surprisingly pervasive seeing it comes from such tiny, insignificant blossoms; and a fuchsia with its waxy white pendulous bell, guarded by its brilliant crimson calix. A right pleasant bower in which to spend a calm, quiet hour or two. Calm and quiet among the blossoms! Not a hope! Life can push problems before one, even when one lies with one's girl among the bluebells.

Some two or three miles to the south sits complacent Torquay, meeting-point for visitors in summer from all parts of England; sits then plumped out by the largesse of the visitors; sits like an old goose fattened for Christmas; a ramshackle town, scattered over many beautiful hills, and brimmed delightfully by a lovely sea. Crowned at night by a multitude of colored lights, admired by a young Russian friend-visitor, Boris Izaacov, one of the simplest and gayest lads I ever met; although he had lost a foot in the war, his artificial substitute was so cunningly made that he could gambol about like a sensible March hare. He spoke fine, jovial English, and now, sitting in the gloaming, I wish he lived nearer so that his sunny nature might bring a clearer remembrance of my own younger days to me; another gay young Russian was Elena Silantiev, who came on a visit with her husband, Vladimir, and their son of three, busy, ebullient Andreev, immured within his love for motor cars. Many dear American friends have come and gone from Torquay, having fulfilled a visit to the O'Caseys, leaving roses of memories behind them, blooms that fade not, remaining for ever as rich as the Rose of Sharon or the Lilies of the Valley.

It is odd to move through Torquay's hurly-burly of summer money-making, raking in the dough from the visitors spending more than they can spare, and to give one's thoughts to the time of the Armada when a great Spanish galleon, captured by the English, was towed into Torbay, and all her Spanish crew imprisoned in the olden-time Tithe Barn of the monks, now known as the Spanish Barn, perfect today as it was in the time it was stuffed from floor to roof with the spoils of the monks, wrested from the blood, sweat, and tears of the toiling peasantry of the districts. The saint who watched over, and blessed, all this good work was one Norbert, who was famous for never taking a bath because it was a vile way of coddling the vile body with comfort, and who was shown a vision by the Blessed Virgin of a great train of monks in white garments carrying lighted candles, marching about a sweet valley, chanting praises to God the Father Almighty. Norbert found an identical and sweet valley all laid out and ready for him, north of Paris, near Prémontré. There he sowed the seed from which sprang the buddies of the Premonstratensian Order, some of whom, smelling out a grant of land from the Devonian devotees, came over, and piled up the great monastery of Torre Abbey, the wealthiest one in the whole of England by far. The wealthiest, and just as full-follied as most of the others, and soon the spotless white robes had stains on them, especially the Priory Church of St. Mary Virgin attached to the major house. There the clerics strutted about in gay military dress, cuirass and gorget, baldric and sword, with flaming crimson boots, with toes curving upwards like a cow's horn; the vicar 'storing his wheat in the church, and leaving the tower floor littered with his malt. It is said he preaches well, but is too often in the Manor of the Lord Moreton'. Even the deacons went about in sky-blue gowns, with knives attached to embroidered girdles; and quite a few of them, vicars and deacons, were blithe and bright and early and late with the local lassies O, and who's here to blame them, for what signifies th' life o' man an 'twerena for th' lasses O? It hasn't changed a lot either, for hasn't the present Pope John, in his recent tightening of clerical discipline in his own diocese, mocked at the 'moaning and groaning' of the younger clerics at not being allowed to have at least one wife, like Saint Peter? A laddo of the Pope's years can easily find time to mock at the natural and inevitable sex urgings of the young; not even a Pope's prayer, threat, or beseeching can banish this delectable urge from the physiology of man or woman, be they queen or maid, priest or peasant, or even Pope—if he be young enough.

This great Abbey ruled religiously, and fiscally most efficiently, over the surrounding districts and beyond; the valleys of Favor and Westhill; St. Mary-church, Manors of Coffinswell, Coombe Poffard, Shiphay, Hele, Barton, and Brixham. In the Torbay district, St. Marychurch was the centre of population then, the village, where the peasants grouped together in their tiny shelters, though many of them lived farther away to till the more distant fields, and bless God for life. Torquay was but a collection of fisher-men's huts. The Abbey fixed the Priory Church of St. Mary Virgin in St. Marychurch so that a close eye could be kept over the villeins and serfs who daily went in dread of Reeve, Bedell, and of him who kept the Pound; for the stocks were ever ready to pin to a place any peasant offending; and, if impudent, a whetstone to hang around his neck, the one ruff a peasant ever wore there. One of these named Trum-lands rented a number of fields from the monks, and rented these out to fellow-peasants, but at a higher rental, or employed them to till the fields for him, giving a slim share to the labourers, a fair share to himself, and a plump share to the monkish owners of all bodies and souls within the rule of the Abbacy. Through these fields, the fields of Trumlands, the peasants trudged on Sunday mornings and on the mornings of holydays, along a winding way, the low-ing herd winds slowly o'er the lea, down along, all along, right along lea, to Mass, walking east, turning south, then turning east again, tired after a week's wild work for monk and master, on to Mass to beg the grace of strength to begin again on the morrow working for master and monk, to north now, and semicircling towards the gateway, their slow and dragging steps chimed by a quicker bell, and entering into, graced by the sign of the cross, the mawlike porch of the Priory Church of St. Mary Virgin. All dead now. Eternal rest has been given them, but does perpetual light shine upon them? All dead and gone these more than a thousand years ago; a millennium of rest already. Men and women gone; the monks of the Priory Church gone with them; Trumlands himself mixes his dust with those he mastered; gone, too, are the fields; but the winding path remains. The Trumlands Road of today winds its selfsame way this very day, the way, the very way, the peasants trod to Mass is trod by me day in, day out, almost all the year, separated from it only when a winter's day is too fierce to let me go abroad.

Trumlands — who was he? What sort of a man? Had he a wife; had they children? How old was he when he died; where is he buried; and who fell into the property? No one knows. He just came and went, leaving nothing but his name on a road behind him. The name seems to have disappeared with the man, for I have never come across it, never heard of it in County Devon. I, too, wind my way along his road, but not to Mass nor to Matins or any Evensong. The trees, birds, and flowers around give all the prayer and praise I need. The powerful Abbey of the Premonstratensians itself is gone; a few buildings held now by the Corporation, the massive gateway, and a few bulky butts of ruins pointing to where the great Abbey Church stood, remain; and no one gaping at these relics has the faintest idea who the Premonstratensians were; or cares a damn anyway. The old Garth is a garden where old ones sit, the lawns are where children and their parents play, where honeymoon couples stroll and whisper, the monks unknown; the girl thinking of the power in her boy's loins, the boy of the girl's trim body which excites a passion in them. The Tithe Barn stands there still, squat, massive, where the monks hived the plundered corn and wine and wool, the hard-earned produce of the toiling peasantry. And this was often spent in riotous living, for old accounts show that many of the Premonstratensians bewandered far from the Rukes, enjoying themselves at feasts, banquets, fairs, taverns, and got to know how trim many a lassie's legs could be; so the honeymoon couples strolling about the long-gone cloisters may not disturb the rest of the dead and gone Religious, for these old holy places here and almost all other holy landmarks aren't quite so hallowed as some of our pietistic champions would have us believe: many of them, like Justice Shallow, knew many a Bona Roba and heard the bells chime at midnight. Closing our eyes on the old sitting in the flower-decked garden, the children running on the lawn, the honeymoon couples strolling around, and thinking only what was once here, we see decay and death, and ne'er a sign of resurrection which an Anglican Archbishop told the world was an idea that could be accepted 'on general grounds'. Not here, dear sir, not here. The kids at play, the kissing honeymoon couples, certainly share the soaring chant of the lark, but the derelict gateway, the stone coffins, and the poor abject

ruins, give no inkling of the soaring flight of any
Gerontius. This halting nebulous apologetic of the
Anglican prelate collides with the bold, assured asser-
tion of the Resurrection made by Dublin's Roman
Catholic Archbishop in his long Pastoral issued during
Lent's long wail of weeks, in 1961, where he asserts
that the body, though after death it disappears completely, assembles itself again at the Resurrection.
What a long, busy assembly line there will be then!
It flits together again, and the more it gets together,
the happier it will be. In this Pastoral, this Dublin
Archbishop tells the world that it is so declared in all
the three Christian Creeds; 'it is declared by Council
after Council in the Church, symbol after symbol bear
witness to the unchanging faith in the bodily Resurrection of the wicked and the just'. He brings St.
Augustine to the phone to back him up by saying
'Lads and lasses, take this down: "This flesh will
rise again. This flesh that is now seen and felt. This
flesh that is buried and dies; that has need to eat and
drink to live; this flesh that sickens and suffers pain,
this flesh must rise again; for the wicked (the goats)
that it may undure enending pain; for you, however
(the goodies), that it may be transformed." '
It is odd and surprising that this moss-covered
meditation, more savage than the awful yelling of the
Vandals besieging his episcopal city of Hippo, should
be a front-window show in modern churches blathering about being in step by step with Science; that
clerics should still sprinkle their flocks with the dark
hyssop of this horrible Christian conception of eternal
torment tearing and burning the flesh of resurrected
bodies of men, women, and children. It seems to me
that this horror of physical punishment for the 'wrong-

doer', young and old, has flowed far into life following
medieval days and is seen today in the prisons, schools,
homes, colleges; in the tortures of the Gestapo, by
the Black and Tans, by the pious Irish Catholics
themselves upon each other throughout the Irish Civil
War, and the appalling abuse of the fine Jewish race
by exulting Nazi savages, the uniformed Christian
Gentiles, the tortures in Algeria by French bullies;
not injuries inflicted in a moment of passion, but
injuries meted out after earnest calculation and careful
thought. A foretaste of this divine punishment eternal
in the next life is given in the temporal life we live by
the chopping-block at Eton, the cane in the Catholic
and Protestant schools, the cutting blows of the cane
given by the prefects to the little arses of their fags in
the English public schools, and the red weals raised
on the hands of the young by the straps of the Christian
Brothers, and other religious orders everywhere. This
savage doctrine blossoming out of St. Augustine's
gloomy mind, applauded by Dublin's Archbishop, has
had a damned long life and a savage one; but modern
knowledge and scientific civilisation are gradually
grinding the dark life out of it. This brutality, lust
to be well-off, setting honesty and integrity aside, in
business and in art, in politics, in the Church, are
the plumb-lines by which merit is tested, shown in
television, heard over the radio; so that at the last
judgement (if there be one), not the criminal or the
delinquent shall be judged, but the hypocritical and
self-satisfied society which bred them. Punished by
God, punished at home, punished in school, in college,
in prison, and, after death, punished eternally. It is
near time the young rebelled against it all!

Archbishop explains nothing. Do the wicked —

since their bodies will again be as they were in life —
eat and drink to keep alive? If they haven't to, then
the bodies can't be the same as they were. If they
still have to eat and drink, they will have to work to
get the corn and wine; and, if they suffer such un-
ending pain as the Saint and the Archbishop allege,
damn the day's work they'll be able to do; and, if
God feeds them automatically, then, again, they won't
be as they once were. To me, it seems a very irreverent
thing — to say the least — to imply that God, all the
time between death and resurrection, is patiently and
grimly waiting to get his own back on all who were
'wicked'; though Science has demonstrated that what
is called sin by Saint and Archbishop is largely a
matter of nerve, cellular, and gland formation of the
body, the 'flesh'.

Very eloquent about the body, though without
Archbishop or Saint every body knows a bit about
itself; but few words about the soul; what it may be,
what it looks like; how it goes — nothing in fact,
though, if I remember right, the Archbishop says that
a single thought can bring a soul to any spot in the
Universe. A kinda heavenly, self-flying, supersonic
paratrooper? Fact is, any query about the soul brings
silence. Not always, though, for only a while ago
(1961), a drama critic writing in De Valera's daily,
the *Irish Press*, said this of the characters appearing
in a play: 'I couldn't believe in them, for I knew
nothing of their true thoughts. They seemed ready-
mades (there are a helluva lot of ready-mades in the
Irish Republic!) which no character is. Each should
have had that discovery of themselves, each seen the
nothingness of their own personal lives, and been
brought face to face with their souls. Those who

listened should have felt the unreality of everyday reality.'

Be God, a shattering critical revelation! From a Donal O'Conaille. He musta spent a long time thinking! A real Dunce Scotus. He saw the poor soul, ethereal essence trapped within the vile body, squirming to get out, like Ariel tight within the cleft of a tree. Soul, come out for a minute or two till we have a decko at you. Doppelgänger. Two in one siamtease twins. I hope, Soul, you won't need propping up. Your knees wobble a bit. Body-blow? Punch-drunk? Try to stand steady, and don't shame your poor body. There you are in, looking out, and here I am out, looking in; a most embarrassing contratempts. You find it hard to stick me, and I find it hard to stick you; for when you're up, I'm down; and when I'm up, you're down; you like the madonna lily in your mit, I'd rather sport the red rose in me bosom, so, though bound together, we're for ever divided. Why such a sour look? Life's too short to quarrel, so shake hands, and let us be friends for old time's sake. Surely you'll be your pint stoup and surely I'll be mine — Auld Lang Syne, you know. No? You're against the world, the flesh, and the devil. Well, so'm I, up to a point, but I'm tired hearing you telling me that, an' it gets me down. I can't scoop myself outa me flesh, can I? An' go round, like as a skeleton, can I? An' I have to stay put in the world, haven't I? I can't do it either without me body. What's that you're muttering? Good God, man, I do regard me soul above me buttons! But while I'm here, I have to mind me buttons and me muttons and me tuttuttutons, haven't I? That doesn't satisfy you either. Oh, you despise the world, do you? A snob, eh? Well, I'm in the world, and you're in me, so two of us'll just have to do our best with it an' each other. Wha'? I don't do anything like a best? What d'ye want me to be? A poore soul sitting sighing under a sycamore tree? And for what, may I ask? Make war on meself to conquer me appetites and bring peace to you? My sins? D'ye never shut them eyes of yours? Me sins! What sins other than them me glands provoke? Wha'? Letting me eyes follow the comin' in and goin' out from short skirts of ungodly legs? And how'm I going to escape them? Follow the advice of St. Augustine, eh? Oh, yeah! And what's that now? Whenever I see a short-skirted lassie coming, I'm to flee? Oh, yeah! An' where the hell am I to flee to? D'ye imagine I'm ready to spend me life going at a gallop from one place to another? Oh, I don't want to flee, don't I? I find the sight enthrancin', do I? An' if I managed to get far enough away from where there was no short skirts, I'd come across nothing but bikinis! You'll just have to stick a few things, if you're going to live with me. Here if I'm to live at all, I've got to be master of me soul, and the way you go on, you turn yourself into a menace, even when you try to do your duty to your neighbour, for they don't want you poking your nose into their private affairs. Bad enough to make me miserable, but you want to make it impossible to live. As a body, I'm not going to let you bully and blast me out of existence. It's you who'll have to suffer — they say . . . in the end? You have, have you? Well, who the hell are you? You're me, see? Though I'm not you — not entirely, see? We're mixed together, and when I dissolve, they say, all that's left of me is you. Now, while we're unseparable, you're short of being a genial buttie, so I'm going to have a nice time when my body is absent, and I have to hang on to me soul. I've often bettered meself to make you feel more comfortable. I've climbed up Croagh Pathrick, and crawled down Croagh Patrick, half skinned alive be the sharp stones, hoarse with praying, facing snow, hail, rain, and Connacht winds, with you whispering, Go it, Charlie, don't let me down, be a man, lift your knees, keep your head up, you're working out an exceeding weight of glory, if you stick it to the end! Battered, forlorn, tattered and torn; and when I did stick it to the end, and the ambulance men were bringing me out of a torpor, you kept whispering, You cursed three times going up and four times crawling down, and spoiled, spoiled it all!

Give up the use of bad language? Don't you see me putting me hands over me ears, can't you hear me weeping when you let loose language unfit for a soul to hear? It's sinful and this means death to me. And what about me? I die anyway, don't I? If I spent me whole livelonglife climbing up, crawling down Croagh Patrick, like that fella Sissypuss, I'd still have to meet with the last fall and the tumble, like a falling leaf in the deeper time of the autumn, while you live on gay and ghastly, deprived of your buddie who gave you legs to dance, arms to capture a girl, eyes to see her face and figure, ears to hear her sighing, lips to kiss her, and a tongue to coax her into the thrills you so often yearn after.

Body, you're dodging the whole issue. Whenever you meet with what you fancy, you're off, dragging your pore Soul along with you, and I have to do the suffering; watch you while you work me ruin; wait till you get tired of blasting me, and start on your penance again. I'm an old shrivelled thing before me time. Often when you're trying to pile up your good deeds, you make things for me worse than ever. How do you? Well, what about your pilgrimage up and down Croagh Patrick? For weeks before you got within sight of it, you were acting like Bronco, going to do wonders. Odd wonders they were! Aw, I heard you — you can't cod your soul. I heard. I hear everything you say to others, and everything you whisper to yourself; and I heard you going up the mountain, heard all sitting aghast in me little cubicle inside of you. You cursed the stones going up, you cursed the heather that tripped you, the bracken that splashed rain over you; you cursed even the little flowers here and there that tried to cheer you up, and when a poor woman bumped you into a hollybush, your blasphemies kindled a flame round me for weeks afterwards; and I had to listen, I couldn't get away. You boasted you'd bring down a big spiritual bouquet of muttered and murmured prayers, but, instead, you dumped a load of blasphemies on me back. Then I have to take up the chore of getting you square with heaven again, suffering on your behalf to get you any-way presentable, till you feel fine on the right side of absolution.

Haven't I to suffer too, grit me teeth, disjoint me joints with kneeling, bore meself stiff with penances, struggle to the surface again after near drowning in a sea of sermons? After much penance and prayer and a bit a fasting, I get face to face with you, me soul, and, honest to God, I don't think much of it, just as you yourself never did like the look of me. The soul against the body and the body against the mind. We have to live a life of co-existence, while remaining ideologically different, always in a wrestle of Greco-

Roman style or rough-an'-ready catch-as-catch-can. It's all such a wasteful weariness! What on earth is either, and what on earth is both? Is there any connection between *res cogitans*, me and me mind, and *res extensa*, me and matter? Does matter mind mind, or does mind mind matter? Is mind itself, indeed, matter too? Is you, me soul, insubstantial, consubstantial, transubstantial, or circumstantial? What does the Sorbonne say? Salamanca? Maynooth? Billy Graham or Johnny Walker? Are you an eternal jewel or only a dream Gerontius? Are you king over the body, or a princely clown of pundemonium? What are you — where, why, what, are you? I can't see you, hear you, feel you, smell you, touch you. To the searching, often bitter and poignant question of immortality, are you only the dusty answer?

'My mind', said Edison the scientist, 'is unable to conceive of such a thing as a soul. I may be in error, and man may have a soul, but I simply cannot believe it.' Nor can I, though, God knows, I have many dear reasons for desiring it to be true; and, 'fore God be it said, maybe, remembering the bad things said, the bad things done within the years of my life, and the good or brave things left unsaid, and the good things left undone, a fear that the claim of immortality may be true, so that in the day of wrath I might find myself acting the goat, entirely and for ever separated from the gentle little baa baa lambs. Science seems to have shown, and so proved, that what is called 'Sin', or a large proportion of it, shows itself, not because of man's natural depravity, or by some evil thing taking possession of him or her, but is provoked or persuaded by the cellular tissues of nerve, gland, and brain-cell; how these have come together and have intermingled, so that no act of contrition or many penances can alter gland, nerve, or brain-cell; and that healthier and saner conduct and mood can come only through social amendment, aided by the many wonderful discoveries of medical and surgical science, aided further by the genius and skill of those who practise these humanist sciences. This, too, is the one way to bring Jerusalem to England's green and pleasant land: the calm, but irresistible, evolution to a higher life, which alone, if there be a God, can bring humanity close to his right hand or to his left one, with understanding and a deep and independent reverence, shown, not in loud-voiced hymn or wailing prayer, but in brisk, affectionate, and self-expanding life. The way of the talents; the diligent use of whatever gifts or gift, talents or talent, may be given us; to some five, to some two, to some but one, as terribly important as the ten or five given to the others, to be used to the full, and not, through fear of any kind, to be hidden away so that it perishes, or is taken by one with other talents to be used more effectively. So in my reverie here, beside the crimson hydrangea, the white dahlias, the fading petunias, I imagine if there be a God (which, God help me, I cannot believe), then he is as the man travelling into a far country, and called his servants and delivered unto them his goods, to one five talents, to another two, and to a third one; demanding when he returned, after a long time, from each an account of how they had used them. Only the man with one failed the test, having buried his talent in the earth, afraid to venture his talent in the service of one who reaped where he hadn't sown, gathered where he hadn't strawed; so instead of developing into a fuller soul, he dwindled into nothing. So, if God be, he is one who gathers where he hasn't strewn, reaps where he hasn't sown, and can do so only through the talents and their insistent use by men. He looks to man. Through the sciences, art, literature, music, technology, sport, social growth, we go towards heaven (if there be a heaven), and not through pastoral (unless it be the pastoral poem about charity by Paul) or prayer, by nun's bonnet or monk's cowl, cloister or cathedral, bishop, priest, or deacon; but only what we do with mind, imagination, and by hand. All have been given a talent, but half are prevented from using them by privilege, the accident of birth, tradition, and cupidity; and our way of life must first be moulded so as to sweep these obstacles off the face of the earth, so that all may start and all may go, and all may hear, when the end of life has come, the well done, good and faithful servant, thou hast served humanity well, and God (if there be one) is glorified.

It is acceptable and fine when symbols enter into life within the form of legend, myth, and fable; we welcome them, and hang them up as delightful colored pictures on the delicate walls of the mind; standing before them at times to admire the colors, the line, the form, learning from them that the simple and ordinary can very often be beautiful. How beautiful a field of wheat can be, either in the green leaf or in the golden ear; wheat from which the common bread is made which we all eat to live; and Whitman composed his stirring, bugle-call poems from the simple symbol of common leaves of grass! Solomon in all his glory, said Jesus, couldn't rival the lilies of the field; the colors of the anemones abloom in the field faded the hues of the king's rich robings; and the blue of the eyebright is more beautiful than the blue of the dress adorning a belle of the ball. So fable, legend, and myth are often charming, touched with beauty by some early poet. It is innocent fun to watch God modelling the first man from red earth or the woman from a bone out of the first man's body; to lie with Adam in the first garden under the beech, the fern, or the bamboo tree, to be lulled by the music of the two streams watering the garden, as we are lulled by the music of Tennyson's brook sparkling out among the fern, and brushing by forget-me-nots that grow for happy lovers; to admire the strident colors, with Noah, of the first rainbow; to help the good Samaritan to pour oil and wine into the wounds of the stricken Jew; to weep with Orpheus when he lost his dear Eurydice; to enjoy the fantasy of the poet-apostle, and journey with the three wise men, following the star to where the babe was born; to sing Christmas carols ornamented tunefully by some ancient composer so that we see three ships come sailing by, and feel the winter's snow falling on our cheeks as angels, weaving a way among the stars, sing their song of peace on earth loud in the skies above and above the upturned heads of the gaping shepherds; to hear with indignation Joseph's rebuke to his Mary, and then to see with glee the cherry tree bending down so that she might reach the dangling fruit, and cool her dry tongue with its sweet and soothing sap; to weep with Niobe when she sees her children die.

Time and time again, we are called upon, pleaded with, exhorted, to come to God, and how!; that the one thing the world, that man, needs is God; that without his help we can do nothing. A lot of us are sick of it, the call, the pleading, the exhortation. We sweat in all this hot air from pulpit and Press, from

Television and Radio; we are tired of this ecclesiastical skiffle band with its insistent single drumbeat, its twang-twang on one plucked string. Bright and Early gospel messages first thing in the morning, Epilogues last thing at night, Christian viewpoints, Christian meeting-point in the times between, vexing every intelligent ear that hears any of them by accident. It is near time that the blather about man needing God's help changed to the more sensible one of God needing the help of man. This call upon God is arrant mockery, running into some church for a spot o' prayer o' Sunday mornings, while the rest of that day, and throughout the hours of the others, the peoples are rushing after, and adoring, their own foolishness, and God can't pull them out of that condition of mind and conduct. If man chooses to act the bloody fool, God sits helpless in his heaven, their looks on God, their hearts and minds on other things, useless things, dangerous things: on Blue Streaks, on Sky Thunderbolts, on Polaris submarines, on booster power to send handsomer hydrogen bombs cascading down on the heads of enemies whom they are supposed to love; missiles from air to air, from air to earth, from sea to air, the best possible ways of cracking bone and rending flesh from flesh. These things are what are aimed at by those who say they believe the blather about man's great need of God; these are the things that keep them safe, they say; these are the things that give them false hope, that give them false faith, while charity can go to hell. Bombs and blast and cancer! Our future heritage! In April 1960, a picture in a Catholic journal shows the Pope bending tenderly over a pretty girl of seven years, who is gliding down to death. 'She came from Oklahoma to see His Holiness, and the print below tells us that the pretty little girl, Catherine Hudson, is stricken with leukaemia. She received a souvenir from the Pope in a special audience.' Every picture tells a story, and Catherine's is a sad one, a very sad one: your Holiness, I who am about to die salute ye! A more mortal moment and a sadder one for the old Pope than for the young child. However eager he must have been to save, the old man had not the power in either arm to hold the handsome child back from death for a single day. There was no use suggesting Lourdes to the child's father, for in Lourdes there was no cure for leukaemia. How relieved the poor old man must have been when the child had gone, dancing a child's sad minuet with death.

These are some of the ways of bringing us 'closer to God' — by preaching over the radio, from the pulpit, by picture and word on the television screen; but there are also negative ways of keeping us from wandering, from going off on a tangent of sin; moral rectitude in a Protestant way, from occasions of sin in the Catholic way. One of these is the canny or strident censorship of the written word, especially those packed into a book; a censorship that can be national, provincial, or parochial. One thing is certain—that children can never be damaged by reading a hundred horror comics to the extent they can be bloodily pulped by the fall of an atom bomb. The O'Caseys have never prevented, never tried to prevent, their children from reading any comic they might choose. The house had volumes of the world's finest literature ranged on shelves in every room, and these were there to take and read whenever our children choose to do so: no book was banned. It is easy to frighten a child, easy to put the fear of God into one, which, of course, is putting the fear of man into the child, without God having anything to do with it, unless we regard some bishop or canon as God, in a kind of *locis incarnatus*; but it isn't easy to pervert a kid; a child's mind is too simple, too full of enjoying life to be roused into a tendency of evil by any book; unless it be the resentment crushed into his young mind by the compulsive memorising of the Protestant bible or the incomprehensible Catholic catechism. It is the elderly, not the young, who are perpetually afraid — of books, of plays, of poems, of pictures. There is quite a bit of censorship in England (Ireland? Shush!), though we once got damnably hot under the collar about the terrible fate of *Dr. Zhivago*, forgetting all about Joyce, and the desperate assaults made on Lawrence, on Epstein, on Hardy, yea, even on Tennyson. Apart from the Churches, the common law, there is quiet and effective censorship carried on in localities, *sub nosa* and *sotto voce*. The other day Mr. Bernard Williams, a lecturer at University College, London, at a meeting of librarians, warned against the possible banning of books in public libraries. 'We must always be alive to the possibility', he said, 'that there may be powerful bodies in the community who may exercise an informal power over what people can read. The hypocrisy of banning books on the ground that they can do harm, when we can have no notion of what harm they can do, to whom or how, is something that itself is likely to have more serious consequences than the publication of a very great number of dirty books.' These puddlers of purity are a menace to every community.

I have had my share of banning in journals, at meetings, on the stage, in the theatre. I was shoved for ever off the Abbey stage because I ventured to criticise the playing and production of Shaw's *Man and Superman*; when *Purple Dust* came out, the late James Agate flew at it, throwing the book out of a window, tearing at it savagely, and shouting, 'O'Casey stabs England in the back!' Presumably because the play prophesies the disappearance of the British Empire, one prophecy anyhow that has come to pass, so signs on it, the play was never done in England till 1962, except for a few hasty performances in Brighton — of all places. Once, after the first volume of my auto-biography had been published, I was asked by the *Sunday Times* to review a life of Jack London, then one about Robert Loraine, then one of Charles Lever, and all went merry as a marriage bell; then I slipped. Along came a life of John Mitchel, the Irish patriot, transported to Van Diemen's Land by the then British Government. The review was delivered, but it was absent from the paper's next issue, and from the next. They sat silent, possibly disliking praise for an Irish rebel. After more'n a month, I wrote about it, asking why, and was told that the sentiments and the judgements were not acceptable by the *Sunday Times* (I still think it unfair that I was never paid for this commissioned review, but was too proud to demand payment; so ended my career as a reviewer. Though the six guineas a week had added another bolt on the door to keep away the big bad wolf, I was glad the chore had ended, for I had little confidence in myself as a reviewer, and often envied the way Brooks Atkinson in America and V. S. Pritchett in England wrote reviews so easy and so well; seeming to compose a review as easy as kiss hands, writing within an hour or two as I couldn't hope to write in a month o' Sundays. The other fine journal,

the *Observer*, too, found no room for me. A reply
to a review by Dr. Gogarty on a book of mine, and
by George Orwell on another, never soiled the fair
face of the journal; both ignored, and never even
privately explained, though a letter of mine criticising
an article by John Wain was returned, but refused
publication 'because of lack of space'; and another
letter of mine was refused appearance in the *Daily
Telegraph* 'because of lack of space', too. Some time
ago an amateur drama group attached to the firm of
Fisons, selected a play of mine, *Bedtime Story*, and
were so successful that they decided to enter it in the
Drama Festival in which groups entered from Essex
and surrounding counties. But the Education Council
stepped in and the play stepped out; for it was decided
by this Council that this play was too saucy to be
shown to the elderly audiences which might come to
witness the performances during the drama trials of
the Festival. So this little play has never been performed in England, as far as I know, except by the
students for the students of the R.A.D.A., for fear it
might weaken the moral fibres of the elderly, bringing
the land to a decline and fall into the depravity of
whoredom; though this, at least, would be better and
brighter than to decline and fall into the drab and
malicious menace of puritanism. First, then, it is
hypocrisy and humbug for Conservative or Socialist
to go round thanking God for the 'free world'; for
freedom of normal conduct and freedom of speech are
no stronger there than anywhere else, for each Press
Lord decides what shall go into his paper and what
shall not go in, the Editor of each being forced to
worship the totem pole of the views held by the owner,
from the parish magazine up to the biggest and bulliest

of the National dailies. All is done that can be done
to prove that we are very fine fellows, while still
keeping women in their place, leaving wind ws open
for them, but keeping the doors shut; but, all the
same, we are the best fellows, only to be found in the
western world. 'Over there', said Mr. Dimbledee, on
the television screen, a rapturous, angelic look on his
homely face, 'over there', pointing to the east, 'is darkness, and over there', pointing to the west, 'is light'.
The Lord has graciously conferred the illustrious Order
of Lux Mundi upon the western world. We are the
good companions. We have never strayed from God's
ways like lost sheep; we've always done the things
we ought to have done, and never left undone those
things which we ought to have done, and there is
perfect health in us all. You know that, God, as well,
even better, than we do, as we do. So far from following too much, we have never, never followed the
devices or desires of our own hearts; never, or hardly
ever. We love our enemies, especially the communists,
and yearn to take them under our wing as a hen does
her chickens, though we may have to, if they press us
too hard, broil them under the heat of the atom bomb.
Though all men are liars, we are none, so help us God.
Let us hope we are not too good to be true to God.
Pray, western ladies and gentlemen, that we may be
delivered from this stupid superstition of proclaiming
that all truth and righteousness are here, while all
duplicity is over there, over there; that we may rid
ourselves of the eidolon of being one, holy, gloriously
incarnated and dangerous Doxology.

THE GREEN BUSHES: A SONG

Air: The Green Bushes

THERE she stood in her white-border'd dress of bright
    blue,
Th' fairest girl God made or man ever knew;
An upstanding, full-blossom'd firm almond tree,
Down by th' green bushes there waitin' for me.

Along came a stranger, lac'd hat in his hand;
'I'll make you a Dame o'er wide acres o' land,
In a carriage all gleamin' I'll sit you in style,
Like Egypt's great queen in her barge on th' Nile.

'I'll build you a house with high gables an' tow'r,
Maid-servants to trim an' take care of your bow'r;
Rich carpet on lobby, rich carpet on stair,
An' a diamond to shine like a star in your hair.

'White petticoats frail as th' veil of a bride,
Showin' most o' th' charms they're pretendin' to hide,
Silk stockin's to tenderly kiss a white thigh,
An' a chemise as soft as a lover's first sigh.

'I'll wrap you in cloak an' I'll lap you in shawl,
To keep your young bloom from both tempest and
    squall;
All these I will give if you'll only agree
To leave th' green bushes, an' marry with me.'

When th' young lover came, th' green bushes were
 bare,
Not a leaf on a stem, not a girl standin' there;
'She's gone for a life of wild riches an' glee,
An' left th' green bushes for ever, an' me.

'I'll not shed a tear an' I'll not make a moan,
Tho' she's left me forsaken an' standin' alone;
I'll seek out a girl better-manner'd than she,
To seek th' green bushes an' wait there for me.'

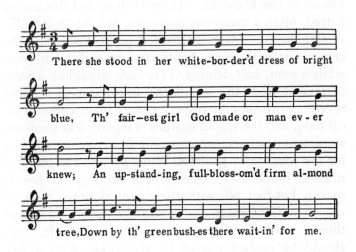

There she stood in her white-border'd dress of bright
blue, Th' fair—est girl God made or man ev - er
knew; An up-stand-ing, full-bloss-om'd firm al-mond
tree, Down by th' green bush-es there wait-in' for me.

THE GREEN CROW CAWS

IT is curious how many folks, pride-full of the knowledge of the world and of modern literature, mock at a trembling tear or a sad emotion in a human eye. Anything in a play, a picture, a song, that tends to start a tear gives a hasty curl of scorn to the mocking mouth of the know-all. There is deep and deadening hatred, often a malicious contempt, for the 'Sob-stuff'. A sigh heard, a tear discovered on a cheek, fills the critical air with jeers, hoots, and resentful laughter, while a poor, half-demented creature strangling a babe to save it from the sin of the world evokes a silent reverence; profound respect dawns upon every cynical mug, and the stupid murder is regarded as a solemn sacramental service. A murmur from anyone sighing for the touch of a vanished hand propels the mighty-minded quick away from where the sigh is heard, to run hot-foot off with their cynical noses high in the air. Gentleness and grace are taboo; diseased things that have wormed a way into life, and should be probed out of it, are hailed with a hey hi nonny O.

Poets, playwrights, and novelists seem to be unaware of, indifferent to, the world of children. They see themselves in every glass, and imagine that life is made of the images they see in themselves: the only life worth living. They ignore the swarming children round about them, laughing at them, and willing them, forcing them, to die. If they stay or stoop to notice the world of children, it is with contempt and disgust.

Often in play, televised show (for example, that monstrous televised show called *Whack-O!*), they show the young as nothing else but stupid boors, barbarians in whom is little but a sense of destruction and cruelty. Yet I've seen an infant hand held out towards a colored flower seen for the first time; I've seen the wonder in a child's eye who meets the sea for the first time; or who picks the daisies from the grass as a first treasure of beauty and of charm. These cynics, ignorant or sophisticated, speak, act, behave, as if their life was the only one, and that all things and thought must be measured by it. Unless ye become as little children — fah!

Recently, a critic reviewing a new play said, 'This is a play about marriage; about what happens when romantic love inevitably gives way to the boredom, fatigue, and sheer brutal routine of living together'. Oh, what a beautiful mourning! So millions of married couples everywhere, after that romantic overture has ended, survive through the rust of the years, in fatigue, and the sheer brutal routine of living together! This is some of the malicious nonsense preached by those who seem to wish this to be so; but it is not so, not even basically so, for the couples aren't always 'living together'. The needs of life, all the activities which have to be undertaken, prevent couples, romantic or disillusioned, from constantly 'living together'. Every day, save perhaps one a week, long periods of time separate the one from the other; and the romance of the courtship — no longer so glamorous as it had been — is usually made romantic again in another way by the birth of a baby. The couple are no longer living together — there is a dividing link between them. Now they have to think of another as well as themselves; another voice is heard in the home, another step is heard coming and going. Then, there are friends, friends of his, friends of hers; they come and they go, relieving — if relief be needed — the one's company from the other; there are the pictures, too, when, though they sit close, they live, in fantasy, each in a different way, maybe, another life with the shadows on the screen. There is sleep, the many silent hours in a dusky stillness, separating the one from the other, forfeiting companionship for a rest, needed to renew the activities of life for tomorrow. He spends hours each day at work, she spends hours in housework, in shopping, in minding the baby when a baby comes. So a couple suffers many hours of separation, from the need to work, to sleep, even from the need of enjoyments, and the quiet breaks brought into their life now and again by the personal thoughts each mind harbors, even during the busy routine of a day; preparations for the year's festivals, too, diversify the time spent in living together as man and wife.

Even with courting couples, Romance isn't always ringing a peal of bells, though the whole world be gathered into every embrace they give each other. Even at this honeyed time, when the couple leave the silent bunnydiction of the moon, they think of bread and cheese, of brick and mortar. Throughout the time of the pledge of wedlock to the morn of the marriage, life makes them dwell on the things of a routine world — what they shall eat, the wherewithal with which they shall clothe themselves, and of a home where all these things are done (and in this they differ in no way from him or her who chooses the lonelier life of bachelordom and spinsterhood). Life just gives them an empty space somewhere, and this space must be given the things that make life livable, so that the 'routine' and the 'drudgery' begin even in the glamorous time of the union. There is no escape, except for the few; and so a beginning must be made at once after the first swift passionate embraces have folded themselves away. A home has to be made, and it takes time and work and patient waiting; drudgery and routine go with the building; but there is excitement, too; the bringing to the home of a new rug with a nice pattern, a picture for a wall, a chair, a shining pan, crockery, gay-flower'd or speckled, for special occasions, are moments of excited enjoyment; another thing done; something else, useful or ornamental, added to the growing glow of a home. Courtship and the first days of marriage aren't all given to the laying on of hands on a white breast or a white thigh.

Then there are the millions of couples living together the whole world over, rearing families till time sends the young on their own ways, leaving the couple to live alone together again, till death takes one of them away, leaving him or her lonely indeed, no longer feeling life so happy, when, indeed, the drudgery of loneliness shows itself, for ever seeing a streak of mourning in every flash of brightness; finding that even when windows are wide open, the blinds are still down. So this ghastly gospel of 'boredom, fatigue, and sheer brutal routine of living together' dissolves itself into a dark, dewy nonsense, for man is ever seeking companionship, close in the affection of a friend, close in that of a wife. Hearing this ghastly gospel propagated in a book, a poem, or a play, confirmed by a lonely and a fatigued critic, Life gives a deep threatening belly-laugh, and goes on living with a family or with just two together in a cottage or in a room with a view. All normal humans dread the dreary spirit and pang of loneliness, and hasten away from it whenever it chances to come their way. When life lives to the age of Methuselah, and then only when we are as old as Shaw's Ancient, do we crave to live on the rim of humanity, away from the song, the dance, the banter and the bustle, to go deep into thoughts of things beyond us, stretching out the mind towards them as far as thought can reach.

Most of the 'boredom, fatigue, and sheer brutal routine' is provoked by the present planning out of life, the planning for profit rather than for need; the rotten schools given to children by God (according to the Sunday schools); no room in the living-quarters, within or without, for the children to amuse or instruct themselves, so shielding them from the busy ways of the mother; no place where the children can read, draw, paint, and build their own fancies in peace. Self-development through the many ways life gives to all is a sure deliverance from boredom, fatigue, and sheer brutal routine of living together; to the woman escaping from the children, to the children escaping from the woman. Even without these necessary aids, life usually tries to make the best of what she has, and many a jovial hour is spent, or eked out, within the most trying and crowded conditions. Near London's heart, in Notting Hill, there is a family of seven living in one room for which they pay a fiver a week, doing all things there, except use of a toilet, which is in another place serving seventeen persons (no world's wonder to me, and far from a record). Here are at least seven reasons for a revolt against the fatigue and sheer brutal routine conditions; but I've never heard a critic setting forth against them, for these critics are concerned only, it seems, with those whose fatigue and boredom spring from having too much, and no will to do anything with what they have; content, in a resentful way towards all others, to regard self as the centre of all things. My own daughter, Shivaun, lived for quite a time in a miserable little flat in this same district of Notting Hill for which she paid five pounds a week, and ne'er a thank-you when the money was being handed over. These conditions in Notting Hill were shown over British Television on the evening when the Russian poet, Alie Surkov, Secretary of the Soviet Writers' Union, was visiting us, and he arrived shortly after the television revelation. During our talk the matter of England's higher standard of living was brought to the fore, and both the poet and his companion were surprised, even doubtful, when I told them of the sorry conditions of life in Notting Hill, where there are no MacLeishian golden combs, or golden spinning-wheels, or even a golden apple on a golden plate to be found. Nor is absence of more sensible things than these so uncommon in other places within Blake's Jerusalem: I know of a young sensitive girl, who has had a baby recently, living in a top-floor flat in one of Bristol's higher houses. It is indeed a poor flat, almost worn away from living, but she and her husband (possibly a survival of the war-time mend and make-do brigade), with no help other than their own hands and minds, have made it a colorful and a much gayer-looking flat than it was or really is; but though its look is more bearable, it still is almost worn away from the standing world. When this courageous girl has to seek out groceries, she has to go down many flights of stairs,

cold and draughty in spring and autumn, fiercely cold
in the winter, carrying her baby with her; climb up
again when she comes back, carrying her baby with
her; going down to collect the milk of a morning and
any letter that may be lying addressed to her on the
bottom step; while, when it rains, in an odd corner
here and there, one may hear the slow drip . . . drip
of raindrops wending a way down from some leak in
the roof. When the west winds blow and the rain
falls, the old wrinkled roof springs a leak or two, maybe
three, and soiled water trickles down a wall, or drops,
quick drop after quick drop, into bedroom, kitchen, or
lounge, hurrying her with basin or bucket to catch
and keep them from giving rug and floor a soaking.
I know the house and I know the stairs, for our
daughter lives in a similar flat opposite, and I've been
there when buckets and basin caught the lusty drip-
ping from a ceiling in this room, and another ceiling
in that one; saw it in the evening of the day before a
Christmas dawning. By hard work done by Shivaun,
her brother Breon, and her mother, the face of the
flat has been greatly brightened, and color in cushion
and curtain, and color on the walls, have made it
smile, made it livable, and — if its inner nature be
forgotten — made it a cheerful and charming home,
where sleep can come, where meals can be enjoyed,
within gay color and good light. Long-playing records
and wireless set can bring art, literature, music, and
good taste to a place long careworn with dilapidation
and decay. The irony of it is that those who live here
are thought to be fortunate, for places in which to
live are few and far between, and hard to get, and only
half-derelict houses can provide a sort of a home which
is within the possibility of a wage-earner to pay for.

Half-dead places like these in millions are in England still, doped into further languishing life by the rents gotten out of them, at times roused into a drowsy attention by a cosily-sympathetic reference from some half-dead pulpit, or a brief, sharp criticism from some sleepy Parliament bench. They are found, trying to hide their heads, even in the flaunty, übermensch districts of Mayfair and St. John's Wood.

But the odd and good thing about it all is that so many of these gallant youngsters beginning life in earnest fail to carry out the despairing instructions of the playwrights to sit down and moan and lament the dimness and dereliction around them; but set about, with aprons on, coats off, and sleeves rolled up, to change the face of decay and gloom into one of cheerfulness, color, and charm. They bump difficulties aside, blow away dirt and dust, bluff squalidness into hiding, and fill out vagueness with stimulating life. They are the brave ones, and they are a great multitude. They work for themselves and they work for others, for their younger kin who follow on, giving them an encouraging push towards human resolution, to a refusal to take things as they are, for in coloring a drab wall they take from the treasury of the skies. Their hopeful work, done in time, goes forward into eternity. The young couples who give color to some, indeed, to many, of these places, color on wall, color in curtain, color on floor, are stars in these drab skies, and they give hope and spread a sense of charm into the minds of those who come to spend a chattering hour with them over a glass of wine, a simple meal, or a genuine cup of tea. These decorators of life are of those ones who give light to darkness; who by imagination and effort shed forth the light of the Holy Spirit of man, leaving the institutional altar cold and the pulpit empty.

It is these who are the costume-colored bodyguard of humanity, the ones who are never publicly announced, whose names are unknown to the newsmen, but whose names are written in the book of life; silent heralds whose tabard is the resolute urge to drive away the drab, the insolent dirt, and the lassitude of resignation, so that room may be made for the dancer discontent; to stamp out all things around them, within and without, that tend to hurt the health of body and mind. It is these, with others still more humble than they, who stretch Apollo's bow of burnished gold, and shoot forth his arrows of desire into the hearts of men. We look forward, not only to a comfortable life, but an active and gracious one as well.

Those are heroes of quiet determination, and they give a pungent savor to life; they have to fight alone, they are not helped, but they are tolerated good-humoredly. The present habit, however, in poem, play, and story, is to show humanity as helpless, despairing; saying silently or vehemently, that life is futile, and nothing can alter it; the Christians giving this futile manner the name of Original Sin. If anything should happen which apparently bears out this sad philosophy, many big mouths bawl it out and write it down. The more we change, the more we remain the same; the same to you, sir; the same again. God may be, but man is not, thank God, the same yesterday, today, and for ever. Everyone changes, even during a lifetime; the community changes during a generation, and nothing remains the same; even the land we happen to live in changes contours made by nature, and other contours made by man. All who happen to be as old as I am can look back to the days of their youth and see the changes that have come over life in England. The young of today looking at a picture or a film of London, not so long ago either, wonder at its oddities. Look at the pictures of American manners, dress, and life of 1863, year of my own mother's marriage, time of Lincoln, and a present-day American would hardly even guess that he was looking at his own town-land. These are but recent changes, but, if we go back a much longer way, we find that everything is utterly changed, and they shall never be again such as they were before the change came.

Today, it seems the last drop of the milk of human kindness has been burned up by the sun of unrighteousness; and poet, playwright, and storyteller have become hot dogs, fanged and yapping, biting too as they run around loose. The island is full of sour noises. Caliban is king, Ariel is fast in the tree-cleft again, and there is no Prospero to release him. Where the cowslip grew, the cactus grows now, a cactus without its often lovely blossom. Oddly enough, there were more murders, suicides, torments in the Elizabethan plays, and even Shakespeare had his share of these; but there was music in them all. Sad music often, but sadness can give out sweet noises, as in Cherubini's *Requiem* and Verdi's *Requiem*, too; as in Webster's

> Call for the robin redbreast and the wren,
> Since o'er shady groves they hover,
> And with leaves and flowers do cover
> The friendless bodies of unburied men.

The tiny, timid, and the shy little wren with the hotspur robin-redbreast, do a deed better than any done by a conscientious Boy Scout; do a Christian

67

charity, they bury the dead. We do, too, but not so much for charity as for the fact that we damned well have to get rid of them; or so the modern poet, playwright, or storyteller might cynically hiss from the compression of his tight-lipped contempt for things living or dead. Shakespeare, too, in his land-dirge for the handsome Fidele, opens his heart to pity and resigned compassion, flashing light on the gloomy face of Death by encouraging mortality to remember all it eludes when life dreams her darkened way to the end, and droops to clay again:

> Fear no more the heat o' the sun,
> Nor the furious winter's rages.

Bitter, even savage, as Shakespeare so often was, he never lost the lovely power of emotional compassion; nor, indeed, did the other Elizabethans, though they could be as realistic, as fierce, as dire, but much more so, as any bitter and cynical writer of today; whose savagery, bitterness, and cynicism is always sly, mean, and commonplace; with the exception of Beckett, who, alongside the greater Elizabethans, never loses the emotion of a great compassion. Ready for tears, as ready for laughter, how bitter Shakespeare can be when he is in the mood! As even in the sylvan play, along with a fine love story, we find him setting a song sung in the Duke's company beneath the greenwood trees of Arden; an indignant, bitter song declaring,

> Blow, blow, thou winter wind,
> Thou art not so unkind
> As man's ingratitude . . .
>
> Freeze, freeze, thou bitter sky,
> Thou dost not bite so nigh
> As benefits forgot:

Though thou the waters warp,
Thy sting is not so sharp
    As friend remember'd not.

Heigh-ho! sing heigh-ho! unto the green holly:
Most friendship is feigning, most loving mere folly:
    Then, heigh-ho, the holly!
    This life is most jolly.

Here is Shakespeare weaving the green-leav'd red-
berried holly into cynical and bitter beliefs! Holly,
mind you — the emblem of the joy of Christmas.
Shakespeare was an angry young man, as, indeed, were
all the major Elizabethan dramatists; just as the present-
day dramatists are; with this difference — that they
of old had gaiety in them too, a song, much laughter,
pity and compassion, and never abandoned the blessed
feeling of human emotion: these wore their rue with
a difference. Still, no modern playwright, be he or
she never so young or new, could write as bitter and
biting a phrase as did those of the long ago and the
far away. Take Shakespeare's compact and terse description of Life: read his woeful outcry of 'Tomorrow
and tomorrow and tomorrow', ending with the frightening muted shout of agony—

           . . . It is a tale
        Told by an idiot, full of sound and fury,
        Signifying nothing.

God Almighty, could any saying be more terrible
than this one! In a play of today, gone away west
now, a disillusioned mother having stoically watched
her bruiser-son leave for Australia, and the easy Lolly,
her daughter, leave for London and love, her feeble
husband for another woman, makes a desperate effort
to be bitter, and cries loudly to the roof-tops 'Eh,

Life's a beggar, isn't it?' Yes, mom, it is, but this final line is a squeak. Better, even, had she said 'Life is a bugger, isn't it?'; but that would have been too much of a bad thing; but, at least, there would be a streak of bitter humor in the exclamation. Even when these writers are determined to be bitter at all costs, they often go the wrong way about it.

There is all complexity of human feelings, harshness, tenderness, joy and sorrow, blasphemies, devotions, fierceness and the gentle touch of love, song, and laughter in all the older plays. There is often, if not always, a good morning after a goodnight spoken, as in *Hamlet*, when young life enters to take up the burden where Hamlet laid it down; and as the sad scene ends, the beautiful committal of Hamlet to the dust and silence by his friend, Horatio, murmuring from a mourning heart:

> Good night, sweet prince;
> And flights of angels sing thee to thy rest!

As for an expression about life in a minor key, we have

> Life is as tedious as a twice-told tale
> Vexing the dull ear of a drowsy man.

No present-day writer's most bitter or savage snarl at life that I have ever read can equal this cold and contemptuous dismissal of life by Shakespeare; yet the same plaintiff poet can set out a few of life's minor forms for a worshipping admiration; a few simple flowers — not those nursed and amazed into a gorgeous distortion for a flower-show, but simple plants ornamenting a meadow or sprinkling color and form over a dusty or a damp wayside. Not Proserpina's flowers dropped in fright from Dis's wagon, but common ones we've met and admired many times in wonted walk or a wandering one: daffodils that take the winds of March with beauty; the violet, in color sweeter than the lids of Juno's eyes, in scent sweeter than the breath of Cytherea; and the pale primroses, dying unmarried before they behold the sun in his strength. The simple daffodil, primrose, and the violet — so simple, so lovely; these giving lovely patterns to the earth, the darting swallow weaving fantastic abstracts over the sky. And Shakespeare looked, saw life, and pronounced it good and lovely.

Man is fearfully and wonderfully made; and what present-day writer could give man a better description than Chapman, when he wrote

> Oh of what contraries consists a man!
> Of what impossible mixtures! vice and virtue,
> Corruption and eternesse, at one time,
> And in one subject, let together loose!
> We have not any strength but weakens us,
> No greatness but doth crush us into air,
> Our knowledges do light us but to err,
> Ornaments are burthens; our delights
> Are our tormentors; fiends that raised in fears,
> At parting shake our roofs about our ears.

Chapman's dirge, not for the dead, but for the living. Man the unhappiest of living things, always wondering why God made him; still wondering because he refuses to realise that man made himself. Is any of today's angry young (or old) men angrier than Chapman or Shakespeare were in their day? Consider, too, one who was, and still is today, reputed to be the gentlest of men; whose whole and full nature was love for others, of kindness, whose words were a balm and a blessing: yet this man's emotion could be a flame and a blasting. Thrice the gentle nature flamed into anger: the loving words became a curse, the voice that fluted forth thoughts of salvation and of hope, hissed out threats of biting torments to prominent and holy persons of his day. Yes, Jesus Christ was, indeed, an angry young man when he cursed a barren fig-tree, when he denounced the Scribes and Pharisees as a generation of vipers, hypocrites, and whited sepulchres; and the gentle hands that blessed, and, it was reported, often lay softly on the diseased, their healing power lifting misery away from all whom they touched, made a whip of cords, and drove the money-changers out of the Temple. There were angry young men in every age, even, I daresay, among the cave-dwellers. There will be such till time ends — the cold, careless anger of cynical playwright and poet webbed within the lacquered vision of themselves, where every prospect pleases and all outside is vile; and those of us who see a world wonderful whose anger would drive fear from its wonder, forcing want and disease to join fear in his frightened flight from life.

So it is nought but notable nonsense for reviewer or critic to hail this shriek or wail of the despair and futility of life in play and poem as a new signal in the heavens, a dark, dead comet giving the coo sinister to the world, proclaiming by its sign that life is a mass of false hope and no promise. To some, at times it is; at times, even to a whole people, as it seems to be to a nation suffering defeat (and, at times, even when a victor) in a devastating war; but these de profundises are man-made, and grow not within the wonderful fibres of a sensible life. The long-ago poets knew this as well as we do, and displayed its misery in a far more wonderful way; and reviewer and critic should have known this before they conferred upon the young writers of today the order of the Angry Young Man.

Of course, life is as tedious as a twice-told tale to each of us some time or other. There are many sad and weary in this pleasant world of ours; there are those who wearily pass through the tedium of what the Irish call *A cur an lá inniu cuig an lae i marach* — putting the day today towards the day tomorrow, with a sullen soul and a weary body; but life is no less wonderful to the others. It can be as tedious as a twice-told tale even to children, as I'm sure it must be the time the British Broadcasting Corporation decide it is time for 'children's prayers', when old fools torment the youngsters with such pathetic lies as 'Since God looks after the wild flowers, how much more will He care for you'. Looks after the wild flowers! He goes an odd way about looking after them. Of course, He does nothing of the kind, and wild flowers have to damn well fend for themselves; as we have to do, too, though with the flowers it is an everlasting fight for existence, with us now it is a perpetual struggle forward towards educational and social development.

Life becomes a tale of an idiot when nation is set against nation, and war flames in our face to a clamor of sound and fury, signifying nothing; and life becomes an idiot's babble when we watch the few having so much, while many have so little.

There is a great difference between the writers of yesterday and those of today. The ones with us now live in a world where all the dragons are alive again, and all the knights are dead. They have rent every strip of finery from life's garment; finery of laughter, of joy, of sentiment, of courage, of romance, and of the right to tears when sorrow comes; they have dressed life in a shroud, and have spotted it with the spits of fleers, frustration, futility, and derision. But they cannot get rid of the jewels; they glitter everywhere, and hack as they may, they remain where they are, for they are woven into the very texture of life itself; courage, generosity, sympathy, tolerance, and devotion to others, known and unknown, even to the giving up of a life. These noble gems — rubies, sapphires, diamonds, onyx, beryl, and chrysolite — gleam everywhere, in all places where man lives in social union or disunion with his fellow-beings: into a blustering sea goes a Wexford lifeboat to a bunch of rocks where a ship is breaking up, while the crew cling to the shrouds. A rope flung to them is always carried aside by the powerful wind; the Cox waits for a suitable wave lifting the boat high; he jumps, lands on the ship's deck, carrying the rope; it is fixed to a mast, and, one by one, the crew climbs to the boat, the Cox the last to go; a man sees a young lad struggling in a millstream, getting carried into a river; he jumps in, grips the boy, but the rush of the waters is too strong to let him get to the bank; hours after, the bodies are recovered, the boy surrounded by an arm of the gallant man; smallpox breaks out in a Scots city; doctors and nurses unite to fight it; a doctor and two nurses die who, having saved others, couldn't save themselves; up in Belfast, a little girl of four, wandering in a garden, disturbs a wasps' nest, and is attacked by the whole hive; a girl of ten rushes to her aid, flings her coat over the child's head and shoulders, and flails away the wasps with her hands till other helpers come; she and the child are stung in many

74

places, and a doctor says that, but for the girl, the child would certainly have been stung to death. No derision of life can ever shame out of humanity the inner urge of courage and kindliness in their concern for others. Man is, at least, as kind, kindlier in fact, than God is preached to be, for man isn't responsible for most of the major disasters periodically afflicting the comfort and security of his own kind. Famine comes from Him. We are told in the hymn, 'We plough the fields and scatter the good seed on the land, but it is fed and watered by God's almighty hand.' Not always, for how often do we hear the cry that the harvest is in danger, or the harvest is lost: God burns it up with the sun, or buries it all under floods of rain and whirling winds, and the Churches pray for mercy. Tornadoes, typhoons, and tidal waves sweep over the Pacific or the Caribbees, the moon, maybe, looking on, sweep over the American lands, taking life and scattering to tinder the home where a life had lived. His hand shakes a city or a town, and an earthquake levels the town or the city into a huge, tumbled-down funeral pile. He blows on a flame in the earth beneath, and a bursting-out volcano buries a village, maybe a town, under a load of flaming, stifling ash. Pestilence, too, like the swift epidemic of 1919 that laid low in less than a year double the number of lives that were lost within four years of a bitter and bloody world-wide war. All these, by common consent, with legal recognition, are called Acts of God, and War alone is the one great calamity fashioned by the more stupid mind and fumbling hand of Man. In all these instances of calamity from Acts of God, we see the rest of the human family, who have escaped for the time being, rushing with all the help they can gather to those who need it. In all accidents, from the air, on the sea, on the land, squads of devoted men and women are ready and waiting to go to the assistance of those in need of it, often, very often, at the risk of their own lives. We have no reason whatever to be ashamed of our humanity; we have many good reasons to be proud of it.

In spite of this manifestation of concern in the core of kindred, present-day writers deride tenderness in all feelings of man, sneer at any emotion man may show in any sorrow in life, any prompting of kindness and good nature; play, poem, story, fix their thought, it seems, into making life a masque of gloom. There is no institution in the world today so rigid in its rules, so merciless in expulsion from its circle, so petrified in its dogma, as this literary institution of life's futility and despair. A sudden laugh would be a shocking heresy, a smile a thing for a warning to whatever face dared to wear one. Yet those things despised by the Latter-Day Faints of critic and author go on living, as immortal as the brook, the tree, and the lovers on Keats's Grecian urn.

How the present-day critic-godjets hate the older feeling and the older melody with a venom that seems to be partly pathological. So much so that even melody-minded Verdi in music was cast out for years, and Tennyson, the poet, cast out for ever. Such a song as 'Where is now the Merry Party?', which I one time could sing with the best of them, would be hooted out of hearing, were it not completely forgotten. The song after describing a merry party around a Christmas fire, or, during summer, among the hay, asks where are they all now; answering 'They have all dispersed and wandered, far away, far away'. It is sentimental, but it happens to be sadly true, having in it the same sad melody and feeling of

> We twa hae paidl't in the burn
> Frae mornin' sun till dine,
> But seas between us braid hae roar'd,
> Sin' auld lang syne.

Both tell us of the same sad sentiments; the same longing, conscious and subconscious, for the renewal of well-remembered things, of joyous days so far away and long ago; and, in despite of the frozen heart and cynical mind, it lives on in the warm human mind and heart of the common man. The silver bells of memory will for ever ring in human ears, the silver bells of long ago. The honk of a motor, the whirling rush of a jet-plane overhead, the rhythmic hum of a thousand machines, can never sink them into silence.

Then there is the adoration of the Mother, a cult that is unhappily overdone, and has painted many a repulsive line and gaudy color on her image, though the image in its purity stays gentle, self-denying, and influential in all classes of life. But its loveliness depends utterly upon the kind of woman the mother may be. She isn't ideal, but a human being of flesh, blood, and feeling; and is often, as I well know, a heartless, selfish, and venomous bitch. But, by and large, the mother is the greatest defender of life that life owns, both in the animal and the human kingdom. Though the need of the mother, if she be a worthy one, never dies within the feeling of a child, the child shouldn't be expected to be what the mother (or father) was, or is, remembering Shaw's remark that children, so far from regarding parents as an example, should look upon them as a warning. Parents, to be true to their children, should leave them alone. The hope of the old is never the hope of the young. The eager young are anxious to fix new stars in the sky, which, to them, shine more bravely than the stars beginning to fade.

Still, however we may regard it, the mother-image looms large in life; it is so in the painting of Picasso as well as in Raphael. I remember an uncle of mine who had a fine baritone voice, singing at weddings, even at a wake, a tender song about a young lad dying from a fatal wound received on the battlefield; and as the singer sang, I saw the tears trickling down his cheeks. Hear the loud laugh from the modern big minds! Sob-stuff! The opposite to a good-natured laugh, too. Isn't the song true, all the same? Whitman, who attended the wounded in the American Civil War, wouldn't laugh; but he was an emotional fool. To be honest, I felt it hard to keep the tears back too as the song was being sung; but then, too, I am another emotional fool:

Lying on my dying bed, Thro' the dark an' silent night,
Praying for the coming day, Came a vision to my sight,
Near me stood the forms I loved, In the sunlight's mellow gleam;
Folding me unto her breast, Mother kiss'd me in my dream.
Hopeful, I abide the hour, When will fade life's feeble beam,
Every pang has left me now — Mother kiss'd me in my dream,
Mother, Mother, kiss'd me in my dream.

Isn't it true that under such circumstances, in a time of imminent death, a boy (or a girl) may return to the memory of childhood, and, as he did then, seek his mother in the time of fear or great agony? How many young Americans, how many of our own lads, Irish and English, in the terrible moment of dying on a battlefield, may have seen the vision seen by this fictional young soldier dying on a battlefield, as they did in Europe, in Korea, and in the islands of the Pacific? I hope many, I hope all, of them did. If the mother had been one who had run to him when he was hurt, nursed him when he was ill, soothed him when he was afraid or anxious, then in his extreme hour his thoughts were bound to fix fast on her, and a vision of her would readily form a comforting picture in his terrified mind. Horrifying sentimentality to those who scorn emotional experience, yet the tears that moistened the eyes of those who listened to the song were justified and honest in that they were outward and visible signs of a full feeling of sympathy with a dying youngster fighting away the dread loneliness of death.

Feeling can be banished from play and poem, but it can never be banished out of life. It begins when a new-born child first nuzzles into the breast of its mother, and it goes on in that life till the time comes when it is transferred to another closing the eyes of the dead, once the new-born babe. We would be curious, cold beings without feelings, and a poem or play without them is just as strange, and more than cold. Bitterness, cynicism, and despair are, in themselves, feelings, even though they be born in the brain; but so is hope, so is sympathy, so is love. They have all the same birthplace, and are not bastards; so none can say those are more aristocratic than are these. We have you there, gentlemen and ladies. So he who keeps a tear tightly in its place is no more eminent than he who freely lets it flow. Hope, sympathy, and love are abstract terms; no one can even imperfectly define them, but we know what they mean, for they, at one time or another, are within us all. They are all eternal, lasting as long as mankind lasts; born even

among the robots, as was documented in Karel Čapek's
play of *R.U.R.* Feeling is a faculty common to all
living things. Even the vegetable world feels in its
own way; they shrink from physical cold and expand
to the heat; they feel any rupture to their form, a
broken stem, a hacked-off branch. So we, too, feel
physical shocks, sudden cold or sudden heat, the wound
from an operation or an accident; but the definition
of the physical feeling is as inexpressible as those of
the abstract ones from love or from hope. So since
we can't take this feeling away, this emotion that is
common to all things — even to those who taboo them
— to banish it from poem or play is to banish it, not
from life, but to banish life from the poem and the play.

There is the emotion of sorrow tingling the nerves
at the death of a loved one; felt by the greater poets as
well as the less in the weepy verses of the Victorians, the
one just as true in its feeling of sorrow as the other.
Shakespeare's outcry for a child lost to a mother:

> Grief fills the room up of my absent child,
> Lies in his bed, walks up and down with me,
> Puts on his pretty looks, repeats his words,
> Remembers me of all his gracious parts,
> Stuffs out his vacant garments with his form,

is much more lovely, but no more sincere than the
Victorian song mourning a dead child:

> Under the willow she's laid with care
> (Sang a lone mother while weeping),
> Under the willow with golden hair,
> My little one's quietly sleeping.
>
> Under the willow by night and day,
> Sorrowing ever, I ponder;
> Free from its shadowy glooming ray,
> Ah! never again can she wander.

Soppy sob-stuff, of course, to the literary hierarchy of principalities, powers, thrones, and judgements. It hasn't quite got the poetic beauty and swing of Shakespeare's lines, but the passionate sorrow of the woman whose little girl lies under a willow tree (or any other kind of tree, under grass, or under clay) is as deep and genuine as that of Constance for her Arthur, though then only a prisoner in the hands of John. So goes the terrible uniformity of grief, knowing nor race, nor class, nor creed; and the sorrow of the American mother mourning for a son lost in Korea is neither more nor less deep than that of the Chinese mother mourning another, lost in the same wild place, both of them denied even the agonised blessing of murmuring a sad farewell to either boy.

Feeling, rather than thought or detachment, seems to dominate the world of life. It was not thought but feeling that led the way to human development, for the meaning of the word is based on the word 'to grope', and life, in its first stage of withdrawal from the world's waters, must have felt, groped, its way in to the land. When hands grew handier, we groped our way forward more accurately, and, even today, with all our knowledge and our dependence on mind, the fingers retain an amazingly delicate sense of touch. We usually trust our feelings. How does one feel towards this or that? How often the question is asked! 'I felt sympathy towards him or her: I felt obliged to do that or this; I felt it was time to go; I feel something is bound to happen': the examples of the use of feeling are a multitude, and there is no escape from them, even in a snarl of a poem or snarl of a play, for cynicism itself is prompted by the feeling that there is little or no hope in humanity. Feeling isn't always good. There are feelings of hatred as well as those of love; the feeling of Caligula was very different from the feeling of Christ towards humanity. 'How often would I have gathered ye to me as a hen gathereth her chickens under her wing, and ye would not!' What a passionate blend of the feeling of love and regret was there! How He used feeling as an argument too — 'Reach forth thy finger and thrust it into my hand, and thy hand, and thrust it into my side; and be not faithless but believing.' Think how we may, emotion plays a tremendous part in the good or bad development of our humanity.

Seeing that emotion can be so evil or so good in determining our outlook on life, we shouldn't be so damned ready, even eager, to thrust a dagger-jibe through a simple sentimental mind or heart composing a sentimental song, or singing one. These had in them a commonplace pathos that was deeply felt by the ordinary people who heard them sung, or tried to sing them themselves. Such songs as 'The Anchor's Weighed', 'In the Shade of the Old Apple Tree', 'My Pretty Jane', had a deep feeling within them, which, when they were sung, flowed into the breast of the listener. And it wasn't much of a wonder, either, for they were earnest, though far from poetical, easily understood at a swift hearing among beer-bottles and tumblers of lemonade, or tea with a slice of currant-tinted cake. Take the song, 'When your Hair turns to Silver, I will Love you just the same': is not its implication similar to that of the more elegant and lyrical one by Moore, 'Believe Me if all those endearing young Charms'? They were appreciated in most Irish homes long before the lust for popular success beclouded the land darkly; before the pops or the juke-box were born; before that ghastliest of all musical events was brought into being — the International competition for the best popular song of the year. These old Victorian songs were the best that their composers could do. Except as sheet music, they had no way to success, and they depended on the feeling they aroused in those who sang them and in the minds of those who heard. Beyond a tiny royalty on the sale of the sheet-music, they got little from them. The biggest reward they got, or could ever hope to get, was the pride felt in their wan but honest creation; and, remembering this, we need to give them a little more honor than a jibe.

The superior ones, plumed with and primed with higher aesthetics, scorn more than these simple rhymers: they have cast as forcibly as they could the American poet Whitman, and the English poet Tennyson, into a Hades where grows no asphodel, nor any rosemary of remembrance. Even these, even they, are banished by the big shots, the pashas of literature. Whitman the big yawp! Ay, but what a yawp! One that has become the yawp of all humanity. Tennyson, leaning on Whitman for support in Hades, has to listen to Sir Something Nicolson calling him something like a posturing puppet; while the poet Auden is reported as declaring that 'Without a doubt, Tennyson was the most stupid of English poets'. Since Auden was Professor of Poetry at Oxford University, it follows that his genius becomes an authority in criticism. However, it is a pity, a misfortune, that Tennyson was so musical in his stupidness; a sad thing that Tennyson should be so lusty in his graceful enjoyment of, and his hope in, life, something, possibly, that Auden couldn't enter, and, even if he did, couldn't understand. In spite of the fact that Tennyson would dance a minuet while Robbie would be doing a Highland fling; in spite of Tennyson's grandiloquence and grace, there is something of the heartiness of Robbie Burns in Tennyson; none whatever of this spirit of the Scot in Auden. In spite of Tennyson's grace and beauty, he has a joy of life that would grow cold entering the poetic mind of Auden. For long, I myself thought little about Tennyson, less about his work, and he was known to me — told to me by others — as 'The Rectory Lawn Poet'. Well, he did meet, did know, the visitors to the rectory lawn, but he also knew the farmer and worker of Lincoln, knew the fauna and the flora of places where he strolled; was intensely curious about the politics of England and the birth of a dragon-fly; he loved them all as Shakespeare did, peering into many things, and trying to understand them all. Tennyson kept an alert ear cocked to the science of his day; a prophet, too, who saw in a glass darkly, warning us of armies grappling in the upper blue, teeming down a ghastly dew upon our English homes. Now we silently dread a ghastly dew showering down upon our own heads from high up, or lobbed upon us from a long distance away. He understood a great deal, and the story the brook tells of her life is very simple and very beautiful — in its rustic way, as great as Joyce's curiously talkative Anna Livia Plurabelle. It was one of the few poems I learned in my boyhood, and the years have not faded its loveliness for me. When in Coole, Galway, Lady Gregory challenged me to find the source of Coole River, which, she said, bubbled up from a spring, half-hidden by abundant growth, some four or five miles away from Coole House. Day after

day, while staying with her, I roamed about seeking
the spring that gave birth to the river and afterwards
spread out into the wide Coole Lake where wild swans
swam. One day, going down a narrow channel,
flanked on either side by a loose-piled stone wall,
entering a wild field, dense with tangled shrubbery, I
heard the gurgling of bubbling waters, and down in
a foxglove, ferny hollow, I found the spring that became a brook, grew into a river, then widened into
the broad-breasted Lake of Coole; the sparkling water
surging up now in a rush, bending down fern and
foxglove, covering the loosestrife, and laying it flat;
then dwindling to a gentler outflow, so gentle at times
that the attentive ear alone could hear the murmur of
its purling push upward; and in among the fern, the
foxgloves, the loosestrife, were great clumps of long-
stemmed forget-me-nots, round about as well, forming
an enchanting little valley of bright and cloudy blue
and pinkish blossoms. A little way from where it
rived the earth to come to life, it stole away, rippling
against stem of foxglove, meadow-sweet, and fern,
swaying them aside to trickle out among the farther
forget-me-nots, and further on at a distance I saw
the gleam of its waters, showing that it was
strengthening into a Tennyson brook, later to
become a river, and, last thrust of all, to sigh and
surge itself out into the wide and womanly Lake of
Coole.

After days of searching, I had come upon it, suddenly, for I had no thought of finding it a few steps
beyond the clumsily-clever, stoned walls; and the
beautiful spring had revealed herself, not by sight, but
by sound, for I had heard her song, her gentle song,
before I had seen her; there she was in her veil of

blossom, showing her sparkling nakedness between them all. Seek and ye shall find, Lady Gregory had said, and if you come to where it is, you shall find a jewel that no hand can ever take away. Willie Yeats, she went on, searched for it several times, but never found it. No visitor yet can say he saw it. Seek it, Sean, and, if you find it, you will be glad in your heart. He had found it — the well at the world's end of Coole. He followed its winding for a while, till he came to where it was a narrow brook across which an active lad of twelve could jump. Yet Willie Yeats had never seen it; he had seen the lake, some of the river, but had never seen the brook or the spring that made them all. I wonder why? So enchanted with the white thin bone of a hare, or with beauty of an evening full of the linnet's wings, that he couldn't find time to go on a pilgrimage to find a spring, bosomed in a mass of foxglove, fern, and forget-me-not. Strange to think that Yeats had come to Coole, had gone again; had come and gone again, and yet had never seen the spring or the brook. Yet here were both of them in front of me; beautiful, and never to be forgotten. I had never looked at the world through the white thin bone of a hare, but I had enjoyed more than one lovely evening at Coole, sitting on a bench outside Coole House, a fig-tree behind me, watching a red-and-green sunset on a far horizon, evening full of the linnet's wings; but this here was a discovery, something lovely found after a long, deliberate search, and I felt as Cortez felt when he stood on the peak in Darien. I felt — emotion again! Feeling — sentimentality, but very lovely and very enjoyable, and one of the finer parts of life. Just as, when I looked ahead, the brook awoke in me memories of the brook I knew only from the words in an old school-book:

> I come from haunts of coot and hern,
> I make a sudden sally,
> And sparkle out among the fern
> To bicker down a valley.

What a simple and lovely description of the birth-place of a brook! The haunt of coot and hern, and here it was before me, though here was lonely loveliness, for there were neither coot nor hern among the fern, the forget-me-not, or the foxglove. I doubt if there be any among the modern, haughty-browed poets who could compose such a simple and so charming a song about a brook as this one by this scorn-crowned Tennyson. The fact seems to be that this bosom of beauty, seen in Coole, would horrify most of them. They would call on Hades to get her away, did they see Core picking the flowers from plain or river-bank: away with her — she and her flowers are too lovely for this life! We know the facts of natural life; that fern, foxglove, and forget-me-not push and writhe in a strife for the perpetuation, each for its own species; but when they do it in their finest clothes how beauti-ful each of them is in its own way in the midst of a struggle for existence! In spite of its simplicity and country color, there is a voice here, and a way, too.

In prescent play and poem, there is a Voice, but there is no way, except it be a way to the tomb. Prob-ably the best known and most praised poet in England today is Mr. W. H. Auden, who long seems to have searched for a way, but never found one, though he has never lost the Voice. There is no more color or light in the voice than in a firework blurring or bloom-ing a second-long shape before a sullen sky, fading away into the sullenness of the same indifferent sky. As soon as the one flashes, it fades; as soon as the other is read, it passes into the shadow of something that has never lived. The stars are pinched from the sky, and no home fire is left burning. There is no tear in it, no sobbing aloud or sob in the silence; no anger, lust, no courage, neither sigh nor yelp; nothing but a faint feeling of a passing touch from a wispy exhalation. The ghost of Petrushka without its squeak. The sparrows have certainly well failed to make him feel at home. His Muse seems to be ever doing a dance of the seven veils or a burlesque strip-tease (intellectual) carousel. Poetry and all first-class literature seems now to be entirely intellectual, too elevated to defile, even to smudge it with heart or bowel. Recently (November 1960) Mr. Stephen Spender, judge of a poetry competition, said 'the works submitted (3000 of them) showed that intellectual poetry was still predominant'. *Predomine dirige nos!* If this be so, then Mr. Auden is the feathered chief of the intellectual poets, for I have heard it said several times by high intellectual authority that Mr. Auden is the predominant poet and has had the greatest influence, in fellow-forms and fellow-outcries, upon the younger poets now flooring the literature-land: he is a visible and aural choice, for the best of them even lag a long way behind. It's a long, long way to the skill and word-choice of Auden; so in considering him, we take the whole, for the whole is greater than the multitudes of perts. It is a strange swarming of poetry, each poem wearing the same tartan of woe is me, woe is you, and woe is all, like a one-note siren warning life against itself in a never-ending wailing blow; and a bevy of saint, scholar, critic, and school-tie townies keep ears cocked to the carrying wind, and, when the wind blows the wrong way, press an ear to the ground so as not to lose a whiff of it. All those whose nerves thrushes cannot soothe, listen, and say How lovely! What Swinburne said of the pale Galilean, the world of poetics says of Auden: Thou hast conquered, the world has grown grey from thy breath. Yet the world sings; yet the sky is often blue; and wherever we may go, we hear the sound of dancing in the glide of the waltz or the tap-tap of Variety; life cannot believe in death. This sort of poetry has a dark philosophy, altogether opposed to the urge to live; a wordy world of Hieronymus Bosch, but life makes her own pictures, and though the purple of joy at times changes to a black hue of sorrow, there remain the crimson and gold bordering every horizon. It is, all the same, a sad thing that these clever young upstarts in poesy should labor so hard to turn the world and all its thought to a land of condors, sick cattle, and dead flies. Reading these poems and thinking of them as they are read, it would seem that all, or almost all, of them are bummed from what the poets conceive to be Freud's psycho-analytical philosophy; but are they Freudian or fraudian facts? Is Auden's mind a mirror of Freud's? Is he (and they) holding the Freudian mirror up to nature? Present-day playwright and poet have made for Freud, as wild-minded fans rush at this film star or that fluffy-haired crooner; they have torn the shirt from Freud's back, and would, if they could, do the same with his shroud — any sort of a relic so long as it gives them a touch of his magic. They skim over his *Interpretation of Dreams*, and off they go! Lackaday! There is more in the human mind than even Freud found. These poets and playwrights know so much; Freud knew so little; that one is pushed into believing that they are the supreme Ids and Egos of modern literature. They ignore the fact that the science of neurology has a lot to do with all these things, the material structure of the body's nervous system that carries all feeling to the brain — even those felt by these poets, playwrights, the woe-filled word-forms that flow (emanate?) from their spectacular brains; from the deepdown void of Id, Ego, super-subconsciousness; taken from airy nothing, but never yielding a local habitation and a name. Each seems to have a special electronic eye in the centre of the mind.

Indeed, Mr. Auden implies that Freud did not know enough, in his poem, *In Memory of Sigmund Freud*:

> But his wish was denied him; he closed his eyes
> Upon that last picture common to us all,
> Of problems like relatives standing
> Puzzled and jealous about our dying.

'The world', says Auden, 'is an oyster with nothing in it.' An empty shell! Nothing in it for him or for any of us? An empty shell: this seems to be the cap-badge and pennon of almost all the poet-tribe today. None armed with a burnished bow; not even one of ash or willow; and no desire to shoot into the air or wind or rain; not even a wish to let others try their hand with cloth-yard and yew bow; none of them armed even with a burning pestle. The world's oyster is a big one, a wide one, and has something for every man who dips into it; and the lucky dips are as many as the unlucky dippers fingering out gifts that disappoint. To use a gift gotten out of the world's oyster isn't easy, but how should we grow in strength and wisdom if all things were easy to do? There is happiness in things done: in the fixing of a fuse, the cooking of a meal, the hanging of a door; but these are probably things so insignificant as to be beyond the poet's notice. He has never seen the pride on the face of an apprentice-carpenter when he first realises he can use the hammer, the chisel, and the saw; or on the face of the apprentice-bricklayer when he steps back to view his first brick-course well and truly laid; or even the laborer when he feels that shovel and pick are at home in his hands. These in their simpler ways are as triumphant as the creation of art in any form, and it is by these gifts that we live, move, and have our being; and it is these that have placed the walls around, corridor and arch, and roof over the very building where the poet himself parodes around and about his own art. If Mr. Auden thinks as he says

> To talk the dictionary through,
> Without a chance word coming true,
> Is more than Darwin's apes could do,

he might well remember that he himself can make a damn fine try at talking a dictionary through; and also, if a chance word be true, the apes are in themselves extraordinary creatures, and he and I and all of us have a kinship with them; nor is there shame in regarding an ape as a distant sister or brother. The Logos is what is done as well as what is said; the Logos is flesh and blood, and good things done by the hands are words, though the poems written by most up-to-date, fashionable writers seem to be but words, sounds only that flit into one ear and out of the other of any common reader who is still in a state of activity. His volley-fire thoughts have little power of piercing; they

pass by and vanish like the rippling airs coming from
the flutter of a fan.

Within the Reith Lectures, broadcast over the
B.B.C., under the title of *Art and Anarchy*, Edgar
Wind, Professor of the History of Art at Oxford University, deals eloquently with the present art habit of
dehumanising painting and literature; and he seems
to believe that its influence has lost power and
penetration; it is no longer dangerous. It has become so diffused, so widespread, so common, that
humanity, reading or looking, shrug it off; though
they find it interesting; they may admire the genius
of that painter, this poet, but the influence of either
lingers with them for the moments through which
they look or read, and then weaves a way into the forget-
fulness of a calm indifference. The cocks and cockerels
of despair and futility crow, but the call stretches their
own necks only, only their own wings clap; the blackbird and thrush sing away, and the crow caws as the
crow always did; and man goes his way untroubled.

God and Everyman know that O'Casey is no fit judge
of poetry. He has never studied it and never wished
to do so. Indeed, he has studied but a few things such
as geography, the first three principles of grammar, a
little arithmetic, and left the rest to God. All the same,
he has read a lot, among which was a large part called
poetry from Langland to an attempt to read Ezra
Pound's *Cantos*. So he has opinions, and courage or
audacity to blurt them out before all who stay to listen
to them. These are some of them, a kind of a *Dance
with Kitty Stobling*. There is no question that Auden is
a poet, for the world proclaims him so. As with film
stars there is a pin-up girl, so in poetry there is a pin-up
poet, and Auden is he — a chief among his tribe. He

is, I imagine, a first-class representative of the present-day trend in the formation and philosophy of verse. He is the greatest Jeremiah of them all. To me the method, the rhythm, as apart from the philosophy, is very monotonous and very dull. The poetry seems to have no more variety in tone or in measure than a war-siren sounding for hours; the siren played or blown in a minor key; a continuous roll on a muffled drum. It doesn't rouse, it doesn't sadden, it doesn't enrage, it doesn't lull: it deadens. It has nothing to do with the prosodical method of the verse — if this be the correct term, — for Tennyson's *In Memoriam* is in the same rhythm throughout, but it saddens, it lulls, and, to anyone who has lost a beloved one, it is often very dear; it has in it the music of a clarinet. The same can be said for Byron's *Childe Harold*, played on an augmented orchestra, on violin, clarinet, flute, trumpet, and drum. But Tennyson and Byron are now *non grata*, exiled from living literature to make way for the despairing poets who remind me of a verse by some American poet which says — if I remember right:

> A ship alive becomes to him a hull
> Charred and undone; the fumble of a wreck;
> His dreams are but the droppings of a gull
> Caught in a noose of seaweed round his neck;
> And crying like a maniac towards the sky,
> He pulls mankind in after him, to die.

These deadening poets are budding out in thousands. In the recent Guinness Poetry Competition (the great brewery firm of Dublin), the entries, 3000 of them, were judged by John Press, Stephen Spender, and Patrick Kavanagh, who, it seems, were worn out before they finished reading the lot. What a lot! John Press said of this 'unrelenting flow of verse' that

93

it was 'insignificant, and there seemed to be little new poetic talent'. Spender said 'the verse submitted showed the dominance of "intellectual" poetry. He had looked for energy and brilliant imagery, giving force to ordinary humane feeling'; and Patrick Kavanagh said, 'he was depressed before so much competent but uninspired verse, and felt that the versification obscured the work of the real poets'. Looks as if Guinness's poetry wasn't good for him or the two other judges. Uninspired intellectuality! Now, who showed these 3000 aspirants the way? Who showed them the target they must aim at? Where is the energy and the humanity in the poetry of our major poets today? Life with them seems to be either rushing to destruction like the Gadarene swine, or running headlong down a hill. 'The dream', as Auden says, 'always leads to the nightmare garden'; or as dull as 'Mrs. Dale's Diary'. As for being 'humane', or even human, full of 'ordinary human feelings', there is not a touch of them in any poem, because they don't seem to know what ordinary human feelings are, or what they are like. How would the poets mentioned respond to

> All the world seems sad and lonely, Nellie Dean;
> For I love you, and you only, Nellie Dean,
> And I wonder if on high
> You still love me, if you sigh
> For the happy days gone by,
> Nellie Dean?

Or I wonder if these three Poet-Judges would take a tea-break from their scrutiny to sing lustily in unison such a humane ballad as 'I'm one of the Ruins that Cromwell knocked about a Bit'; or would Mr. Auden throw off his academic robes while lecturing, to have a go at the singing of ' Daisy, Daisy, give me your

Answer do', calling on his students to have a go with him, too? It might — you never can tell — put a bit of the energy, human feeling, and imagination, seemingly needed, according to poets themselves, in the verses coming and the verses still to come. They are, in a way, a comic lot, misery-mes walking the world like those evangelists who warn us that hell is all around us. Yet, at times, they seem to say nay one minute, yea the next. A play has been mentioned wher'in we are told of the 'boredom, fatigue, and sheer brutal routine of a couple having to live together'. Again in a poem entitled *Les Sylphides*, the poet describes a young gullant taking his donah to a ballet. They sit close, watching the white skirts whirling, each girdled with a red sash; calyx upon calyx like Canterbury bells in the breeze, incensed by the sweep of the music, and so they married to be more together: the more we are together, the merrier we shall be; but they were never again so much together, separated by morning tea, by the evening paper; and waking at night, she wondered if it was worth while, and why the river had flowed away, and where were the white flowers. So one is miserable (according to the playwright) because they are too much together; the other miserable (according to the poet) because they're not together oftener. These misery-mes have it both ways, and we have never had it so bad.

It is a comic tease to the mind to regard the curious coloration of the conceits of the modern writers; how they so obstinately and truculently insist in play and poem on inflicting their own views of life and its futility on every other mind, insolently saying, This is the life all know; you've got to take it; there is none other.

Not only that, but they would bomb with many words romantic poetry or romantic novels, and make a Guernica of the whole of them. Even Shakespeare doesn't go scot-free, and we have Auden's *Caliban to the Audience* in which a bulldozer of leaden sentences ruthlessly demolishes the romance and fantasy, along with Prospero, Miranda, and Ferdinand, leaving not a wrack behind! It reminds one of a lad acting the aggressive cowboy shooting down fantastic enemies with sharp and loud shouts of Bang Bang Bang! It was followed by a Third Programme broadcast of reflections by Alonso, songs by Trinculo and Stephano, Miranda, and the rest, who tottered into and then out of the recesses of the poet's mind, whispering to him, presumably, what to say, what they are really thinking; shove Shakespeare aside, and give the world the Real McCoy. Young Ferdinand lying in the arms of his Miranda is warned by Alonso:

> So, if you'd prosper, suspect those bright
> Mornings when you whistle with a light
> Heart

(How could mornings be bright if he had to suspect them?)

So passes the pageant of dejective dullness, bullying us, or trying to bully us, away from the bright morning of Shakespeare's play. I wonder what this poet would make of Yeats's magic 'Lake Isle of Innisfree', with its evening full of the linnet's wings. We have been bullied away from Milton, Shelley, from Tennyson, now an attempt, apparently, is being made to bully us away from the greatness and beauty of Shakespeare! Life takes a sip of tea with these thinker-poets, nods her head, and goes on to have a deep carouse with Shakespeare and the other auld-lang-syne poets, feeling that the modern poetry may be grand, though dull, realising that a dull grandee is as dull as a dull tramp; and feeling within herself that many a brave heart, though not light, can still keep whistling when the dark morning dawns. Life cannot take as valid the lipso dixit of the poet-judges sitting atop of the high green hill, sitting always by the sea, and they donning their black caps to pronounce a death sentence on the world. We shall dance the bright mornings out and thrust forward through the dark ones while we whistle the brighter mornings back.

It's no go!

It's no go the gloom or the pessimistic bawl,
It's no go the death-cry, it's no go at all;
Life saunters jauntily, life always has her say,
Plays her games, has a dance, and wears her ribbons gay.

It's no go the poet's round of ever-present doom,
For her laughter's heard in London streets and in the Devon
    coombe.
It's no go the lesson teaching ev'ry step's a fall,
For life gets quick up on her feet, so it's no go at all!

It's no go the chanting of the poet's Doomsday Song,
That everything that's right becomes just everything that's
    wrong;
For life can even sing of life twixt St. Peter and St. Paul;
So it's no go thinking differ, it's no go at all (!).

So life comes back to the simple folksong and sentimental ballad, abandoning with a nod and a wink the dark mumbo-jumbo memento of the prostrate poets bowing to the god of ruin, and returns to the urge of life, of building, to the call of our common humanity; to the activities of community struggle, its work, its sorrows, and its joys, its fuss by day, its calm by night

— refusing to stay under the banner of the Weary-
Willie poets and the Tired-Tim playwrights; back to
human feeling and human emotions — tinker, tailor,
soldier, sailor, rich man, poor man, beggar man, thief.
We wheel away from the dark vision from Prime to
Lauds, and go back to the emotion of a moon behind
a hill, love's old sweet song, the dark-eyed sailor as
his ship weighs anchor finding that parting is such
sweet sorrow as he kisses his girl goodbye; away
from the self-exalting obscurities of pompous poetry
to the young soldier dying on a distant battlefield,
almost happy as he goes from life because his mother
has kissed him in a dream (oddly, in the roughening
and poet-handling of the old Greek play, Jean Cocteau
makes Oedipus call out for his mother when in the
grip of the Sphinx, in his *The Infernal Machine*, and,
again, when he stabs out his eyes with the brooch
from Jocasta's scarf, and is a lost man, a vision brings
his mother to help and comfort him); back to the
sorrow of 'Alice, Where Art Thou?' and the rollicking mood of 'I'm One of the Ruins that Cromwell
knocked about a Bit'. Even soldiers marching towards death could sing 'Pack up your Troubles in
your Old Kit Bag', and Shaw's soldier goddamns
marching to down Joan and the Dauphin of France
sang, too, Rum tum stumble dum, bacon fat and
rumpledum mid the thunder of the guns and the
flutter of a kingfisher's wings. The wonderful verve,
resilience, and carry-on courage of our common humanity! And it all springs from simple thoughts and the
love of simple things. Let these woe-filled poets of
the defunctorum consider the lilies of the field, simple
in color, simple in beauty, yet Solomon in all his glory
wasn't arrayed like one of them; and in all great art

of music, literature, architecture, painting, these simple thoughts and love of simple beauty are vividly embedded, for from these simple things all great things are born and blossom. What are these great ones in science and all arts but taller-stemmed and more brilliantly-colored blossoms shining above the myriad others thronging them round, all springing from, and receiving their life out of, the good earth. But the new poetic and playwriting minds will have nothing to do with these, have forgotten them, their voices lost in the noise of the bell the poet pulls; but he for whom the bell tolls is not life, but the poet who pulls it; dong dong dong! Life is far away from its sound; life hears not, cares not, too busy with her own tasks, her own joys, her own hopes, her own great achievements.

> It's no go the squealin' or the megaphonic call,
> The big ship of life slips by the doomer's little yawl;
> It's no go for doomsday buskers, no go at all.

> It's no go the fun'ral bell to halt the march of man,
> For all that nonsense now is but a horse that also ran;
> Ye may twist your academic robes to make a coffin's pall,
> But it's no go, ye doomsday buskers, no go at all!

Sic transit gloria scripta lugubrisium poetica dullorosa.

For a' this an' a' that, Auden remains a magical weaver of words; it is only before the philosophy of the poetry that I try to stand and give challenge. T. S. Eliot and he, side by side, claim the poet-primacy of all England; the rest follow twenty to fifty verse-miles behind the pair of them.

99

UNDER A GREENWOOD TREE HE DIED

*To all mothers and fathers mourning loved
ones who died too young.*

THAT is all he is now: a hand of greeting falls for ever
upon a sad sweet shadow.

He had come down from London bringing his
sister, Shivaun, with him, in the little red Ford van,
to spend Christmas and the holidays at home. He
looked somewhat tired, but there was a good reason,
more than one, why he should look a little pale, and
feel a little weary. A week before, he had come down
in the red van, bringing some friends with him, to
attend a party given by the Bursar of Dartington Hall
School for his daughter's coming of age; and had
driven back to London the next morning, taking the
friends with him, so that all could end college or school
term before the bells rang for the festival, before the
holly was carried in to hang on a wall or crown a picture. Before that, he had rushed into busy activity,
with Shivaun, preparing for the great meeting in
Trafalgar Square, carrying a banner in the procession,
while Shivaun at his side carried another; all to show,
and all to prove, that peace rather than war and aggres-
sion was the present and the future ideal of the young.
So Eileen and I whispered together that what with
his running around and his biological studies at
London University, he had overdone it, had wearied
himself, and what he needed was a good long rest.
God knows, he has gotten it. Never again will he
shout in a demonstration for peace; never carry a

banner. But, for the moment, he was just a little tired. We little knew, nor did he know, that he had already drunken a deep glass of Mr. Weston's Good Wine.

The next day, fifteenth of December, he went with Eileen to Dr. Doran, who said he had a very acute attack of anaemia, and that he would know its depth and extent when a sample of the lad's blood had been tested in the laboratory. On the eighteenth the disease was declared to be leukaemia, and Niall knew that he had been sentenced to death with a scant chance of any reprieve; a chance in ten that he might survive for a month or two longer. The ambulance would come in half an hour to take him away, away to hospital; the second time the ambulance came here — first for me exactly a year ago; now it came for Niall, our darling boy; came to bring him on his way to death; not here shalt thou die, but in London where thou wast born. I went in to him while we waited for the ambulance to come. He looked up at me, no tear in his eye, but a wistful look asking me something silently. I took his hand in mine, and felt the pressure of his, a pressure that was wistfully asking me something, something I felt to be Why and Whither? I pressed his dear hand as lovingly and as encouragingly as I could; again, he returned the pressure.

'It's hellish', he murmured, very lowly. He said no more, so we stayed together, hand in hand, he in bed, I sitting on the bed's side, close to him as I could get; leaving him but for a few moments to see the specialist, Dr. Haddon, who had come down to examine him, and who was to follow him to Exeter Hospital to do all science could do to soften a disease science knew very little about. He told us that he dared not give any comfort; that the most science could do, with its present knowledge, was to try to keep the boy with us for a month or two longer. Only another month or two — oh, Jesus, and our boy would be no more with us; never come in, never go out, never sit at table, never lead us in a bright and reckless laugh, never inquire what I thought of a book I, or he, had just read, never drive or ride in the red van again, never drive his mother about in her Minx car, never wear the bright blue jersey we had gotten him for Christmas. In another month or so he would be gone, and already he heard the rushing of the dark river across which he would soon have to go, leaving the rest of us on the farther bank; away from our sight for ever. But there was hope: those doomed by doctors did not always die. He was a vital lad; he had an intense desire to go on living; he would fight against death to the end; so there was still hope in our hearts, but hope herself was ever murmuring within our minds, there is no hope.

The ambulance-men came into the room and gently lifted Niall from the bed on to the stretcher to take him from the home he loved, the home he would never see again. I bent down to kiss him, and his lips clung longingly to mine, as if he would gather back again from my poor breathing the life he was losing. 'My young darling boy,' I murmured, as I kissed him again, 'May God go with you'; and, oh, I could not guess the agony that was in his mind as he could not guess the agony that was in mine. The evil bud of an anxious dread was alive and growing in the heart of mother, father, brother, and sister, and growing, too, in the beating heart of our sick boy.

For Niall, the active and delightful communion with family and with friend would be lost for ever: never again would he play treble on the piano to Shivaun's or Breon's bass of some piece by Beethoven or Mozart; when I mentioned the great lizards' failure to survive, never again would he tell me that they were far from a failure, that they had roamed this earth for a hundred million years, and, if man could live so long, it would be well; never again would he put on cricket-pads to go out to bat, or don shorts and crimson jersey for a football game; never again would I hear his merry and prolonged laugh in the next room, so hilarious that it made me join in alone in my own chair in my own room; never go out again, alone with him, or between him and Breon, to stroll along Dartington Drive, by the river Dart, through a summer evening, returning in the deeper dusk, the gentle evening star aglow within the colors of an opal and amethystine sky; walking together while it was yet light before the darkness came upon him, came upon our young and darling boy; a few brief moments in the garden of life, going where the primroses go, and then the night came, and we lost him, lost our boy in the midst of the darkness. As he entered the darkness, the little subdued cry of 'I must confess, I feel a little frightened'; and then the quiet resignation, and, last, the rambling, broken by clear periods, and then the rambling again, and lastly, the quiet, calm disappearance. Our darling boy, our dear, darling boy was gone. But this last had not come yet: he was lifted into the ambulance, Eileen, dry-eyed and cheerful, a bruising ache in her heart, went with him, holding his hand, ready with a loving pressure to help him on his wan way, while I sought the solitude of thought to will with all the nerve-power, all the vitality left in me after just seventy-seven years of life, that our boy would not bow before the doctors' judgement, but would be able to mingle his young life with the life of the family and the life of the world again; my mind following the ambulance to Exeter, looking at the boy stretched in it, his mother lovingly holding one hand, death grimly gripping the other.

For the next few days, Eileen stayed close to Niall, her shadow falling on the hospital walls, her saucy presence, pressing down an aching heart, strolling into the ward where he lay, his finely-formed hand fluttering out to warm itself within her enclosing clasp, his eyes alight, for the bed for a while checked its growth into a tomb. Silently, the boy's eyes said Mother, and, as silently, hers said My darling son. For the next few days, Breon and Shivaun went to Exeter to keep in touch with Eileen, and on the eve of Christmas Eve I set out with them, watching the blurred forms of tree and house hurrying by as the car journeyed through the fog and the misty rainfall. He had had a number of blood transfusions, the blood coming from a vessel above through a tube and then a needle into a vein in the arm, tightly bandaged so that no movement might upset the slow and silent drip, a young lad being buoyed up with the richer blood of another, someone, a brother or sister unknown, who had thought 'Silver and gold have I none, but what I have, that I give unto thee'; the blood flowed into the waiting vein, drop by drop, slowly, taking hours to spill out its last drop of healing virtue, Eileen holding the boy's free hand during the buzzing discomfort to vein and feeling from the blessed intrusion of a comrade's blood, till the restlessness eased, till the boy grew drowsy, till the drowsiness strengthened into a painless sleep, and the finely-formed hand of the lad no longer sought a contact with the mother's. Oh, the sad shadow of a coming event when no contact could be sought, no contact could be given. Lulla, lulla, lulla, lullaby; the restlessness of body and of thought is hushed in sleep, but it is a hush more dead than any sleep, unwilling sleep for one so young, so active, and yesterday, but yesterday, his mind was so quietly thronged with ideas of what the future would bring him forth to do.

So within the car I swung into Exeter for the first time, an old city knowing many names from the time of William the Conqueror and King Alfred, still a little rueful from the bombs that shook its walls during the last big war, known to most for its cathedral, to me for its hospital; a city that will for ever now give an ache to my memory, for here our son made his first stop on his way to death. A huge building where many find healing and many find the end. Visitors went in two at a time, and Breon and Shivaun were the first to go, Eileen and I waiting till their allowance of time had ended. Anxious to see Niall, we moved slowly to the doorway, entered, going slowly down the corridor towards the ward where our son lay.

By the door of the ward where he lay we waited; still we stood, silently waiting for Breon and Shivaun to come out so that we might go in to stand where our young son lay dying. Motionless we waited to go in and stand beside where he lay, our hearts aching, minds thoughtless, refusing to believe that our boy was bound to die. At that time there was but one life worth saving — the life of our dear boy. Nurses flitted by us, efficient, unsparing of themselves.

Doctors, white-coated, strode by, cool, sure, for ever facing pain and death, fighting to remove the pain, fighting to keep back death from coming too soon. Two of these were giving our Niall ever and never-tiring attention; but Eileen knew in her heart, and Sean did too, that their urgent and constant skill would not do: it wasn't good enough. No doctor the world over could save boy or girl stricken down with acute leukaemia. It was just a question of time, and a very short time, too. We waited between the clean white walls of the corridor, so calm, so dignified, that it was hard to imagine Death would disturb so precise and passionless a place. But Death was there; Death was near, right between the mother and the father of the young lad, almost ready now to take his hand and go.

We met Breon and Shivaun coming out, and were warned not to be shocked to find Niall talking oddly, and finding it impossible to say a full sentence. We hurried into the ward, to the bedside, and found him calm and quiet as ever, but worried that he had to be mute, and could not talk or tell his thoughts to those who had come to hear them. 'Pencil', he murmured; 'I . . . write.' Eileen gave him one, and he wrote down how he felt, how his throat seemed to lock itself away from speech, suggesting that Eileen should ask the Sister why. Eileen hurried away, returning to tell us that the Sister said Niall being in a low condi-tion had caught some slight infection; that it wasn't to worry him, and that it had nothing to do with the prime disease. So Eileen and I convinced ourselves, convinced Niall, that he had no need to worry; but out of kindness, the Sister had deceived us, for the locked throat was indeed another grip the disease was tighten-ing on the bodily life of our boy.

The bed where our boy lay was up at the farther end of a long ward. There was no complacency here, all doctors and nurses were for ever busy healing; discharging those who had gotten better, receiving fresh cases immediately, and quietly removing anyone who had died on them. The younger doctors and most nurses were busy, too, rehearsing songs and carols so that patients might be helped to enjoy themselves at Christmas, to dawn upon the Christian faith within a few days now. A great Christmas tree, its top branch almost touching the high ceiling, had been dressed and shone with glittering balls and segments of all colors and shapes, the sprays sprinkled with frost, some of the tree's long side branches stretching out almost over the bed where our boy lay along alone with death.

A few moments later, a look from Eileen and a murmur that she would like to be alone for a little with Niall, told me to go, for it was clear that Niall wanted Eileen to be near him more than anyone else in the world. Poor brave Eileen who had had such a long vigil over me a few months ago, but from which there was a fair return, would now have a shorter but a much more bitter vigil from which she alone would return, leaving her beloved boy for ever behind. The boy could not have made a finer choice of a companion for his ending, so I pressed his hand that I had been holding, looked down on the sharp intelligent face with its penetrating blue eyes, its delicate nose, its shock of hair, the firm and humorous mouth; bent down and kissed the lips, a warm touch which he eagerly returned, and murmured that I would be with him again very soon, very, very soon, pressed the dear hand once more, and again as he smiled up at me, and left him alone with his mother. No troubling thought struck me then that this was the last time I should ever look upon that intelligent and delightful young face, smiling up at me from under a greenwood tree.

So we came back home to prepare for Christmas, to wrap up the books and the bright blue jersey to be presented to Niall when we gathered round his bed-side, so that, even in his torment, he might catch a glimpse of the goodness-custom of Christmas Day, an excitement that had been banished from our own anxious hearts; while Eileen remained behind to minister to him, telling us that night she had soothed him into drinking fruit juice and inducing him to swallow a quantity of chicken-jelly; fighting for him, and helping him to fight for himself; adding hope-fully that he was much better and very cheerful. So Breon and Shivaun wrapped up what we wanted to take with us the next day to Exeter — fruit, wine, sweets, and Niall's bright blue jersey, a record, and two books on biology that he had asked for, little thinking that a white shroud would be worn by our boy instead of the bright blue jersey, while I sat by the fire filled with my own thoughts that draped a mourning badge round every thought of Christmas; filled with the thoughts of what Niall had been, and of what we hoped he would have been when a time came to do things.

Alone with my own thoughts? nay, rather alone with what I thought to be his, wondering what they were now. Before, his boy's way was the wind's way, and his young thoughts were long, long thoughts; but now? My own thoughts had all gone into a will; a will as strong, as determined, as the nerve and vitality left in me after seventy-seven years of life could make it, that my boy should live and return to the glow and murmur of our family life. My thoughts were all of him. Looking idly through an old black-covered, blue-lined day-book in which I had written scraps of thoughts for biography, or jottings for plays, I came across a dated reference to our Niall. It read: On the twenty-second of January, nineteen hundred and forty-nine, Niall arrayed himself in a brilliant crimson football-jersey, blue shorts, and black stockings, barred with vivid red stripes, for a match on Dartington Hall's home ground. Solomon in all his glory wasn't arrayed like this young lad, minding me of the day when I donned a jersey of blue, barred with green hoops, white shorts, and running shoes, to go forth to play my first fast hurling match, and to play well and play fast for the honour of the club. Eileen had marched through many streets, had visited many shops, had searched high and low, before she had managed to pounce on the jersey and the stockings that alone would fit our Niall for the fight in defence of his club and his school; then he was fourteen years old, and it was but seven years ago that he had first worn the crimson jersey, and now it was very likely that he would never, never wear the blue one.

Two years later, another casual note in the same old book tells me Tonight, October the twenty-second, Niall spoke enthusiastically about his partnership with the Dartington Hall Choir who are to sing Handel's version of Milton's *L' Allegro* and *Il Penseroso*. He read the libretto from the score first, read it splendidly and enjoyably so that it was plain that he knew and understood all he recited, though he had to guess what a Rebeck was meant to be. Then we got out Milton's works, and read and re-read the two poems, discovering the parts and phrases that Handel had left aside; reciting them together, I finding beauties in them, marked out by Niall, that I had never noticed before. I was surprised and gladdened that Milton could appeal so delightfully to such a young mind. A little later, he acted Mark Antony, and we plunged into *Julius Caesar*, he and I acting the bigger scenes with all the energy we had within us, and it was a lot; later still, just before he entered the army, he played his last role (but one) — that of General Burgoyne in Shaw's *The Devil's Disciple*. Oh, had I known, had I but guessed, how I should have lingered over all this singing, these recitings, fondling every phrase he tried to sing, every line he spoke from Shakespeare and from Milton! Now, he was playing his last role, silently singing a swan song, under a greenwood tree.

A wide-mannered lad who ranged in sound from Jazz to Beethoven, from Dickens to James Joyce, from biology to football. He was a fine cook, hardy and active at family gatherings with our guests, his mother's right hand at birthday festivals, or the bigger and more blatant one of Christmas; could play the trombone, and often did, in any amateur dance band; knew all the families of all the plants of Europe; used some of his last hours studying algae and fungi in Smith's book on *Cryptogams* (botany was a wonderful link in the unity of our children, for they were almost three in one and one in three); was gifted with a fine sense of fairness to all outside of himself; the penetrating blue eyes peered into all sides of life, peered fearlessly, with sometimes a deep sigh, and often a rollicking laugh. Oh, my darling lad, when you went, we lost a lot, but life lost more. Perhaps he would pull through; he was so vital; he had been busy to the last, rushing round, pushing tiredness away from him so that his doctor said he must have done it all on his abounding nerve strength. There was hope still.

So we parcelled the few presents, hoping Niall would be better, and looking forward to spending an hour or so beside his bed, trying intangibly and gropingly to graft a little of our own assurance of life into a young mind that was soon to sigh out its ending. So Breon, Shivaun, and I set out in the Hillman Minx that Niall loved so much and drove so well; to Exeter, to join Eileen at her hotel right in front of the Cathedral, and then go with her to spend what we could of Christmas Day with the dying boy. It was a shocking day, the wind blowing fierce and the rain slashing down with vicious insistence, and the wind was a bitter one. A lone road, with scarce a car passing; big pools through which the car plunged sending spray over the bonnet; the trees bending before the wind, and every house passed seeming to huddle itself closer to its own walls. Fear no more the heat of the sun, nor the furious winter's rages. Cold comfort: Niall feared neither. He revelled in the summer sun and the snows of a wild-cat winter. Oh, the changes of the seasons are a joy to a young mind within a healthy body. There's no voice or even whisper in rain, wind, frost, or snow that says 'die' to a young heart. Let the greenwood tree be bare and bony, or lush with leaf and blossom, the young heart sings beneath it.

The Minx slid into the Cathedral Close, and halted outside the hotel. We were close to him now, and soon would be beside him, be beside him. A few lonely cars jutting from the pavement's edge, and the

Cathedral lifting its bulky towers up to a sky so dark and lowering that it seemed to touch their tops, were the only signs of life standing silent beneath the pelting rain, and against the panting, pushing wind; an unlit Christmas tree beside the Cathedral's wall heralded no happiness to a soul, but dripped disconsolate where it stood. A lonely crib with the hulking Cathedral in its centre, the wind's fierce blast and the rain a-pelting: little Jesus wouldn't like a day like this. We hurried into the hotel's hall, away, away from the cold wind, to seek Eileen, and to set out to carry good cheer to our stricken boy; but Eileen had left word that she was with Niall, and she would be back as soon as she could; that we were to go to her room, to light the fire there, and to wait for her coming.

Waiting! We had a lot of waiting to do: Waiting now for Eileen's news; waiting to go to the bedside of our Niall; waiting till he had gathered enough strength to go from Exeter Hospital to St. Bartholomew's in London; waiting for a possible smile from a dour hope that our boy might be able to be with us again for a year, for a few months even; while the boy himself had to bear the most agonising wait of us all. In Eileen's little bedroom, with its little gas fire trying to cheer away the yell of the wind and the whip of the lashing rain on the window-panes; Eileen's bits of things scattered over the bed, hanging on the chair, and a few in the wash-basin soaking there till she had a minute to wash them clean; our few parcelled presents placed among Eileen's things on the bed, looking as if they too were on the way out of the world of Christmas merriment and good cheer. Then Eileen came in, her fawn mack black as a mourning gown with the slash of the rain. She was in a hurry.

Her face was pale, and lines of anxiety had been strengthened into lines of determination, her blue eyes had a soft light of battle in them. She had to go back at once to Niall; she had just run over to tell us that he wasn't too well, and that the Christmas gathering couldn't gather to his bed. He wasn't able again to speak more than a few words, and each word meant an effort of nerve and will. The best thing we could do was to have some tea, and then go back home, leaving the chance of seeing him for another day. She would just have a glass of wine, and then run back to the bedside. 'We can't bother him with presents just now. He knows the danger he runs, but he is very brave. I have to wash out his mouth every so often, and when the doctor comes to give him the drug that relaxes his throat, I have to be ready with the fruit juice and the beef essence, so that he may swallow as much as possible before his throat stiffens again.' So she drank the glass of wine and hurried down to the car for Breon to drive her to the bedside of her boy. Kind, indomitable Eileen battling for her boy's life; the pelican opening her breast to give life to her young, careless of the life she needs herself. Oh, mother, mother, mak' my bed, to lay me down with sorrow; and we all felt that the bleakness and cold of the merry day was making a deep home in our hearts.

There was no use, Eileen said, of us waiting there longer. The hope of Christmas Day was gone. Breon would bring us home, and would come back to stay with her. So we went into the foul evening again, into the car, and away, the wind as strong and harsh as ever, the rain heavier, leaving our boy with the knowledge that death was nearer, but welcoming the thought that he would have Eileen beside him till the last sigh came. Through deep pools the car plunged, and through the headlights full-on we saw the sheets of rain falling on road, hedge, house, and field. Ten miles on we came to a car halted on the roadside, blinking its lights as a signal for us to stop. The driver warned us not to go on, for, he said, he had just managed to come through, with the waters over the bonnet. We pushed on, however, but soon found we were plunging into swirling waters, rising higher as we went, and the wind shook the car when a gust came sideways, with a sight of roughly dancing waters fronting us as far as the eye could see. We turned back towards Exeter, crawling down the hills, for the waters had loosened the soil of the roads, and the inclines were dangerous and slippy. We were glad to get back to Eileen's hotel where we got rooms for the night; and later on, when Niall had slipped into a sleep, Eileen managed a hurried dinner with us, before she fled away again to the hospital. Niall's home now, and her home too, to stay with him till the drugs made him drowsy and indifferent; then creeping out, ashamed to leave him for fear he would awake and seek to look into her eyes or grope for the soft and encouraging touch of her hand. She, too, needed sleep, a wan sleep, a sleep that but helped to make her fit for another day of helping her son on his sad way; rising from bed every third hour or so to hurry to where he lay, staying there, if he were awake, till he sank to sleep again. I went to bed at two of the clock, but turned and twisted, wide awake, till after I had heard some bell chime the hour of four, and then the sleep was fitful and full of foreboding. The next day, St. Stephen's, Eileen was early at the hospital, coming back to tell us that Niall seemed a little better, but wasn't fit to see us yet, but was looking forward to a visit when he became stronger; and that his mind now leaned to the hope of being well enough to make the journey to Bart's Hospital in London tomorrow; tomorrow, if he were well enough, he would go; and Dr. Haddon was doing all that science could do to make the journey possible.

Leaving Breon with Eileen, Shivaun and I came back home by train through a flooded country to wait for news; Shivaun and I to wait for news. Yes, he could make it: he had gone on the journey the next morning, travelling with a nurse and Eileen in a special compartment, the long journey to London and Bart's, through a thick fog that delayed the arrival for over an hour; cheerful, he went, with renewed hope that science there might preserve him to the world for some time longer. The Lord God had been good to him. He had arrived. Breon hurries back in the car to garage it, and let it wait too, like us all; snatches a quick meal, and away with him again to catch a train to London to be at Eileen's side; to be her guide, her prop and stay, a very present help in her present day of trouble: a gallant lad who rarely left her side since Niall fell; while Shivaun and I went on with living at home, I getting the breakfast, she cooking the other meals, I washing things up, she drying them as they were washed; at night, seeking in the stupid face of Television a way out from anxious fear, but seeing there only the young face of my boy, her brother, and within the young face the sad pain of having to go away from life so soon.

All that could be done was being done for him, said Eileen. He has had drugs which allow him to talk more freely, and he is as vital as ever in his thoughts for things outside of himself; of the sad happening in Hungary which distresses him; of his belief in the future; and of Eileen herself, vehemently counselling to be always true to herself, always; she was a great woman, and he begged her to be always true to herself; that she mustn't let more prosperous times shift her from where she stood; that nothing within her must be lost, but all things, all her fine qualities must be strengthened by her sense of honour for them; that she must never fear to hold her own opinions, never fear to be herself: she must never lose sight of herself. His searching mind was still searching; the crusader's spirit was still vital within him. 'Dear Eileen,' he said, 'I love you deeply, we all love you, and you should hold fast your ideal for ever.'

Dear kid, in a rationalist form and fancy, he preached the kingdom of heaven to Eileen and to Breon; declaring to them in his human mystic, that the kingdom of heaven is within us; he was using his last moments to mould a world nearer to his heart's desire; a ray from a spirit moving over the face of the darker waters. Dying old men in the same ward had called for priest or parson, had cried out loud that they didn't want to die; bawling that they were afraid of hell, while the priest tried to calm them; but the young one had held his peace, though God knows, he didn't want to die either. He held silent about his fear, except once in the darkness, an hour or so before the end, with Eileen and Breon beside him, he had murmured, 'I must confess that I feel a little frightened'. Dear, dear boy, there is no dishonour in feeling a little frightened; but when Eileen put the light on, and pressed his hand, the boy was calm again. Unaware of them in a credal form, he had within him the cardinal virtues of justice, prudence, temperance, and fortitude, bearing the lost loveliness of life without a moan. Oh, my lovely boy, woe is ours that you were taken away so soon! Once only had he seemed to show how bitter the loss was: when he saw Breon distressed, and tears in his soft eyes, he said, 'There is no cause for you to worry, Breon, for it is I who have to die, and not you'. It was hard to resign himself away for ever from the many things he longed to do; to go from the companionship of young friends who thought so much of him, and looked up to him for advice in any problem; for even in the midst of dancing, he had a mind ready to comment wisely on a problem presented by a young friend.

So Eileen kept close to her younger son, anointing him with her calmness and her courage; washing out his hot mouth every few minutes, giving him a little less discomfort; changing his pyjamas when they got wet with sweat, and helping him to put on fresh and warm ones; while Shivaun and I waited at home for whatever news grim time might bring. Niall had gone to Bart's on the twenty-seventh of December, and doctors were busy doing all they could for him, distressed that one so intelligent and so gallant should die so young; though there was fine hope that he would live for some time, maybe for three months or longer. Breon rings up on the evening of the twenty-eighth to say that Niall is not so well, but he is cheerful, and the doctors have relieved his throat so effectively that he has been talking away, and still has much to say; he has taken a cup of tea, the first for weeks, and has eaten an orange, given carefully in tiny fragments, Eileen foreknowing in some curious way that he might like one, has brought some with her, and is able to hand him one when he asks for it. Perhaps he may live longer. The next evening, we are told that Niall is cheerful, and even a little gay, but hardly ever lets his eyes stray from his mother's face. And Breon is rarely more than a foot or two away from Eileen ministering to her son. Poor, gallant boy with his poor, gallant mother.

On Sunday morning, the thirtieth, Eileen rings up, and tells Shivaun, first at the phone, some news, I waiting impatiently beside her. Shivaun hands me the receiver, saying, 'I have terrible news, the most terrible news in the world', and hurries to her room crying. It is indeed terrible news, that Niall died at nine o'clock the night before; died quietly, swiftly, and bravely. Up to the last, nearly, he had talked seriously, and had spoken about us all during the day, a painful one, a day of battle indeed, for at times his body went cold, his teeth chattered, and blankets had to be piled over him; while, later on, his poor body burned so that Eileen had to strip all off, to let him lie beneath a sheet only, and kept going to the kitchen for ice-cubes to put over his eyes to soothe away the burning of his brow; but in between, he talked to her about herself, about Shivaun, making shrewd remarks, and giving that advice that was so characteristic of his great, gay, and prudent nature. Eileen hadn't rung up the night he died to tell Shivaun and me that he had gone away from us, that we had lost him for ever, so that we might sleep quietly unaware of our Niall's end. He had slept soundly, God knows, slept more deeply than he had ever desired or intended to sleep; slept more soundly than we had ever wanted him to do: a sleep from which he would never awake.

That evening, that very evening, Niall had seemed

to be decidedly better; more restful and settled. The doctors said so and the nurses thought so too. Doctor and nurse advised Eileen that she could safely go, have a quiet meal, and rest for the best part of the night. Eileen had felt doubtful, and she hesitated. Didn't they think she should send for his young friends? Not just now, they had replied; no need for haste; it will be quite safe to wait till Monday. So Eileen left Niall sleeping calmly under the glittering greenwood tree, for there was a great Christmas tree in the ward at Bart's, taller, more wide-spreading branches, and with a greater glitter, than the tree in the ward at Exeter Hospital, and left with Breon to get a quiet meal which both badly needed. She was still doubtful; some odd feeling within her urged her to go to where her boy lay. She told Breon, but he assured her it was but imagination. It lingered, and she had hardly begun the meal when she told Breon that she must go. In a taxi she hurried away, urging the driver to go quick, for her boy was dying. He did his best, and his fare had to be pressed upon him at the journey's end. She ran into the hospital, up the corridor where the ward was, meeting the Sister, who hurried her along, saying how glad she was Eileen had come, for Niall was on his way from the world; on a swift way from all he had loved.

He had had moments of delirium during the last hour, and strangely his thoughts crossed to America, calling out gayly that we must get the Minx car, and get to America to see Sean's play, and where he could hear the genuine jazz played. At the last, he had asked for his young friends, and was told they were on the way to him; he had flung his legs from the bed to be on the way to America, and it took Breon some effort to get him back again, for Niall had never lost his swiftness and strength of limb, and his vitality still surged through his soul. He had called for Shivaun and for me, and Eileen told him we were just around the corner waiting to come in to him; while the young nurse was visibly affected that such a gallant lad should have to go, and the doctor who had attended to him was distressed that his greatest skill and knowledge could keep him alive no longer, for the swift end was rare, but it occurred occasionally, and it came to Niall. The fight was over for him, but the fight was not over for poor, brave Eileen.

At home here, with me the struggle began to try to forget that Niall had ever lived. I set my mind down and up to it: I help Shivaun about the house, keeping my eyes off her face, for its occasional quivering upsets me; I try to work, tear up letters I don't wish to keep; tidy up the table I work at; but the effort at relief is a dull bubble that swiftly vanishes, and Niall is the fullness of my mind again. I find myself, against all my forcing will, crying out, Oh, Niall, my Niall, my darling son. Let it be called unmanly to show and voice the quivering of the heart. I cannot help my grief, and, God knows, I know no shame in feeling it, or of letting the lips quiver, the heart shake, the voice cry out against the darkness of the hour. Every now and again, when I have imagined I have forced myself into quietness, a convulsive sob shakes me; Niall's loveliness and youth fills my mind, and I cry out against the darkness of the time, on the eve of a New Year that will remain for ever an old one for Eileen and for me. We go about the flat, Shivaun and I, trying to hide our feelings from one another. From here, he went to his death; in this

room, where he had been first told of his probable
end, I had given him the first kiss of my agonised
love for him, in Exeter Hospital I gave him the last
kiss, till, maybe, if there be such a thing as a second
life, I may give him the third kiss when I meet him,
after I, too, have gone the way of all flesh.

My bitterest pain of remembrance is not of our
loss, not of mine, but of his: it must have been hard
and agonising to suffer the thought, the knowledge,
that he would have to go; go from life just as he had
fully entered into its rich vigour and its youthful
beauty; so hard to be always thinking that he would
have to go. Oh, my darling boy, so lithe, so jovial,
so full of humour, so thoughtful in the midst of his
enjoyment; you knew you had to go away from all
these things gave you; away from life, and for ever.
My boy, my heart-loved boy, death came to you like a
damned thief in the daytime, when all was young and
everything was bright and brave, and life was dancing.

So poor Shivaun and I waited for Eileen and Breon
to come home; waited, trying to forget Niall and ever
remembering him, and all our little world went slow.
Dr. Varian, who had been our family doctor for near
twenty years in Totnes, came today to give us his
sympathy. He had known Niall well, but he had little
to say, though he cursed and exclaimed most bitterly
that this damned leukaemia was one of the few things
about which medical science knew little or nothing.
Little or nothing, yet the young are dying from it
every day of the year, and science is checked in its
studies by the legal insanity of those who care more
for mobile missiles than they do for life. Dr. Varian,
dear man, and I embraced and parted, for there was
little to say.

Eileen had loaned Niall's body to the doctors to be examined and explored in the hope that they might see something to guide them in the treatment of future sufferers, while she arranged to have it cremated the day after they had found whatever was to be found within it. That night, she told me, by some curious and irresistible impulse, she had gone alone to where he lay to have her last look at him, a long last look at the dear, dear young face. He had looked, she said, strangely like me as I surely looked when I was young, peaceful, very peaceful as if asleep, and she had laid a bunch of flowers beside his fair young cheek, the last token of her deep love for her dear young son. My poor darling Eileen, you have had a wondering woe encircling you. Her pilgrimage of pain stretched out a long way before her still. She had gone all along with her boy to the gateway of death, where they had to part, and parting was such bitter sorrow. Farther, she could not go; he had to go alone the rest of the way. His was indeed a short journey into night: a few swift days, with the sun of life going farther and farther away from him till the darkness was reached. Goodbye, my darling mother: Life was but a swift hail and farewell to me. The sunset came too soon for me, and I never saw the evening star. My lovely rose of youth faded when it promised to be full-blown; the petals all fell away together, fell to the chilly earth, and the bloom was gone. Goodbye, dear mother; the music I hear now no longer tells of youth and home.

He had been sorely distressed by the tragedy in Hungary, by all its desolate confusion, and couldn't understand the Soviet Army's methods in quelling the semi-popular, semi-fascist revolt. He had come down from London to talk with me about it, for he had a great regard for my review of things political. We had talked long about the upheaval, he from his viewpoint, I from mine; he very vehemently, I very gently, for I loved the boy's intense sincerity, and grieved at his agitation. But we couldn't agree with what had happened, which to him was a blunt and clumsy interference, and to me a sad necessity. I got up out of my deep armchair and stepped to the austere and simple one in which I sat when I wrote or typed, and in which he sat then; I put my arm around him and pressed him warmly to my side, saying, 'You must cling to your own opinions, and not be influenced by mine, for your intelligence is, at least, equal to mine'. Then I pressed him to my side again, and, bending down, kissed his bushy head of hair as he smiled up at me. How glad I am now that I didn't get testy — as I occasionally do when what seems plain to me seems obscure to others — How sadly glad I am now that I had caressed him then, for within a few more bare days, my boy was dead; he had gone, and had left the distress of Hungary far behind him.

Why do I write like this? Before God, I don't know. The impulse moves me; a proud urge to silence guards the impulse, but the guarded impulse overcomes the guard, and the moving finger writes. As I write, I hear the swift wind shaking the crowded line of cypress trees along the margin of what is called the drive. Kinder their greeny gloom, softer the rasping of their sighing, than the cynical silence and the glittering bauble-clad greenwood tree that houseled the last hours of our beloved lad. The wind blows strongly as it often does here, and I hear it loudly. This wind is not the wind in the willows, but a dark wind and a brazen one, filling the room with sharp, violent sighs. The wind bloweth where it listeth, but we know not whence it cometh or whither it goeth. I stand for a few moments on the balcony outside the front door watching the cypress trees bend back from the wind, each a rustling black smudge beneath the lesser darkness of a starless sky; the rain gentle when the wind falls for a moment, then slashing the face sharply when a gust of wind whips by strongly. So I write as the wind goes, knowing not whence the impulse cometh or whither it goeth; but strive as I may, the guarded impulse overcomes the guard, and the moving finger writes the words pressing down agony within them. Life's day is a short one, but Niall had but a dawn, a false one, for the dawn faded before he knew it was there.

Niall's body was cremated today, the third of January, two days following the first one of the New Year: his merry Christmas and his happy New Year are over and done with; at two o'clock, he passes through the midst of a fiery furnace, and is utterly consumed. There are no miracles these days: Meshach, Shadrach, and Abednego have ceased to live. He had gone the way he had lived — as a flame of serious vitality, gaiety, and glee. He is now a handful of dust scattered over a Garden of Remembrance; a handful of purple dust — good God, the irony of it. No, no; golden dust, for he was a grand lad, serious when it was time to be so, gay when it was time to be gay. However hard I try to quench remembrance, a flash of agony sweeps through me, the tears fall, and I hear myself crying, My boy, my darling, gallant lad. However hard I press my lips together, the cry comes; but only when I am alone; maybe, occasionally when Eileen is present, but almost always when I'm alone.   Surely nothing dies but something mourns.

The calendar is useless, and the clock's tick has lost significance: no more shall I mark a calendar-day as one more through which my son liveth; no more watch the hands of the clock moving, waiting for Eileen or Breon to tell me of hope or a deeper despondency: no need to be anxious now, for all signs of a living Niall have gone from the world, from the family who loved him; our eyes shall see him no more, no hand of ours shall ever touch his again, neither shall any hear his eager animated voice in a room or by the laburnum tree in the little garden.   As I write this, our boy will have been a week dead.   A fortnight or so ago, he was dancing and delightful; now all that was dancing and delightful has been a week dead.

A little Ford car, an Anglia, had been a great family treasure for ten years, bought when our income from America increased; but, like all simpler and poorer things, it had been often over-burdened with work.   So when income from America increased again, when I returned home from hospital, the family decided to buy a new car.   After many talks, it was decided to get a Hillman Minx.   There was pride in the heart and joy on the face when the car came — thro' the valley and over the hill in the Minx!   Happiness in all hearts, but indifference in mine, for I always felt better and more important getting out of a car than getting into one.   I enjoyed a drive only when I had to pay a visit to a doctor, and illness made me disinclined to bear the burden of going to his surgery in a bus.   Eileen decided to give the little Ford to the boys, who were fine drivers, and they at once swopped it for a light blue-black van which they got painted a brilliant orange-red instead, typical of their bright feeling for life. I felt that way, too, and I looked with more liking at the cocky gay orange-red van than was in any glance I gave to the more elegant and dignified Minx in its sober silver-grey coat. It was owned equally by the boys, and they made much use of it, bringing Breon's material to the room he used as a studio, carrying their lunches and swimming-gear to the sea when the summer came, returning old books and bringing back new ones from the local library, Shivaun delighting in the journeys as much as the boys did. A gay time for the three of them, and well it was, for none of us had an inkling that though two would be left, the third would be taken. But they lived and laughed as if death did not exist, and indeed, death didn't exist for them. They had heard of it, but the very idea of it was always enveloped and lost in the gay glow of life. The boys had gone to Cornwall in the orange-red van with tent and food in September; Niall had driven in it to London, carrying a few things for the room he had there; he had brought Eileen once to a London theatre in it; he had carried friends down to Dartington that they might have a good time at a party there, and had taken them back to London again in the little orange van, the little orange van. Then came the London University Christmas recess, and Niall took his last voyage home, carrying his sister, Shivaun, with him in the little orange-red van; he stepped out of it in the evening with his sister and never set foot into it again, for a fortnight later he began to be but a memory: the one who took life, not only with eagerness, but with glee, was gone; he who took life as daffodils take the winds of March was dead.

How well I remember him even before he came, for this was the boy Eileen was having when I was in New York, and he came forth to the world less than a month after I had returned. I had followed his whole growth, as his mother had, remembering how when he was two or so showing him with hands and fingers the miracle of

> This is the lady's knives and forks,
> This is the lady's table,
> This is the lady's looking-glass,
> And this the baby's cradle.

The times I played with him in Battersea Park, the time we first saw the Dart together when we went to Devon; the times I met him, or Eileen and I met him, coming home from school along the Dartington Hall Drive or along the Plymouth Road, the times I played hurley with him outside of the house of Tingrith, or cricket, or football, on the lawn; or golf with him and Breon on the lawns by the sea in Goodrington, near Paignton; the questions he had asked me about the Soviet Union, about plays, books, and politicians; about the queer ways of Ireland, the tinsel chatter of the many, the mighty thoughts of the few; but silence sits now where once an eager voice spoke, and I shall never be puzzled by a question from him again. I remember how nervous he became when the bombs fell near, and how I held his shaking little body close to my own, and kissed him warmly, though I, too, was sore afraid, while the calmer Eileen looked after the baby Shivaun, and the calmer Breon looked after himself. How Eileen taught him to read — as she taught them all, Breon before him, and Shivaun afterwards — quietly coaxing him into effort through an infant school-book or an infant comic, leading him to the way wherein he found the joy of Shakespeare, Dickens, Milton, Shaw, and many others; sowing within his mind the seed that developed into the keen, questioning mind that later on had to reject the myths of Christianity, and made it hateful of Christian hypocrisy and humbug that were ramping and ruining the world.

Remembrance — all the joy that is left to us now; a poor joy, but our own.

How, later on, he had forgotten his fear of the bombs, and had handled the guns as a gunner, doing his National Service in the Field Artillery. How on account of his knowledge of books, he had been made librarian of the camp up in North Shropshire; how, for no specific reason, he had been taken away from the library, and sent to Germany; how there, the Adjutant of the regiment had liked him, and had needed the sharp and accurate mind of the lad to help in the work the Adjutant had to do; how it was necessary, before he could do so, for him to have a stripe, and how puzzled the Adjutant became because of objections that came from higher quarters; how the officer had had a private chat with him, and Niall had told him frankly about his father's left-wing views; how the officer had said that it was the son he wanted, and not the father, that it was all very farcical, and that he needed Niall's steady and accurate intelligence, and made a Lance-Bombardier of him, in spite of the objections from the gold-braided amadauns of the British Army. I remember how he shuddered telling me about a visit to Belsen Camp while the regiment was on manœuvres, a place where thousands of bearded Jews, wrinkled women, handsome young Jewesses and vigorous lads, and crowds of little Jewish children died; destroyed so exclusively and terribly that even remembrance died with them: nothing there now but the wind to tell of the sorrow and the gloomy silence to cover the dead.

I remember how he visited me stretched out in Torbay Hospital, and the anxiety that welled up in him when he saw the thinning body and haggard face of the old man, praying that I would rally back into life, never once having a thought that within nine months he himself would be dead; going himself where he hoped his old father would not go. Oh, my Niall, my darling boy, I am ashamed that it was not I but you who had first to make the journey into night. Now I and Eileen have nothing but remembrance with which to touch an absent hand, to hear the sad echo of a silent voice, a brief and a bitter consolation. Never again will Niall tell me how many runs he made at cricket, never ask me if I think the weather will stand that the match might go on; never; never tell me of his search in Dawlish Warren for some rare herb or some uncommon grass. Useless now is the Pelican book on *Grasses* by C. E. Hubbard that I made Shivaun get me in London for the Christmas just gone, that I might be able the better to talk to him about this widespread and life-essential plant. Never again will he show me the fossil shells and worms embedded in the granite forming the two piers to the gateway of our home; fossils that lived sixty million years ago; never again will he pounce on the *Scientific American* coming from New York, and delivered by a Devon postman; or finger the letters lying on my table and comment on what some of them said; never listen again with me to a Mozart, a Beethoven, or a Haydn symphony; he will never rest a hand on my shoulder again, watching something showing on the television; neither I nor Eileen will ever speak to our boy again, nor shall he ever speak to us.

Ah, Niall, amhic, never again shall you stand with Eileen and me beneath the awesome trilithons of Stonehenge, or pause beside the stretched-out stone where poor Tess of the D'Urbervilles slept her last sleep of freedom in this world; never again walk along the Avon with us, or stand under the mulberry tree in Shakespeare's garden; never come into my room again to talk about a beetle or about a bird. To go so young, and life so much within you and around you. Oh, where was the Lord's deliverance?

> He delivered Daniel from de lion's den,
> Jonah from de belly of de whale,
> The Hebrew chillun from de fiery furnace;

but he never delivered you. God wanted him, and it pleased him to take the boy, says a voice from Ireland. Oh, God, oh, Ireland! We wanted him to stay far more than God wanted him to go. He was needed and so God called him away, said another voice — from Ireland. God must be hoarse calling to heaven all the young lads and girls who die far before their time. Hear what comfortable cancerous words these canting Christians speak unto the sorrowful; God called the lad up to heaven though the lad was more than content to stay pat on the earth; sweet poison doping us against any effort to keep death away before a life's ending is due, and Science alone can, like Hercules, stand between death and the dying young. It is Science alone which can mend God's image, when the image is hurt; and when Science fails in its mending, then God's image falls away into dust. It is Science we must try to help, Science we must encourage, if golden lads and girls are to safely claim the heritage of life, and pass through the allotted span of three-score years and ten.

His worldly wealth he left behind him wasn't much: a good gramophone, a few pounds in the Post Office Savings Bank; a wristlet-watch which he wore for the last few days, his last present; a bright blue jersey he never saw; a fine collection of records — classic and jazz; a three-speed record player; and a much-loved trombone; and a number of books, one of which, *Story of Living Things*, presented to him when he was fourteen years of age by his sister, Shivaun, was a gorgeous gateway to the knowledge of how life had come, how life had grown all the world over. They are very dear to us, but the dearest of all is the memory of a beloved boy with a warm heart, a penetrating mind, a gay long laughing sense of humour; a lad who was as brave when death came for him as he had been when life was brimming in him, so that Breon said, 'I always loved him, but I will revere him now'.

I cry a caoine for my Niall, for though I may bear it like a man, I must also feel it like a man, and cannot feel ashamed that my sigh will be in the winds that blow where'er his dear ashes blow, for he had very gentle, loving ways within him; but the caoine, as he would wish, goes out for all the golden lads and girls whose lovely rose of youth hath perished in its bud. The bell that tolled for him, when he was going, tolled for others too, and will toll for many more of darling young ones departing before their due season, till Science teaches fools that a breaking heart above a young and silent body is more sacred than a bursting bomb set to kill ten thousand old and young and children, too; till Science comes to deliver the young from danger, and takes the victory from the grave and the sting from death. Science has done wondrous things for the young, but at times Science still has to stand helpless by while young and lovely ones go from life for ever — like you, my lovely darling lad.

And all the thought I had, the plans I made, to try to live a few more years at least till Shivaun would be sweet and twenty, till you had ended your college course, and were facing the world, then I could lead the way for the family into darkness after a long, rugged, and exciting journey, a natural scheme for the oldest mind to fashion, but

> The best-laid schemes o' mice an' men
>   Gang aft a-gley,
> An' lea'e us nought but grief an' pain
>   For promis'd joy.

As mine did, my darling boy, as mine did; we were close together in love and understanding, and when you were wrenched away from me, your young life took away with it a great part of the pride and joy of my own old withering one.

Death cut down the vigorous young sapling, and left the gnarled old tree standing, left the gnarled, old, withering tree standing.

Clearly, I can hear what she said, what Eileen said, what she said brokenly, when she came back from committing her darling son's young body to the flames: when she put her arms round me, she said, 'Oh, Sean, Sean, what a terrible thing has happened to us'.

Yes, a terrible thing to us, and terrible to our dear Niall, too, taken away in the fair spring of his youth as he was opening the gateway to the sweet meadow of summer. The broken cry of Eileen will ever be an echo in the home. His voice too; the voice that tried so bravely to tell his thoughts, his last brave thoughts, spoken while he lay dying under a greenwood tree.

THE LARK IN THE CLEAR AIR
STILL SINGS [1]

THE intelligentsia in the western world have become weary of well-doing. They go about clogged with a sense of sin, and frown upon any inclination of the heart to sing. They have tried in novel, poem, and play to frighten hope from the human heart, but all find it hard to coax it away or to root it out, though, God help them, they do their best. To these writers hope springs infernal in the human breast, and they mock down any writer who ventures to guard and cherish it still: they don't like the lark's song. Present-day writers of poem, essay, play, and novel, seem to set them down as they stand before a wailing wall. They write thumping their chests in despair, murmuring the sad song: 'Oh, willow, tit-willow, tit-willow'. The brightest and best of these sons of the morning totter through time as if Life had fixed a mill-stone round their necks, and faltering feet could go this far, but no farther. Their characters in play and novel, their ideas in a poem, drag their feet like the spirits of the hypocrites shod in lead shuffling wearily along in the depths of Dante's Inferno. They keep their eyes closed to show that man was born blind; they hold arm and leg limp as if power of movement never reigned in either of them; but their mouths are never shut, but for ever wail out the warning given out by Shawn of the Glen that man has been worsted in the fight, and that life has taken a false turning and a false name. To them, life is a drunken

[1] From *The New York Times Magazine*.

sailor, a roaring, sly staggering misery, with nothing living knowing what to do with him; and more a bloodier villain than terms can make him out.

> Love not, love not, ye hapless sons of clay;
> Hope's gayest wreaths are made of earthly flowers,
> Things that are made to fade and fall away,
> Ere they have blossom'd for a few short hours.

This is true only in appearance, for earthly flowers are beautiful, and, like man, they never die: a flower dies here and there and others take its place to bloom as fair, and so sweet flowers shall last till time has ceased to be.

Caroline Norton wrote this verse and died three years before I was born to sing a different song, facing those singing the same song in many different keys — Kafka, Beckett, Ionesco, Greene, Eliot, Genêt, Orwell, Aldous Huxley, and Camus, leaders of a host of worshipping intelligentsia — a great galaxy of darkened stars dulling the human sky. Many of these are very fine writers indeed, but to me they seem to be setting down the history of life as a Doomsday Book, though Samuel Beckett wears his rue with a difference. He is a poet, and there is a sly humor as well as music in his writing. One has but to listen to good actors speaking it within a monologue or a play to hear the music, at times to feel the deep, gloomy compassion, and to be touched by the humor in the sad recital. Gloomy and full of expanding doubt in humankind as they may be, indeed, as they are, they remain fine artists, and can be stimulating even in their darkened vision, as James Joyce is above them all, and a very few others: but they are not for those in the Spring of life, not for the young who are seeing visions of great things in the future, as I do, even though I be old and grey.

It is the minor spirits who follow the stronger ones, cribbing their ideas from their masters, who spread despair and what they call the woe of life over the western world, without any of the stimulation found in the work and style of their betters; it is these minor, small souls, dead souls, really, who labor to persuade life that life isn't worth living, that the good earth is but a madhouse, a jail, and a morgue. They even try to teach light to counterfeit gloom. Every sentence they write abandons life, yet they cling to it as the ivy clings to the wall; they grip life with all their might, and call a doctor when they feel a cold coming: they refuse to live and try to stop others from living either.

It is not a new thing, this angry rejection of the greatness of life; its stresses and its joys. Many a time a hasty shout has been given, an indignant fist shaken at God and at the world for the many trials man has to meet. At times, the lusty and ever active Elizabethans rail at nature, at God's way, and at the many disappointments of life. Thus Chapman's Montsurry,

> Since all earth's pleasures are so short and small,
> Th' way t'enjoy it, is t'abjure it all,

and another Elizabethan poet exclaims venomously

> What is the pleasure of life
> But the good hours of an ague?

Life often puts on the black cap for Shakespeare: in many a part of his plays and sonnets, he rails at fortune, mocks life because of the dangers life must meet, its uncertainty, its rare joys as uncertain as the uncertain glory of an April day; rails blasphemously even at the God he is said to have believed in:

> As flies to wanton boys are we to the gods,
> They kill us for their sport.

But Shakespeare does not stay very long with his sorrows; he sings and dances even in the midst of them —

> Come unto these yellow sands
> And then take hands . . .
> Foot it featly here and there —

and already he has forgotten his dejection. He can weep following Hamlet's or Lear's bier, but can soon hurry away to the Boar's Head to drink a flagon of wine with Falstaff. Shakespeare met difficulty and despondency in the theatre, on the street, halting him to say gloomy words into his ear, but the poet was always in a crowd of fairer thoughts, and he soon broke away from his dismal advisers, and hurried away to his gayer and holier activities. Milton, too, had his dark moments; pensive souls spoke to him, lost spirits troubled him; he saw Samson in deep and angry misery, but among these he saw laughter holding both his sides. Keats was assailed by many, a bed was his home for a long time, yet the dying poet sang like a lark in the clear air of the day; and when night fell, the stars came, and the lark slept, the nightingale made her melody through the quieter and sadder hours of the night-time.

In most plays, written yesterday or today, there never seems to be room for a laugh, or for any rough or gentle belief in the greatness of life or the common goodness of man; no admiration for, no laughter at, no enjoyment of, the strange wonder of his ways. The writers think only of their own importance. A book has just been published packed with English plays of the immediate yesterday; they are faced by a preface by the English drama critic, Kenneth Tynan, who thinks them to be 'plays of rebellion'. The plays show no interest in politics, and rebel only against what they think to be conformity, ignoring Capitalism and Communism with all their implications. The characters use a cult language, wear eccentric dress, exult in a private philosophy, separating themselves (as they believe) completely from the communal society in which they live. This is a very safe form of rebellion; a rebellion of personal bawling. Any one man can escape from the society in which he lives, and a man or woman who thinks he plunges into rebellion because he dresses differently from others, isn't armed against an oppressive power in society even with a blunt pin. Anyone in America, here in England, or almost any other civilised land, can wear the gayest of colors, if they so desire, without any danger of being hurried off to jail. Myself when young wore a gay kilt, a gayer shawl, pinned with a big brooch at the shoulder, and a bonnet sporting an eagle's feather, without exciting any alarm wherever I happened to go. An old man, now, I still like bright jerseys and gay-colored caps, but I never feel separate from the doctor, the scientist, the worker, or the business man who dress in conformity with the manner of their professions.

One play tells us that 'everybody's wedged in; nobody can move; nobody counts'; and another shouts, 'Rules, laws, guides, promises, terms, guarantees, traditions — into the pot with the whole damned lot of them!' A third asks, 'Have you got your permit and your promise? They will prove to you either that you live in the best possible world, or that you *will* do, and they will prove it either by dialectic or the Bible. But can you wait that long? Have you ever given your instinct a chance to say whether you are happy or not, or whether you want to kill or not?'

A grand gospel! A nice lot we'd be, a fine condition of life we'd live, if there were neither rule nor law! We might exist, but we could not live without them. At present — till we get to a far finer way of thought and emotion — they are necessary for our civil and social salvation. Our problem is, not to do away with them, but to make them better, more sensible for all: National rules and International rules. We take our cue from Nature that has her own laws. It would be a nice thing if the Earth suddenly got stubborn, saying, 'I'm sick and tired of moving, I'll stay where I am'; and halted in the winter solstice: then would seed-time and harvest end; cold would be here, but the heat would be gone; and everlasting night would be for some and everlasting day for others: it would not do at all. We should never again see the darling buds of May! We are under rule when we go to work, when we go to church, when we go to hospital, when we go to play, and we'll be under rule when we get to heaven or go down to hell.

Rebels! These playwrights aren't rebels against any stupidity, any injustice, but merely runners-away from life. The fault is not with life, is not in the stars above them, lies not in the earth beneath; it is not with the people with whom they live, but in themselves. They seem to think the rhythm of the universe starts from them and that the tick of the clock of time goes only with their own heart's dead-beat. Frustration, disappointments, grief, are, at times, the portion of all: every man knows what these are. They are personal trials, and life takes little notice of them, but goes on living. Like pain, these things must be borne by each who has one or more, must be conquered as they come so that we can leave the sense of loneliness they bring with them, and enter again into the grand fight for a safer and a brighter life.

Man is the only life on earth that can see its form and love its grandeur; he has enriched the world, for without him it would have no meaning and look dead; it would be dead. He has ennobled the star we stand on; exceptional souls give things exceptional beauty. When Christ saw the lilies of the field, he said to those around him, 'I say unto you that even Solomon in all his glory was not arrayed like one of these'; he gave the blossoms an eternal beauty; and when Shakespeare looking at another flower in an English field, said, 'Daffodils that come before the swallow dares, and take the winds of March with beauty', he gave these flowers a loveliness and a courage unrecognised before.

Mankind teems with brave men and women; ay, and good Samaritans, half-hidden away in distant points and odd corners. However rough the sea, the lifeboat goes out to deliver perishing men and women from stormy seas and battered ships; when cholera appears in Egypt, planes from every nation fly in to fight the curse; in a bombing-raid on London, a young nurse stays in a ward from which patients could not be shifted, and dies there with them; there is a threatened epidemic of smallpox in Glasgow, so doctors and nurses isolate themselves with the afflicted ones —

a patient, doctor, and nurse die, but the danger is over; a lad of thirteen sees two girl-swimmers sinking in the sea; he goes out, brings in one, goes again, and, after a fine fight, brings the second girl safely to the shore. Life will never want for heroes, mostly unhonored and unsung, but always there and ever ready to act.

It is argued that Camus, Genêt, Kafka, and such writers 'give us the ugliness of life to raise us to higher stages of moral insight and to more genuine emotions of gaiety and joy.' Oh, they do, do they? They seem not only to try, but to struggle to make ugliness uglier than ugliness really is in life. They seem to believe that if they pull the gay-colored wings from a butterfly, it will look lovelier and fly higher. No one could be more bitter and sadder at times than the great Strindberg, but there was always deep compassion in his poetic plays and the gentle gong of hope was always sounding. There is nothing in the works of those drearier writers like the huge haunch of beef that Rembrandt painted with glowing color and elegant form, or the sight of the bud on the roof of Strindberg's gloomy castle, Strindberg's flaming dismal castle opening into a gigantic chrysanthemum flower.

Our world has grandeur and life has hope. In spite of the despairs of the American beats and the European wailers, the lark in the clear air still sings the melody of hope; and hope in action will do great things everlastingly, till, a thousand million years from now, maybe, Time gives its last sigh, and all things go.

IMMANUEL

GOD with us: that is what this is said to mean. He is
with us, they say, but how and where and when? He
is everywhere, among all peoples, at one and the same
time; he hasn't to travel, he is just there. Even where
there is nothing, Yeats tells us, there is God. But is
Yeats right, are the others right? Sheltering in the
cleft of a rock, Moses saw him though God's shadow
alone delivered the prophet from death by the force
of his radiance like the radiance of a hydrogen-bomb
Moses saw God's back-parts as he passed by swift as
the swiftest wind. God dwelt, it is said, in the Ark
of the Covenant, and everywhere the Israel people
went the Ark was sure to go, and he went with it.
Even when he was busy, and one of his own needed
help, he sent a deputy, like the angel who flew down
into the den where Daniel was, and muzzled the mouths
of the lions; and, as the circumstances warranted, he
showered down gentle manna on the Israelites in the
desert, and thundered down brimstone and sulphur on
the sorry inhabitants of the cities of the plain. Always
either thundering or chirruping. Nothing was, or
could be, hidden from him. But everywhere? Is he
among the clowns at the circus, with those who ride
strangely on the swift horses? With the football fans
bawling from their stands and the players on the field?
With the poets and playwrights, bad and good, and
the audiences who read, hear, and bear them? Is he
there whispering advice even with the critics? Is he
to be found in the potting-shed as well as in the

cathedral? Or is it that he appears only during the honouring of the rubric of the Anglicans or the missal of the Roman Catholics? Does he listen to the drivel of the television and radio, to the music-hall song as well as the Gregorian chant? With the soldiers, muddied and bloodied, on the battlefields as well as with the mother with her baby on her breast? No mother's son can tell, and only God himself knows. He may be nowhere just as he may be everywhere: you never can tell.

Christians (and, sometimes, non-Christians) have an odd way of explaining his presence and his ways with puzzled man. In the *Sunday Times* of 1st December 1957, the drama critic of this journal, commenting on the play *Requiem for a Nun*, said, 'I have never known the Bible quoted on the stage without making the writing round it, judging it as literature, look shoddy. Faulkner performs a miracle; for he takes words from the Bible at one of the supreme moments, and puts them in a setting entirely worthy.' Then follows the quotation from the play: 'When he said "Suffer little children to come unto me", he meant exactly that; he meant suffer: that the adults, the fathers, the old in sin and capable of sin, must be ready and willing — nay eager — to suffer at any time, that the little children should come to him unanguished, unterrified, and undefiled. To hear Zachary Scott speak those words quietly, like a man who knows the precise weight of every one of them, is a wonderful experience.' Shall we kill off our cattle for fear they'd get foot-and-mouth disease? Farmers stay silent. Shall we then kill off our kids to deliver them from falling into sin? Rachel rejoicing for her children because they were not childermass!

Since the play has as one of its chief incidents the killing of a baby by its nurse to save it from the stain of sin, we are forced by the inference to assume that the death of a youngster untouched by sin is a fine thing, to be embraced in feelings of comfort and joy. Bad theology, for no human being can save a child from being touched with sin (*à la* Roman Catholic and Anglican dogma), for every mother's son and daughter is born in sin, and in iniquity have their mothers conceived them. Neither infant nor adult can enter the divine presence undefiled; they have to be cleansed from all sin before they can see God: so Christian theology says.

But this special command of Jesus to his disciples to 'suffer the children to come unto him' had nothing to do with death, but everything to do with life; not life in the next world, but life in this one. Did not the dramatist and the critic know that it was not the fathers or mothers who wanted to keep the kids from Christ, but the disciples? Had the 'adults' any suspicion that they were ushering their children towards physical death, they would have hurried them far away, out of sight, out of mind.

This word 'suffer' has different meanings according to the context in which the writers use it. In this instance it hasn't the meaning of grief, much less that of the benefit of an early death. It just means Let the children come to me; don't stand in their way, and it was spoken as a rebuke, not to the parents of the kids, but to the disciples. (In point of fact this phrase, if I remember right, is used by the Church, not as an entry to the Sacrament of Extreme Unction, but as justification for infants to receive Infant Baptism.) It was these chaps who were called upon to suffer, not the parents nor the kids. Savvy? Neither were the parents holding the children back, but eagerly guiding them forward, knowing that Jesus merely wished by a pat on the head and a kindly word to show his love for, and interest in, the very young, whom he likened to the Kingdom of heaven. Suffer simply meant don't hinder, as it probably does in the original Greek, and as it certainly does in the translation into the Gaelic, in itself a translation from the Greek. To me, it is shocking to give such a vile and sinister significance to such a homely and delightful scene. Besides, if Jesus thought of sin at that time, he would (as he does in another place regarding his disciples) have prayed, not that the little ones should be taken out of life, but that they might be kept from the evil that may be in it; he would wish these little ones to grow up, to be his faithful servants and soldiers unto their life's end (Faulkner and Hobson should read the Baptismal Service).

Had there been anything of such a nature, stated or implied, in the meeting between Christ and the kids, the mothers and fathers would have gone like hares away from where he was till they were out of sight of him, and wouldn't, for a long time, venture to let their children wander far from the doorstep. A mother doesn't let her child die if she can prevent it. I have seen many a mother battling against the assurance that her child must die; fighting to save a child even when the child is drawing out his last long sigh, as James Joyce's mother battled for the life of her poor and beloved Isabel. And it isn't even the righteous who are always the best mothers either; often a plague to the children who have to live with them, like the Murdstones, the cleric-father in *The*

Way of All Flesh and Mrs. Dudgeon in *The Devil's Disciple*. Clearly God is not present, either in the playwright's drama or the critic's review. Parents suffer the loss of a child only when conditions make them helpless: war is on, and the young must go, or a deadly disease strikes, and a young girl or a young lad tends towards an everlasting sleep, given, it is said, by God to his beloved; the youngsters fighting to the end against the dismal drowsiness, the mother clutching at a hope with a grip unyielding till the last sigh is given, and the young sink to sleep for ever; the parents resenting bitterly for ever after, till the time of their own going, the thing within or the thing without that took their young away from life before their full and natural time had come to go.

What happens when the grey curtain comes down, when the actor says his last line, and leaves the stage for ever? No one knows. One of the last things Shaw said about what was after death gave us all the knowledge we have: We cannot tell. No one knows. For thousands of years life has been coming into the world, and we know, more or less, what happened to it there; then it goes, and no one can tell whither; whether any part of it continues to exist, to live; or whether all is lost, like a lost leaf fluttering down in the fall, gone from the urge of any coming spring, from any further part in the plumping verve of summer; gone, like an old song loved in the long ago, silent now, leaving no echo even of the sound that once charmed every ear that heard it. Even our grief can tell us nothing. No knowledge comes from the abiding sorrow felt for a loved one gone; even one like the sorrow of David when his son, Absalom, died, or when his beloved friend, Jonathan, fell; or like the silent grief of the woman for her lost lover lying in his last sleep under the falling snow in Joyce's stricken story of *The Dead*.

Those who are under grief for lost loved ones continually ask the question of what has happened to them beyond the place and time of their going; a question asked publicly or within the sad stillness of their sorrowing minds: where are they; what shape do they take; what are the beloved ones doing? Are they not really lost, but only gone before? Is there any attachment within whatever they may be now to the world of strife and love they have left behind? Do they know of our grief left with us as an unforgettable memory? This question has been asked for thousands of years, but no one has answered it yet. God who is always with us never mentions it; keeps a dead silence, mum's his word. Early on, of course, various institutional religions have answered it fully, each in a different way, have even given us details, sombre and colorful, of how the dead enjoy themselves, if they have lived in the mood of life expressed by themselves as the way God meant men, women and children to live in this life; or how those who were obstinate, or who hardened their hearts, live on within a circle of punishment, suffering terrible and eternal torments. Pictures of these happy and horrible states in after-life used to hang on the walls of every church, and many hang there still; and they glowed and glowered on the walls of the mind of man, unfadingly, for centuries. These colored glories and growls are still woven into the yielding minds of children in Sunday school and at catechism class — a kind of Tate Gallery of comic horrors, the plush and purple delights as ridiculous and horrifying as the black penalties of deviationism.

Is there any intelligent being, man or woman, who

has never questioned God? Is there one of them, living or dead, who ever got an answer? Winston Churchill tells us that he, too, asked questions. As a young British officer stationed in India, he says, 'In the regiment, we often used to argue questions like whether we should live again in another world after this was over? Whether we have lived before? Whether we remember and meet each other after death or merely start again like the Buddhists? Whether some high intelligence is looking after the world or whether things are just drifting on anyhow?' Well, do we? Did we? Is there? Omar Khayyám asked all these before Winston Churchill and answered them himself:

> One thing is certain, and the Rest is Lies;
> The Flower that once hath blown for ever dies.

It is not hard to know that the flower that bloomed has gone for ever, but when Death snaps a bud away before it has had a chance to come to a full-blown blossom, Death leaves behind the deepest sorrow a human heart can hold.

The author goes on: 'Some of the senior officers also dwelt on the value of the Christian religion to women ("it helps to keep them straight"); and also generally to the lower orders ("Nothing can give them a good time here, but it makes them more contented to think they will get one hereafter"). Christianity also seemed to have a disciplinary value; it made people want to be respectable, to keep up appearance, and saved a lot of scandals.'

My God, what a high order of thinking! Keep the lower orders quiet and content. Well, Christianity did its best, and still mumbles its admonitions, but we have shop stewards now, and no Bible class, sacraments, sermons, or gospel canting can stop or stay the unofficial strike. These senior officer-fellas are small beer now. Looks like God has left them. Churchill nourished himself into a great man; he is an old, white-browed, crinkled man now, great still in his evening glow, but he cannot answer, hasn't found an answer to his earlier questions: Science alone, penetrating the Christian mumble, is telling us more about these hidden things. Odd to think that at this very time of the seniors' satisfaction, there were terrors in the forms of Keir Hardie, Tillett, and Jim Larkin looming into the scene; terrors which would set the epaulettes shaking, and that O'Casey was one who lent a hand to create the power that would force the Church to hand over her crosier and the officer his sword.

After the centuries of this foolishness, hosts of people have come out into the air to breathe; they live by candle-light no longer. Even the songs of Araby have changed a lot. Life, so little a thing for so many centuries, has become the great thing now. Mass-man is becoming more aware of life's loveliness. The body has become more important than the soul (anyway, didn't a Church Council declare that the soul formed a substantial part of the body?), for while we have learned a lot about the body, and are rapidly learning more, we haven't learned a damned thing about the soul for the last two thousand years when everybody began talking about, and praying for, it. I wonder why did man fix himself into a soul, or let a soul be fixed into himself? Probably because, firstly, he couldn't understand why such an important being should be called upon to die. Secondly, man having come out of the dust, had to be ennobled in some way, so minds conceited declared that man could never die, for having been made from dust, he was, all the same, destined to be crowned with glory. So the Hebrew priest pondering by the waters of Babylon wrote the first of Genesis' idea of Creation, setting down that 'God made man in His own image'. Man of Destiny. And so the bugles began to blow, and blow still, but faintly now, like horns in elfland: man blowing his own trumpet.

How many eager minds are to be what they never can become, to ennoble themselves — not in the way of a quiet reason and a kindly heart, but a nobility of importance and of power over others; to fancy themselves towards a condition which with fair conceit they think to be one of exaltation; they want to be gods; if not whole ones, then half-gods. That is why so many, including priest and parson, hate to hear a mention of the activities of the lower part of the body. The body's basement store. Anathema from the waist down. The manner by which the ecstatic thrill of sex comes is terrible to them, and to many genteel ladies and gentlemen; poor frightened people. This, or any other natural and inevitable movement of the belly is hurried off within a chorus of 'Foul, unhealthy, filthy and vile'. These things keep us from assuring ourselves that we are but mortal, and can never be gods. We try to hide ourselves from what these genteel beings think of as hellish indignities of the flesh; as if the higher part of the body held heaven, and the lower part of it hid hell. The Very Reverend Henry Canon Fletcher of Killaloe Cathedral (the young and busy Harry Fletcher mentioned in the earlier part of the biography, who had married a rich wife, and had gone overseas as Chaplain to the British Forces, was now a man getting on to seventy, but sadly changed from what he had been. He had heard about what had been said of him, and, seeking the book from a library, was told it had been banned; but obtaining it afterwards from Trinity College, he had learned of his youth again, and was eager to see and speak with me. He had written several letters to me asking me about myself; but I had had a glimpse of him in London, and this, coupled with his dull and prosy letters, warned me to pass by on the other side) in one of his letters to me, after desultory writing in commonplace phrases, said: 'If it weren't that we had to go to the water-closet, we should be gods'. Who wants to be a god, since the apotheosis is impossible? There is no indignity in being as we are. If God (as Christians say) is responsible for man's appearance on this earth either by actual creation or through evolution, then he built the lower end of the body as well as the top one. Neither chasuble nor cassock can do away with it; nor can the shocked veiling of our hindparts save us from them. The organs bedded in the belly are as important as man's highest one — the brain. When disorders come within the belly, the brain is dulled; when the belly dies, the brain dies on the belly's doorstep. The body is one and indivisible; Orsino and Toby Belch are one person, as are Isabella and Doll Tearsheet.

Man's earthly nature and all within it have been through time bitter thorns in the spirit; it separates them from the certainty of eternal glory, shakes their faith in their godship. The ways man's body uses to keep everything going are a scare, a reproach, and a mocking. So in a dream, they brought down a god to share and endure them. Almost all the thoughts and efforts of almost all men, through the research and discoveries of the sciences, are now turned towards the study of how best to live in this world of activity, of sorrow, and of joy. Life is pulsed with efforts to make the pleasures of life something more than the good hours of an ague; and, indeed, the cardinal and the archbishop make quick and lasting use of all the benefits science has put at the feet of man. Materialism be god! Supernatural phenomena are for the credulous, and they applaud this piety; but they hurry away from the supernatural when a need comes and run for the help of man. When an affliction strikes the body, I have yet to hear of, or to read of, any cardinal or bishop scurrying off to Lourdes, a place soused in the supernatural phenomena of curative quality and power. When either is under the cloud of an illness, the one or the other flies off with supersonic speed to where they know medical or surgical science will do its damnedest to bring either back to correspondence with worldly things.

Dr. Ramsey, the present Archbishop of Canterbury, does his best to link the idea of man's immortality with the time-space thought and speculation of the day. Answering his own question of 'What is Man?' he tells us that man came into existence in the evolution of the mammal species on a little planet revolving round the sun (the earth going round the mulberry bush, and man appearing under it). Darwin told us something similar many years ago, and he or she who reads an evening newspaper knows this without a prompting tap on the head by an ecclesiastical crosier. We know that the present shape of things has evolved from shapes of the past, gone now; what they were like revealed only by picture or fossil in the museums of this and other lands; all things have gradually changed, and will go on changing, in spite of prayer-book or Bible. Even morals change: it was once a moral deed to burn at the stake a one who differed in any degree from the dictates of ecclesiasticism. It was once a moral act to drop an atom bomb upon the unfortunate people of Hiroshima; but man's manly nature — not his inherent divinity — halts at the possibility of such another ghastly fall.

The good Archbishop builds his idea of man's inherent immortality on the 'fact that man can reflect about the meaning of evolution and about the meaning of himself; that man is aware of certain concepts which have an absolute claim upon him: beauty, truth, goodness. If he doesn't respond to the claim wherever he may be aware of it, he experiences shame or guilt.'

But how is man to tell himself what is beauty, truth, or goodness? Since God seems unwilling to tell him, and the good Archbishop unable to do so, man must try to find out for himself, in his own way, something about what any of these concepts mean to him; and immediately he creates around him a world of differences and contentions: caps are flung away, coats are off, and fists are whirling; and this, now, and for centuries past, has been and is no less apparent in his own religion than in any other concept of thought. 'There is "something" Man is "meant" to do and to be', goes on His Grace. This 'something' is a damnably poor answer to an agonising question. Man himself has determined what he is now, and all he is meant to do has been created within himself without any outside interference or help, except by his environment and surrounding phenomena. Divinity that is said to shape our ends seems to have had nothing to do with it. Man may not know what he is 'meant' to do; but he knows a lot about what he means to do to make our future safer and the world a place more fitted for man to live in, work pleasantly, and enjoy his earned leisure among the arts, deep in the roar of encouragement on the sports field, or quietly resting by his family fireside when the days get cold, or under an old apple tree when the sun shows kindness.

We are not going to get any clear conception of truth, beauty, or goodness, by litanising our life, by knowing pat the tables of feast and fast, by hearing the lessons proper for this time or that, or by a weekly wail of cooing out our manifold sins and wickedness, or lugging home within us a weekly rum-tot of Absolution. A large portion of the world's peoples have done this for centuries, and after asking themselves why, and getting no answer, have turned to other ways, other things, other thoughts, to straighten out the way of life. Truth today is found only in the bosom of science, colored gloriously in art, and flowing forth in many-colored robes from music. In the world of men, truth is the centre of battling thought, and those who know her best are often a quarry for the sneering hunter, lots of these clerics busy seeking place and office: the times still show worth on foot and rascal in the coach.

His Grace goes on to ask, 'if these concepts be the outcome of some plan which man has made for his own happiness. This might be so, says the Archbishop, were it not that conscience sometimes compels a man to do things which serve no apparent useful purpose, and sacrifice home, country, happiness, utility, life itself, for the sake of a "must" which is beyond the temporal border.'

When are we over this temporal border, and awa'? For the sake of a 'must'! But this conscience may be born out of selfishness, ambition, the desire to show off, to be a big fellow: these promptings often stab a 'must' deep into a man's nature. We must be careful of fellows going about with a 'must' in the brain or as a badge on the breast. Like the laddo in *The Wild Duck* who couldn't live without telling the truth, and killed others in the telling of it. I 'must' tell the truth. This egg of 'must' in the conscience has slain its tens of thousands. We have had enough of it. This 'must' is doing a lot of harm over the Irish Border; an ideal setting the guns going. The prelate says again that 'the source of the moral life is beyond man's temporal existence'. I wonder how does he know this? And what other existence has a man other than that of this world? A belief of some institutional body, even when bedded into a creed, isn't necessarily a fact; and all research into man's being shows that man's complete existence is wholly contained within the body, and man's bodily experiences prove, or tend to prove, that the source of the moral life is the result of many generations of physical and psychological evolution; and with this the growth of social life, of the necessity to defend one another, and combination to defend the group; the need for safety and for order; environment and influence play their part, differing here, differing there, even among Christians themselves, evolving new codes of morals when the needs arise and man's mind takes a wider view of life. Today any onslaught on, or threat to, Islam isn't to bring them to the way of truth, but to make sure the Christians can hold on to the oil they have in their heathen lands. God has deposited the oil in the wrong places. Alla olla Allah!

The good Christians are now displaying their wonderful moral qualities to the Arab people with tanks, armoured cars, and nuclear cannon. Now the only thing needed to gild this moral life beyond man's temporal existence, and to show it in all its glory, is the Te Deum of hydrogen-bomb explosion.

If this moral 'must' be beyond the man, how did it, how does it get into him? He can't have what may be called moral thoughts, or indulge what custom calls moral actions, without the aid of the temporal body. It encases, or imprisons, every deed, every thought of the fellow. To speak the 'truth' he has to use his tongue; to heal the sick, he has to use the skill study and experience have given to his brain; to seize on 'beauty' he has to use his eyes or ears — and damned hard and often; to go to visit the sick or those in jail, he has to use his legs. The whole temporal man gets busy. If the moral life be beyond him, is the immoral life beyond him too? Is one a good ray penetrating his temporal nature, the other an evil one, so that the one leads feet to a church, the other leads other feet to the jail: afterwards, when both have separated from temporal existence, one going gay to heaven, the other sad to hell. However high and lofty this moral life may be, even allowing that it is beyond the searching mind of man, it is useless, and can do nix without the help and presence of the despised body. Surely, this moral existence is as natural as the natural man himself; developed as all other improving characteristics have been developed through the course of time; and has gone through many changes, here with us, and among other peoples, just as the material nature of man developed and changed century after century, so that the moral existence of man today isn't the same as his moral existence yesterday. For instance, it wasn't long ago that it was a moral act to hang a stealer of sheep or one who entered a house and bolted off with some of its goods, till a different and more humane moral conception among better men brought about a change in the severity of the law — a change which the bishops fiercely opposed, so that now it is becoming almost impossible to hang a man for anything. Were all these developments, all these changes, brought into being by a moral sense so mysteriously superior as to be entirely beyond man's temporal existence? Maybe the Archbishop means that this supernatural force which creates within, or projects into, the nature of temporal man, changes too, and develops into something newer and nobler as space vanishes and time goes by; but that would make the force somewhat inferior to evolution itself, which wouldn't suit the Archbishop's plea, which itself seems to resemble Mr. De Valera's plea that the Republic is, and yet is not, within the confines of the British Commonwealth. The weakness of the prelate's case is that when one begins to probe it, there is nothing there: it seems to be a supernatural vacuum: within and yet without man's temporal existence.

As for the good Archbishop's 'must', though a man may give up everything to do something he feels he must do (enter a religious order, for instance), he doesn't abandon or desert happiness — he seeks it. He is in the condition of never being happy without it, so he plunges away from all things that separate, or seem to separate, him from the object or the condition that he believes may make him happy. Thought for himself is at the bottom of all he does. It is among ordinary people that the greatest deeds are done: the fireman who plunges through smoke and fire to save a grown-up or a child; the doctor who will risk his life to care for her or him stricken with any terrible and infectious disease; he and the nurse who helps him; the mother who in all times of tribulation acts as shield and buckler to her growing family; the men of the lifeboat, who in the fiercest weather seek to deliver a crew from a battered ship; and all the host of these great souls, unhonoured, and often unknown, who, in the danger, the risk, and the trouble, seek no personal gain, no personal happiness, look for no special reward, except that of satisfaction of running to the aid, and of being able to give it, to distressed members of the human family. Heroism outside of this is virtually a selfish, and very often an interfering and wasteful, practice, like the lass in T. S. Eliot's *The Cocktail Party*, poking her priggish presence into the life of a people who walked and talked together in their way. Would she do that with them, walk with them in their way? Not bloody likely! They must (another of them 'musts') walk and talk henceforth as she walked and as she talked, and they were to make no mistake about it. She wasn't going to leave bad enough alone. She was a one-way, her own way, a truth, and a life, and she would make them realise it. We aren't told how she lived while she was driving the innocent people to frenzy by pitting her incantations against theirs; where she slept, what she ate, or how she got all this accommodation before the exasperated natives provided her with the means to reach where she was so eager to go. Souls had to work to provide her with all these things: odd how much these heavenly things have to depend on the things of this world, with not as much as By your leave when they get them or a Thank you when they are satisfied. All waste.

Another 'must' is born within the nature of the artist; a 'must' in many ways more fantastic in its sacrifices than any running after a god. The one who feels within a great gift, artist or scientist, will bear almost any discomfort or pain, any hunger, any indignity, rather than let the gift go; as Van Gogh, the painter, did, and Darwin did before him, to prove the thesis of evolution; Faraday who worked silently with wire and string to find out all about the magnetic field; Gauguin who abandoned a big business position, home, and family; who endured lasting poverty to paint his vision on wall and canvas. Each artist and scientist carries out what he 'is meant to do' out of his own means, and not out of any impulse given by an outside supernatural prod; the urge comes from chromosome or gene, or both. Few have heard of any churchman having a good job, bishop and such, leaving his palace, giving up income from his mensal parishes, and various church fees, giving him a diet above the naked spud and pinch of salt, for a hut of clay and wattles made, preferring the warm palace, the carpets on the floor and curtains on the window, bottle of port, and an odd game of poker, to roving around reading a breviary in any bee-loud glade.

There was Joyce, too: look at what Stanislaus Joyce says about his brother: 'If my brother had abandoned his family to enter the Jesuit Order, that would not have been cowardly; that would have been an obedience to a higher call to a spiritual life — the spiritual life of the Jesuits! My brother had hearkened to a spiritual call, inaudible to their dull ears, and he followed it to the end with an unflinching courage unique in his generation in Ireland, but not without being assailed on occasion by sharp pangs of doubt.' Tremendous manhood! Had he decided to take the higher road, he would have saved himself a lot of poverty, hard labour, and his mind would quickly have come into a routine resting-place. James Joyce would probably have disappeared for ever, and nothing would have eventually remained but, maybe, a bleak name on a bleaker stone, hidden away in a corner, unglanced at by any passer-by. First lost among the living; then lost among the dead. Oh, that 'higher call' or that 'something outside of man's temporal existence', which are exploited to flatter an Order, or add another mouth to blow upon the sinking embers of a dying creed!

Conscience, too, seems to be but a development of the mind, and this development, bad or good, comes not from heaven, but from temporal experiences. Agen-bite of inwit, often a damned hangover from dying beliefs and creeds contentious. It is the propulsion the mind gets from the way we live, the people we meet, the things we do. It is knowledge absorbed within us from all the impacts, home, parents, school, friends, adding on what we experience in field, factory, workshop, and office; but chiefly from the early experience we meet with during the years of our youth; the things that make one man a laborer, another a bishop; the opportunities and necessities of life lived. Examples of personal evolution. This one's conscience may be born of humility, that one born of conceit. It isn't sensible to associate conscience always with what the Archbishop deems to be virtue, both coming out from temporal surroundings. It never makes us certain of what is right and what is wrong, and laws built up on the assumptions of conscience have always been fought by an opposing conscience to persuade or force them to be changed. The conscience of the Albigenses differed so bitterly from the conscience of the Pope of the day that he sent his army to destroy them all, believing that the Albigensian conscience was supernatural, but coming up from below, whereas his came down from above. The patriotic Protestant conscience of the great Churchill, the gentle but indomitable conscience of the great Roosevelt, and the agnostic conscience of the great Stalin, collided with the imperative, Catholic conscience of Hitler and the pathetic, clumsy, conscience of Mussolini. At the Old Bailey a witness was called upon to identify the name on a document, but refused, quoting the Archbishop's sacred scriptures, 'Judge not that ye be not judged'. The Judge sent him away for a day to think over it, saying to him, 'If, when you come here again, you don't feel in a different frame of mind, there are ways and means which may cause you to reconsider your opinion'. Brought before the Judge the following day, the man's conscience was still sound. He refused to answer questions, saying he lived by the infallible laws of God rather than by the infallible laws of man, and he would not bear witness against his neighbour. The Judge ordered him to be kept in custody till he was prepared to reconsider his decision. This 'must', glorified by the prelate, born out of the sacred scriptures, was a nuisance, and couldn't be permitted to hold up the other 'must' in the conscience of the Judge who had to 'administer the law'. Oh, indeed, a 'must' in a conscience will force one to let himself be burned at a stake for a creed, another 'must' will sanctify a man about to be hanged for loving his country; while other 'musts' will kindle the fire for the burning, or

build the scaffold on which a patriot is to die. Looks
as if conscience was born from no airs from heaven
or blasts from hell; but formed itself from the five
senses of man absorbing into his mind the multitude
of activities and thoughts around him, some of them
chosen suddenly or gradually, garnished with customs
and traditions of those who lived in the old time
before us, who left their beliefs to be gathered by
many who followed them, the one giving divinity to
the conscience lasting longer than many others, but
descending into a rudimentary spot in the human mind,
explained, not by holy writ, or a bishop's homily, but
by the newer science of psychology, to be further
probed by neurological electronics which charts the
rhythms of the brain of one man thinking of the football pools and of another thinking of God. Conscience
with its thousand tongues, every tongue chanting a
differing tale, is tightened or loosened by the nerval
wonder of the human mind. It is of the earth, earthy,
as earthy as Hamlet's conscience saying 'The play's
the thing, wherein I'll catch the conscience of the
king'. Play on his nerves with the play, and his
nerves will wilt, and he will show himself a villain.

The Archbishop asks if these seemingly absolute
concepts were thrown up from the processes of the
solar system or the evolution of species like phenomena
which come and go; incidents in the story like the
brontosaurus or the pterodactyl? And what else are
they, what else can they be? After all, the coming of
the lizards was hardly an 'incident'. It is said that
they lived for a period of sixty million years, so seemingly God was satisfied with their appearance and
conduct, however frightful or comic they may have
looked plunging about among the fern and the rush.

It is only when man appears that the row begins. Man hasn't had time even to grow a beard before he and the missus are banished from the Garden, and the gate locked to keep them out of it for ever. A few years after, when man had multiplied, they behaved themselves so much against beauty, truth, and goodness, that, bar a family few, they were all drowned in the mighty fall of many waters when the windows of heaven were opened, and the rains came down. So when the flood subsided, the one family had to begin again to replenish the world with people, God having hung a rainbow out in the sky to tell Noah that it ain't gonna rain no more. But row followed row, and the chronicles are filled with the complaint from heaven about the conduct of man; again a great deal of the turbulent race had to be destroyed, this time by fire and brimstone, an atom bum; and two great cities went up in smoke, all perishing, bar another little family which had to make again a new beginning. On and on and down and down we go, along with the Chosen People who couldn't or wouldn't keep in the straight way, but persisted in offending, chasing beauty, truth, and goodness out of tent and town, sending them flying over the hills and far away.

Such absolute concepts, goes on the Archbishop, are the road to a belief in God and in immortality. 'A baby', he says, 'matters more than a million stars, more than the process of evolution which led up to there being babies at all, because he will presently be able to respond with reverence and love to *That* which gives meaning to the whole.' That's a spectacular rise for a baby on the human stock exchange — worth more than a million stars! Of course, this depends on the quality of the baby born, for it may never grow into

the wit of doing reverence to *That* which had made
the million stars. In my young days, and for a long
time after, devil a lot was thought about a baby, for
the families, at least among the poor, were huge ones,
and the death of two or three was a common occurrence,
and didn't halt the family stride for more than an hour.
My own mother had thirteen children, of whom eight
died—a fair average mortality rate among the children of
the workers. Even today, in Europe, Asia, and Africa,
there are millions of babies who live lives which, if they
had enough wit, would cause them to wish they had
never been born. Of course a bishop's baby would get
a fair deal; it wouldn't have to bother about what it
shall eat or drink, or wherewithal it shall be clothed.
I wonder does what the Archbishop calls '*That*' think
as much of a baby as It does of a star? What system
of theology gave him that impression? Is he sure?
Up to very recently, even in Christian England, babies
have had a damned bad time of it; and today, even,
there are many ill-clad and undernourished tots, born
into an environment which will hardly give them a
chance to grow into reverence for anything. I remember a friend, a doctor who was an authority on
infant welfare, who visited London County Coun-
cillors and members of Parliament, and tried to induce
them to put forward a Bill so that property owners of
flats should be by law forced to add an open-air balcony
to every flat built by them so that a baby could be
placed out in the air, under the unimportant stars, to
help in ensuring a healthy growth of the organs within
the body of the infant life; but he always met with a
refusal: none was interested either in star or in baby.
Madonna and Child among church-goers, mother and
child among those who don't go, is honored in song

and in story, in pictures, bronze, and stone, but the living ones with the living children are often thought of as much as a calendar over a year old. Dogs? Oh, yes; dogs all right. The other day, a daily gave an account of a lunch to which a thousand dogs were invited. In a Piccadilly restaurant, the dogs sat down to a meal of sausages and biscuits, flavoured with meat essence; and we have a Dogs' Bath Club and a Dogs' Beauty Parlour, where well-bred animals living in Mayfair and Knightsbridge go to be clipped, shampooed, and manicured, or to be provided with warm woollen coats, mink collars, with diamonds shining in them here and there. The dog deserves his day, and it isn't easy to witness the death of any loved animal. A babe deserves all the care that care can give, without any need for the canting sentimentality of 'a baby matters more than a million stars': it may, or it may not. What we know is that a babe becomes the child, the child the youth, the youth the woman and the man, an outcome most important, for according to how a life is lived means that life has gained, or life has lost, a little or a lot. Where do you come from, baby dear? Out of the everywhere into here. I'm afraid that not many are led into the Christian belief by any Archbishop declaring that a baby matters more than a million stars just because it grows (if it be unfortunate or fortunate, for there is a multitude, born babies, now men and women, who never develop the faculty of thought beyond their own immediate need and desire, and many, many of them go regularly to church or mass) into the power of reflecting over the absolute concepts of truth, goodness, and new beauty, and so adds to these concepts a belief in a God and its own immortality.

We know now a great deal about the physical reasons for the conception of life and the physical reasons for the phenomenon of death, though whence and whither and why still remain the secrets of nature, hidden alike from the infidel and the believer. We have it stated that to the Archbishop, at least, a baby matters more than a million stars, but is it the same with the God as pictured in those scriptures from which the Christians get their Faith? Does God, or did He, regard the million-star baby with the same valuation given it by the prelate? Let a soul with more authority, however, put the million-star baby question: Dr. Walter McDonald, Professor of Theology at Maynooth College for forty years, in a book asks, 'Was Samuel ethically right in pressing Saul with threats of Javeh's supreme displeasure, for not having put to death even the women and babies whom he had taken from Amalec? Could even God command a King to smash the heads of all the babies he might find in the cities of his enemies?'

This learned prelate doesn't seem to be right even if his babies matter most because they will presently be able to respond with reverence and love to *That*, and the *That* to which he responds is so akin to what is significant in himself that he will name his god not *That* but *He*. The Archbishop seems to be thinking in terms of a Sunday school, for an immense number — continually increasing — have turned away from the response of reverence and love for the prelate's *He* to the condescending and cursory contemplation of the prelate's *That*, and even this yawn of a sleepy interest is fading quick among the multitude of thoughts concerning the amazing things revealed by Science about the baby and about the star, for the star, too, is of the stuff that babes are made on, and Man is eager and pushful in his efforts to find out more about both of them.

The road mapped out by the Archbishop leads us to belief in God and belief in immortality; or so he says. Immortality. A word about which many books have been written, some an elaborate Yes, others an emphatic No; a word that has given birth to much agony of mind and thought to many souls; a word carved deep into many stones that have crumbled away and become themselves as the dust of him or her whose hope they proclaimed so boldly on the stone at their first carving; a word that eased many at the time of their going, and softened the hard sorrow of the farewell of them who had loved the departing ones; a word that found a tidily-prepared place in men's hearts for centuries, now has to fight a way there, and is often defeated and driven out, unhappy, wandering, lost. Many are the numbers of men who, when they come to die, are content to say farewell for ever to those who still remain behind. Life has become an everlasting hail and farewell. For centuries, the committal of the body to the ground within God's Acre preserved a vague sense of nearness of the dead one to those who mourned their going, but this era of cremation prescribes a complete disappearance, and nothing is left to remind the living of the dead one but a fleeting memory. We see with our own eyes that all perishes, save a tiny handful of dust and ashes to be scattered in a river, a lake, or over a blossoming garden. What can live on when all is gone: the soul? Something supernatural in a man, having neither physical nor material existence, but more real and lasting than if it had, lighter than airy nothing, living on and for ever when the body dies. Departing through the mouth, as the Middle Ages believed, a belief perpetuated by the poets, as in Pope making Eloisa say to Abelard,

> See my lips tremble and my eyeballs roll,
> Suck my last breath, and catch my flying soul:

And Yeats in his *The Hour-Glass*, when the Wise Man dies, makes the Fool say, 'Look, look, what has come from his mouth . . . a little winged thing . . . a little shining thing . . . it has gone to the door . . . the Angel has caught it in her hands. She will open her hands in the Garden of Paradise.' A breath; puff! And that is the part of man which is to go on living for ever till the day when it and a glorified body shall be reunited to spend in spiritual and bodily satisfaction the rest of eternity in heaven. Is this Christian theological teaching? Is the body but a tenement for the soul having no integral attachment to the body itself? Divil a know I know, but let us see what a more qualified mind has to say about it all.

In the book published after his death, Dr. Walter McDonald says, 'touching on the possible troubles facing the Church, over definitions with anathema attached, the great test case, I fancy, is likely to be that decree of the Council of Vienne, as to the human soul being a substantial form of the body. That the Council taught it to be so I take as evident from the words of the decree; as also that the definition is one of supreme authority, claiming infallibility. Is it infallible? Is it even true?

'In what sense is the soul a substantial form of the body? Or in what sense is the matter of which the body is composed — chemical ingredients, such as are found in the inorganic world — in need or capable of a substantial form? Is it that the soul acts as a source of energy? But is there any smallest fragment of the energy of the human body — nerves or muscles — that does not come into it from the ether, as to any other machine ? Conscious sensation, you will say; but is there any sensation that does not reside in the nervous system, consisting entirely of material motions, which, no less surely than the movements of a black-smith's arm, arise chemically?

'They tell us now from Rome that this difficulty has been cleared up, by discovery of the writings of John Peter Oliver; which, however it may have de-cided the question in dispute between Cardinal Zigliara and Father Palmieri, S.J., has left the real difficulty precisely where it was [as you were!]. In what sense, capable of being brought into harmony with modern biological science, is the human soul a substantial form of the body, wherewith it is united?' So, here we are, with a theologian of long study, of great theological experience, a man of brave mind, who stood high in his ecclesiastical profession, inquiring into the Church's declaration that the soul is a substantial form of the body; though no precise statement is given as to what parts of the body in particular the soul has her functions in. Nor does Archbishop Ramsey in his short thesis say a damned word about it.

While the Church seems to say that the soul is a substantial part of the body, the psycho-analysts seem to banish the psychic-soul from all material attachment, connection, or physiological touch to the body proper or improper. Freud seems to say that in psycho-analysis all materialistic conceptions of the mind with the material body, chemical, physiological ideas and knowledge of the body, discovered by mental and nerve scientists, are to be set aside, and all ideas of its mystery must be entirely on the plane of psychoanalysis itself, without any reference to bio-chemistry, physiology, or any other materialistic concept. Anyone suffering from a complete inhibition, or any kind of a neurosis, cannot be cured, cannot, it seems, even be helped by any medical, surgical, or scientific skill. Help can be given only by psychological assistance and suggestion that are, in themselves, definitely psycho-analytic. The disease or hurt is too far down in the unconscious to be reached by any purely physical means, and must be brought up into the light and the air only by psychological aid applied by the questions, suggestions, and psychological replies given by the patient: the unconscious must be prised up by the psycho-analyst till it swims to the surface of the patient's mind, is revealed to the psycho-analyst and the patient from God knows where in the sufferer's mind; the revelation in the patient's confessions, delved up from the unconscious by the probing questions of the psycho-analyst, the searching of the mind, normal or abnormal, by any material, methodical means is pooh-bahed aside; put high on a shelf, shoved into a corner, pushed out into the cold. Again, the Irish philosopher, George Russell (A.E.) had the grand idea that in sleep the Psyche shot out of the body, and went flying off on a grand tour into fairy lands forlorn, catching, as it glided over mountain and dale, glimpses of the majesty of man's one-time glory as a god among the masters round the Ancient Light. The Church, theosophy, and psycho-analysis — over-soul and under-soul — defining the nature, the ideals, the destiny, the ills, the frets, shocks of sorrow and of joy, what elevates, what degrades, till we become confused, no longer realising which is which or what is what; forcing most of us to return to the older way, developing into a wider and more definable one, keeping our feet on the earth, our eyes upon ourselves, our minds sifting and solving the result upon mind and body of the impacts of the world we live in and the only one we know. Most of the odd suffusions of the mind, due to what is called the hidden urge of the unconscious, are, by psycho-analysis, I imagine, attributed to sex instinct and sex practices. It seems to be to the psycho-analysts what original sin is to the Christians, seeping up continuously from the deepest and unfathomable recesses of the mind. But sex, even to women, who have to regard it more intimately and seriously than men, forms but a part, an important part, for it is the life-giver, but by no means even the bigger part of human activity.

Looks to me as if this sullen and secret activity embedded in what is called the subconscious, which manifests itself in thought and emotions inexplicable to the sufferer, in the complex and the neurosis, is similar to the demonic possession so fervently believed in in the superstitious Middle Ages, is similar to the doctrine of psycho-analysis that is hummed into the ear of humanity today; and that the exorcising priest of the Middle Ages has been shoved aside to make way for the psychiatrist of the present age; and that the one is just as infatuated as the other. It would seem to me that all these things are within the solid, but marvellously delicate and active organism we call the body, and only by the study of the solid substance (solid, I imagine, in so far as it stays where it has been placed, and cannot flow in the manner of the blood;

that it is tissue however delicate and fragile it may be), with its multitude of semi-miraculous cells, by material means, can we get to know something of the present apparent mystery of the mind and of all its magic workings; by means of the newer electronics, by what we see, touch, and test, can we, using our own special-ised and wonderful minds, get to know the things that are yet hidden from our understanding. Forgive my ignorance, but I cannot help thinking the deeper re-cesses of the mind to be as material as those which sparkle at the top of it; and that the neurosis is caused by a material condition of the material matter of the brain, not yet reached by the probe of the material mind. Is God there, too, down in the deep recess as well as in the upper story?

There are things we should like to be able to ex-plain as well as the wonder, the quids and quiddities of the human mind. The wonder and mystery of the amazing creature, the penguin, that has made the eternal ice its own. A bird! In their mating time, they waddle to the breeding ground, sometimes over sixty miles of uneven ice, to get to the land where they can lay and hatch their brood in cold comfort. Arriv-ing there, they make their nest of stones, slyly, at times, pinching stones from the nests of other birds to heighten their own, so that, if snow should thaw, the nest will be above any water that may form there. One of them sits on it, while the other goes back to the sea to feed, travelling with a waddle back over the sixty miles of uneven snow and ice, staying five or six weeks in the sea, feeding. Then he returns to his mate, over the sixty miles of ice, unerringly reaching the spot where his lonely mate waits; taking her place to allow her to do the hard journey to the sea to feed,

which she does for four or five weeks, returning again
to help her mate bring forth their brood of chicks. At
a certain age, these leave their parents, congregating
together with all the other chicks, who are visited by
the parent birds for feeding purposes, each couple
recognising their young immediately, and feeding only
those who have on them the claim of offspring. Again,
after a certain time, these young return to their nest
and the continued help and protection of the parents,
till the down on their bodies has been replaced by a
full feathering, and the young become full-fledged with
feathers, able to take care of themselves. So parents
go one way, their young another, all seeking the sea
to live again as they had lived for thirty million years;
coming back in due time to mate once more, each
couple with its old mate, for almost always each couple
reunite in mating time, going straight to the old spot
where their nest had been before, never wandering
from it, piercing the identical place out again with a
sure and unerring instinct. One can almost believe
that God was, at least, among the penguins.

What an amazing show of the instinct in the unconscious psyche of the penguin! A vital display of the
psyche's response to the environment in which the bird
chooses to live; live effectively and, apparently, very
happily too. The psyche embedded in the centre of
whatever mind the bird may have forms its impulses
and its actions by the surrounding sea and ice and
snow; while the psyche of the Emperor penguin tells
it a nest isn't needed, so it builds none; that when the
eggs are hatched the male will bring them forth, doing
without food for three months, while the female feeds
in the sea, returning straight to her mate — though
there is no fixed residence — at hatching time full of

food to feed the ravenous chicks till they are ready to go forth for themselves. Everything within and without formed by the pressure of environment — the flippers, the feathers, the beak, the powerful legs with expansive webbed feet, fit to waddle over sixty miles of frozen sea to reach the land where they can settle down to a family life till its function is fulfilled, and they and those born to them set out to swim the sea again; then when the time comes, each dying alone, just like man. So like ourselves going through any life experience, concentrating on the doing of whatever may be necessary at the time, separating our life from the common tasks as much as we can till the need is over, and then gliding or waddling back again to swim about in the sea of everyday social life. The action hidden away and forgotten, in the depths of the psyche, coming to the surface when the need was there, just as the magic crook comes instantaneously to the young mother's arm when she holds the first life born to her so that the utmost ease and comfort is given to the helpless baby.

But man's mind is much more complex than the mind of a penguin; but no less material, and no less a reflection of its environment than the mind of the big bird. Psycho-analysis has become a fulsome fashion among many of the writers and reviewers of the world. One is now psycho-analysed if a head is scratched, a toe twinkled, a thumb bitten. When I myself ventured to criticize A. E.'s ideas on art, drama, and politics, I was immediately set down (in A. E.'s paper) as being in the hollow of a deep neurosis. Maybe I was, but how did this neurosis arise, and where was it placed within me? In the subconscious, say the shoddy psycho-analysts who are without training or experience; deep down among the dead men of the mind. Presumably, however low down or deep down this neurosis happened to have its bed, it still must be a material part of the material brain, since it cannot arise out of nothing, since *ex nihilo nihil fit*. But it is said that these psychic processes — neuroses, fixations, complexes, and the rest, must be thought of as completely independent of the customary processes or activities of the brain; that they don't come from physical or bio-chemical causes; that all physiological theories must be Winnie-pooh-poohed out of the mind, and that only what are called psychological concepts can be used and applied, if an improvement, or better still, a cure is to be effected in some human whose psyche has become upset so as to prevent the thought and habits of the afflicted one being restored to sweetness and light. But where do these psychic concepts themselves come from? These concepts which when revealed, and shown, colored poster-like, before the vision of the curer and to-be-cured, which revelation may (or may not) cause a relieving cure, or even an improvement, in mind and manner of living, surely spring from somewhere in the human brain, and so must, first and last, be due to material disturbances or stimulation in a material organ. However odd or strange a human mind may become, the cause must be a reflection of environment and experience from the brain, some part of the brain, within a man, and however hard one may try, as poet, painter, philosopher, or friend, a man cannot climb out of himself.

While a man is within the glimpses of the moon, he is as alive as one of sweet Molly Malone's cockles; but sooner or later, he dies, and the rest is silence.

And what lives on after all is gone which gives that immortality the Archbishop writes about, and gives him and Christians the ready-made assurance of eternal life? When Molly Malone died of the fever (for no one could save her), what part or particle of her went on living? Was it Molly's subconscious, her soul, that wheeled a wheelbarrow through the streets of Dublin, in the form of a ghost? Did the conscious feminine die with her body and the unconscious masculine live on? The *anima* or the *animus*? When we die, do we live on in the archetypal? Is there some particle of us, intangible, invisible, to us in the corporeal state, that lives on in the shape of one of Jung's fantastic dreams rising like a colored mist from the still-existing unconsciousness? Do we in an incomprehensible way go on having the dreams that are said to be so effective in the therapy of neurosis; or do they change into glorified imaginations? Do those intuitions, intimations that used to come from unknown sources; moods, plans, and hopes that came from invisible causes; still flame in whatever faculty remains alive? But invisibility and unknown sources explain nothing; for another eye may see a thing invisible, and another ear detect a sound unheard by man. The blind bat can feel what his eye cannot see, and can fly without being touched through a close mesh of obstacles. Many viruses remain invisible, but they are there, all the same, as real as the fingers on a hand. The unconscious is as real as the conscious; and both reflect what we have done, seen, heard, felt, all are projections of the material mind, and being so, must themselves be material too; and all that is mysterious in them can but become known to us through the material means of the penetration of science into the material structure of the mind. Science now can, at least, show the vibrations of the human mind by electronic means, showing how different are the movements of a brain thinking of a girl, of a work of art, of a football match: all of them manifestations in a material way of the nervous pulsation of a material mind, but a wonderful one. Sad, too, for this material manifestation seems to do away with any hope even of a minor survival of a human being when death has sealed a soul away from life. So the gallivanting assurance of the Archbishop in a belief in immortality fades off into the tantalising shimmer of a pious pipe-dream.

It isn't a comforting thought for those who have lost loved ones, and who, later on, will go themselves, to think that all is over with those who have gone, and will be with those who go next. The young son or a daughter of a family, ones with a lithe body, an alert mind, a promising future, who died before those who loved them; who had cherished him or her since babyhood, played with them, talked with them, taught them to read, nursed them in illness, encouraged each onward in all ways of life, and then saw either die and come to an end. It seems impossible to believe that all that mattered of either still lives on; that something called the soul survives actively, as promulgated by the Church and indicated in Thornton Wilder's sad and lovely play *Our Town*. But is it so? Day by day, it seems that science is disproving this fancy held so long, and nursed so fondly within the arms of Faith. All is within the body, and when the body perishes, all activities perish with it. Disillusion is not a thing of today; it began long, long ago; even in Ireland; even with a great and courageous priest. The Church still plunges about in the morass of tradition, never leaving the quaking for a firmer path. As Dr. Walter McDonald says: 'On many questions I have found peace of mind, on lines no little divergent from the tradition. I do not suggest that I have been able to clear up all difficulties. . . . Nothing stands entire — not even the theory of gravitation as propounded by Newton. I have reached peace after mighty storms of fear and trouble; but how many other souls are tossed on the waters, or have found peace of a kind only by abandoning all supernatural religion! Comfortable Cardinals, Bishops, Consultors, safe, comfortable men who rule our councils, might think of these, and have some pity. God does not deny grace to those who do not willingly desert Him; but do not plenty deny and desert Him only after years of agonised effort to reconcile the irreconcilable? Why not face the significant and awful fact?'

Near a thousand a week leave the Roman Catholic Church in England alone; fifty per cent of those Catholics who leave school go out of the Church, and wave a hand to her no more. A Graham Greene or a Dame Edith Sitwell enters the Church, a thousand lesser-known, but equally important souls leave it. The present Pontiff, Pope John, has been asking his Cardinals why the Church has lost the workers — as if they could tell him! The salvage corps of Worker Priests sent to convert them failed, and Vatican officials threw fits when they learned the priests were marching behind the Red Flag. Was God with the Worker Priests marching behind the Red Flag, or with the Vatican officials throwing fits? The Church is meeting a challenge everywhere she goes, everywhere she is; a challenge from which the face is hidden, the hands folded either in irritation or in prayer. She is challenged about the ways of heavenly life as much as in the ways of this life on earth, and she is unwilling or unable to meet either. She is as one running hither and thither, like a lost kid, not knowing the way home. Many are asking the questions asked by Dr. McDonald many years ago; and asking many more new ones, and the Church answers not, staying still in a sulk. As Dr. McDonald says, ' There are plenty of men like me, not in Ireland, perhaps, but on the Continent and in America, who feel the pressure of these difficulties, as poor Mivart felt them in his closing days. And the number of such afflicted ones is growing, even, I fear, in Ireland, which, after all, though set out so far from the main currents of thought, yet cannot hope to escape altogether from their action. Those tons of literature which are landed daily at our quays will have their effect despite what Vigilance Associations may be established to resist them. My books, if published, might do a little to withstand the Revolution, which the religious guardians of our religion will not see coming, or will endeavour to keep out with their broomsticks [crosiers?]. Good men, animated by the best of motives, but so shortsighted and so cruel, too, in their religious blindness to such as cannot shut their eyes.'

Shortsighted, cruel, blind, beating back new thought with broomsticks! So thought, and so wrote, Dr. McDonald more than forty years ago. Today, as well as tons of literature, we have tens of thousands of wireless sets pouring dangerous sounds into the ears of the Irish. Now there will be Television displaying shocking sights to the frightened eyes of the maid and the downcast eyes of the man when any reproving eye is on the watch, with the Guardian Angels' wings worn to the last feather, flying round to keep the young man and the young maid from the thousand occasions of illuminated sin. The Devil is going about, roaring like any sucking dove, among the electronics.

So we come back to what Mr. Eliot, the famous poet, would call the desert of doubt, the night of disillusionment; the rejection of the Christian faith as promulgated by the various creeds, and the different traditions each Church uses to expand the deposit of faith handed on by the apostles. One of them is what the former Archbishop of York puts forward as a prime belief, namely, the immortality of man. We here have, in most senses, to think of, and to meditate upon, the Christian conception of immortality, setting aside the colorful heaven of Mahomet, the universal one of Buddhism, the withering away of self, the non-becoming when one has reached the reality of the true self. For many years now, countless numbers of people have ceased to bother much about the various manifestations of Christianity, but a Christian, practising or lapsed, a Christian, or nonChristian, has, at one time or another, thought on, been concerned about, his own personal survival after death; or, if not concerned with his own, has been so when a loved one, a wife, mother, father, son, or daughter, has gone from life. What is called the soul lives on, and, at the last day, is to be reunited with the body; in the twinkling of an eye the body we knew, full of suffering and deformed, will become a glorified one. Too large a vision for the common man; too oddly distant from the possible to the one who knows what Science has told him. A belief held for long, now held no longer: it cannot be so, cries the thinking mind. We can no longer hear like Herbert with the ears of faith the chime of church bells beyond the stars. And, for all her confidence, the Church is puzzled, and, today, stammers her answer to the denial of that no soul exists. The dream of Gerontius is never dreamed by many now. The soul, says the Roman Catholic Church, forms a substantial part of the body; and one of her bravest and most thoughtful theologians asks how much, how many; where does the soul link herself to the human body; what part of the body is to perish, what part of it is to go on living for ever? The questions still linger on in an odd ear, but most of us have ceased to bother about it, except when a loved one dies, and then this old question haunts the ear for a short time, or for a long time, according to the depth of the affection and sense of loss felt for the loved one gone. I myself, six years ago, had to face the loss of a handsome lad of twenty-one, and since had often foraged about in my mind as to what happened to him; where did he go? We know that it was leukaemia, and not God, that took him away; but that solves not the mystery of his coming here, his presence here for a short time, his hasty departure from life. What was, who was, this handsome form of intense activity in human form who was called Niall? We knew him from the day he first came to the day he died; and yet, we knew him not. We knew the eyes bright and blue that penetrated into the life of insect and flower, and into, very often, the hidden motives of men and women. We knew the delicately-shaped ears that were so keen to hear any little oddness in the manner and sound of those who spoke when he was present; we heard him play on the mellow trombone which he loved so much; saw the rather delicate-looking hands make a fine catch at cricket; the lithe leg sending a ball towards the goal

in a football game; we hear still the echo of his sometimes caustic, more often hilarious laugh; and, above
all, we mourn the loss of the keen, kindly, but relent-
less mind, which promised to make the boy a first-class
biologist. Now they are all gone. All these delightful aspects of human mind, of human body, in a
happy and resolute boy, have gone, and, since his dear
body was cremated, not a trace of any of them has
been left. Only a few things that this life, which
walked amongst us, which we knew so well, and loved
so much, which the life called its own, remain — the
books, the gramophone records, a few letters, and the
bright trombone. These have outlasted the human
life, and, as far as I can judge, they have also outlasted
the human soul. It is a grievous and a bitter realisation, for the loss of our boy has left an ache in the
mind that will be there till the mind feels it is itself a
part of the still and silent dead.

It is not a lonely loss, but is shared by others,
thousands of them. A number of my own friends
carry this mourning hidden deep in their hearts;
mourning for young sons, one for a young daughter;
all with an ache in their minds which can never end
till they end with it; for the gnawing question of why
and whither is busy fashioning biting fancies in their
thoughts. Only the other day, as the New Year
dawned, a cleric, Colin Day, from a Scottish Television
station, speaking about the phrase of 'Thy will be
done' in the Lord's prayer, pictured to all the viewers
a mother sitting by the bed of a young son, watching
him die from leukaemia, without being able to do a
thing about it; murmuring, the cleric said, the words,
'Thy will be done' to bring consolation to her dis-
tracted mind. The model words were to enchant her

into a resigned, almost happy, reception of her loss. The mother could do nothing about it; and it seemed that God could not, or would not, do anything about it either. This clergyman couldn't see, couldn't understand, that this woman, if she were a sensitive mother, could go on saying, 'Thy will be done' ten thousand times over but still would for ever be sitting by the bedside watching her son die, without being able to do anything about it, and that no murmur, however pious, however it might be doused in tradition, could ever erase the deeply written sorrow of her mind.

Nothing can be done about it; the boy's soul has gone to heaven; so say 'Thy will be done', and be done with it. There they sit — the stricken mother, and the cleric trying to console her, trying to cod the woman with a mingled murmur of Thy wills be done; for neither could do anything about it: the boy had to be off, and no hand could hold him back. Let the body be hidden in the ground, all of it, the body improper, the soul-sister proper forming substantial part of the body; hide it under the clay, or let it disappear in a flame of fire; but get it out of sight, and whenever an impulse comes to question, or a doubt pricks the mind, scatter both by a murmur of 'Thy will be done', the everlasting and ever-ineffectual incantation to drive away sorrow into silence.

Sorrow should never be silent; it should be resentful, and fight whatever brings it into heart or home; fight in every way we can to abolish war, its ruin, its misery, its barbarism; fight to dispel disease, till every body born is healthy, and every life spend itself full before its end. To attach the will of God to the death of a young boy or girl through leukaemia, or any other vile malady, is not only blasphemy, but the most stupid of its kind. We should join with those, however simple the way must be, who fight to redeem man from the curse of disease. There is always a way of doing a little, and the least of these simple ways is more effective, even towards the way of lessening the ache of personal grief, than sitting glum, murmuring to the idle air a multitude of Thy wills be done. If we content ourselves with this sweet duplicity, thousands of other mothers year by year will sit by their sons' bedsides, with some hedged-in clerical mind hovering over them, watching a child die, without being able to do anything about it. Not only those of our own body, but all children are our sons and our daughters, and we must fight for them. Let us look deeper than a glance can do into this saying of 'Thy will be done', and we can see there is resolve in it, and that there is a fight in it too. Heaven, if it be anywhere at all, is free from disease; so as it is His will that earth should be as heaven is, let us fight to free our life from disease. Get going! It isn't an appeal to lie down and die; it is a call to stand up and live; and so we shall, live within bright bodies and alert minds, fighting and conquering all things that injure either. We must get to know and control, not only the things within our body, but all those within the compass of our earth, adding knowledge of the sky above, and outward, till we know what we can get to know about the circling planets, and even, maybe, some of the circling suns.

Personal and family griefs must remain within us, and, if we be sensitive, a loved one gone must bring many a sorrow, many a tear, though we must compose our spirit as well as we can to face the world, realising that there be few among us who haven't had a sharp

sorrow to feel and face. What happens to our loved
ones after death is hidden from us, and no saving
answer has ever been given to any question asked:
least of all by His Grace the Archbishop. For centuries, life or time had no question; the members of
the Catholic Church, then all the Christian world,
swallowed down, without even a minor gulp, everything told to them, and lived contentedly within the
bliss of ignorance, and the grinning grind of poverty
and disease; when every ill that happened was shrined
within the slogan of 'Thy will be done': everything
seemed to stand still save the stars and time. Heaven
and hell were there before man, but hell opened for
man during his stay in the Garden of Eden. All the
fables were accepted as simply by the Christians, and
as readily as the picture of the Deity, heaven and all,
as depicted in the American play *Green Pastures* was
embraced by a past and gone Negro community;
though the Negroes haloed the childish concepts with
a wonderful beauty and a haunting pathos in their
heart-moving Spirituals. The prayers, sermons, theological treatises, multitudes of them, have perished, and
gone down into the dust; ashes now in the mouth of
man. The old, old story has been told too often. All,
now, as tedious as a twice-told tale vexing the dull ear
of a drowsy man.

Recently, a scientist speaking to a Dublin meeting
about 'Belief and Unbelief in Ghosts' asserted that 'as
particles, invisible to the eye, of a split atom survive,
there is a reason to hold the idea that some particle of
the mind and of the body in man go on living in some
way, somewhere in outer space; that there are sounds
in nature of so frequent a vibration, at so high a pitch,
that no human ear can hear them; and so, from this

fact, it is reasonable that part of the mind, some incomprehensible activity of the human individual mind, may go on living a life of immortality when the physical life we know has come to its end.' Oh, mighty Caesar, have all thy conquests, triumphs, spoils, shrunk to this little measure! A wan exchange for all that Man has lost! A woeful way of keeping on the move through illimitable space, sans teeth, sans eyes, sans taste, sans everything. Manhood and womanhood reduced to an invisible, floating particle!

Professor Arnold Toynbee still goes about carrying his dark lantern of Original Sin, and telling all who are in sorrow that man's greatest understanding and practice grow out of suffering. A hoary old whore of a fallacy! If it were suffering that brought us up into the highest thought and action, we should be by now gods of wisdom and understanding and practise godmanship in our own right. All the wars man went through, jumping with courage or crawling with fear; all the sufferings and the miseries that all these wars brought to man; the individual pain and sorrow, the collective calamities, would have made man a mighty thinker, and would have burnished him into the belief that he had had damn well enough of it for ever. Man's real fight has always been against sorrow of every kind, a fight to banish it out of sight, out of feeling, out of the earth altogether: to abolish the weariness of hard work, the sorrows of insufficient food, the misery of cold clothing, of misery-making homes, of the pains of illnesses, and, when possible, the unhappiness of death to life before life is ripe enough to discard the care of going. His very belief in immortality was mainly grafted into his mind with the idea that the future life would be lived where sorrow was unknown, and tears were wiped away from every eye; to escape from the pain and misery of this world for the serene life lived in heaven: the Negro to get away from his slavery, and for ever more to play sweet music on the ol' banjo; the Red Indian to hunt for ever happily a ghostly prey; the Islamic believer to nestle in the arms of the beautiful houris; the Viking in the Hall of Valhalla to go through his fights again without feeling the pain of a wound, free from a chance of death; the Christian to be striding among eternal spirits, helping them to sing praises to God, with never a fear of a hoarse throat however long a song lasted. Offer your sufferings to Jesus, the nuns in a hospital tell the patients, and lead in a prayer that makes the offer, the patients murmuring Amen; but few hearts are in the pain-ridden offering. Over and over again, the going out of the place of healing, the escape from a bed of pain, is signed by the life that's leaving pain behind with a brighter eye, a firmer step, and a new hope in the heart, and the godlike usefulness of pain forgotten. Medical and surgical science have been toiling over the centuries to prevent and alleviate the agonies that according to Toynbee are to make finer and better men and women of us; and, to an amazing extent, these scientists have suc-ceeded in halving at least the suffering and misery of illnesses during the last fifty years or so; and they are still forging ahead, determined never to rest till almost all we know as pain and sickness has been banished from the bodies and the minds of men and women and all our little children. Are these devoted men and women fighting against God? Is suffering, then, the much-heralded kingdom of heaven that is said to be within us? Like the happy idea that poverty brought the poor closer to God? The poor, said the Jesuit Vaughan, are God's own aristocracy: flatterer of fools, who took care to keep out of poverty, and covered his body in a scarlet robe. Yet today, the world's conscience is working and thinking how to get the undeveloped peoples on the broad materialistic road of enough to eat and the wherewithal with which to clothe themselves. Does Toynbee realise that poverty brings on ill-health, illnesses, and that these bring suffering; and that man is eager to get away from all, however much he may lose of the good that suffering might do for him. There are those, of course, who have passed through many trials, have had their natures drenched with suffering and with sorrow, who have risen above them all; have risen, not because of them, but in spite of them, refusing to be destroyed by the buffets of time, of illness, of loss, released on them by the rotten ways in which present life is ordered; by ignorance in believing in the old tales of joy when life changes to another one; by superstition in believing that illness can be cured by calling on a power called God, or on one or other of those who, by application to a particular life of devotion, have been given — how God alone knows — mysterious powers to banish deep disease in the tissues of the flesh, giving back a healthy growth and activity to the tissues in less time than it takes for a rapid speaker to say Jack Robinson. They are all attempts to disprove that the natural way is joy and well-being; that disease is a corrosion of natural life, for it makes life fade, and kills it altogether if it is allowed to grow; so when life becomes healthy once more, aided by Science, it starts to sing again. The sorrows of premature death, of disease, are not the sorrows of God, but the sorrows of Satan; and we say, or should say, to hell with them.

'Move up', Toynbee is reported as saying; 'move up — closer to God — towards saintliness.' Is this a new slogan? The heightened and original hymn of the toynbee? But it has been said umpteen times, by Church after Church, by preachers everywhere, by the holy whisper of Saints Benedict and Bernard to the roistering bawl of Billy Graham, who at the moment is the star in the Epiphany of the Christian bawlers. Get closer to God! And how? By moving towards saintliness. And how? It isn't easy, and the way set out as told by evangelist and preacher has been tried for two thousand years, and, even according to Dr. Toynbee, has been a failure; for, he says himself, the way of things today is the worst and most dangerous man has ever known, by and large because of the atom being able to split itself, and split the world into the bargain. So that we are worse simply because the exploding atom would do more damage than a shower of arrows from ten thousand bows. He forgets that man cannot stop or stay discoveries because there is danger in some of them. Whatever way a man goes, he must go on searching and finding — one day the power of an exploding atom that can destroy a million; the next day penicillin that can save as many more. There is as much and more safety and even delight in thermo-nuclear fission or fusion as there is danger of universal destruction, according to the choice man is ready to make; and, if the people seize on the way they should go, they will give short shrift to those who would use the power within this wonderful gift for the purposes of death and maiming. The people will banish the bastards who think of nuclear power in any term of injury or destruction.

Move up closer to God! And how? By a sigh or by a whistle? By prayer and fasting or by the song and the dance? Under a bishop's skirt or under the sky? Everywhere or anywhere or in a particular place? Is this place here holy ground, while that place there is not? Is the holigan one thing and the hooligan another? Is this music sacred, that profane? Is all sacred music excellent, or is much of it worse than the worst that is profane? Does God really listen (if He exists at all) to everything that is said to Him, about Him; and does He listen to everything that is sung or chanted to His honour? Which does He prefer — 'The Boys of Wexford' or 'The Boyne Water'? Do the angels lift their eyes in ecstasy when they hear children singing 'I am a Little Catholic'? Or would they be more interested in 'My Luv is Like a Red Red Rose'? Is there worship and love in the one, but human love only, and no worship, in the other? What element of worship is there, how much of a moving up closer to God is there in the minuet, the Irish reel, the tango, or the rock 'n' roll? Will Dr. Toynbee tell us how much or how little?

There is no use telling us how to worship. No one knows how. We just must have a look round life, and choose our own way, the way that seems to suit us best, though one way's as good as another; and to be charitable when we see a girl or a boy doing it in a differing way. To watch them if we like; to wonder if we will, but not to snort with any degree of dismissal, unless the method grows into a unified power bent on making everyone else do it the same way; or if the unified power, on its knees fiddling a rosary, or standing up bawling a hymn, gets in the way of life moving onwards; for it is life that is the real worship of whatever God or gods there may be; and life is the one thing we know something about, and are ever eager to know more. We must deliver ourselves from the fright of seeing our brother Mohammedan, Buddhist, or Jew kneeling in a different way from big brother Christian; and all of these must get away from the fright of meeting a brother who doesn't think it necessary to kneel at all, but worships whatever God there may be through his own vitality, in song, music, paint, stone, science, healing, and all games from the throwing of javelin and discus to the throwing of a dart in a cosy-hearted pub.

Does Dr. Toynbee mean to say that suffering given to man through cancer, poliomyelitis, tuberculosis, and other ills that Shakespeare says all men are heir to, makes strong men and women of us, and that the writhings these diseases bring to mind and body shove us up closer to God? Is all flesh really heir to these maladies? Not on your life, say I! There isn't a living soul that isn't ready, ay, eager, to be cut off from these God-given gifts. Pah! Their very names are horrible. Has he ever felt the creeping lassitude brought about within an ill-fed body over even the first ten vital years of boy or girl; the feeling that slopes and slips away from life, though lingering long, and lasting out; a body that is always within the touch, but never taken hold of by the hand of death? Is this manner of life bound, even haphazardly, to make the victim stronger, or lift the victim up a mile, a foot, an inch, closer to God? Do we hear the rustle of angels' wings fanning the air of reeky slums, its slime soiling the soul as well as the body? No; not even the rustle of a linnet's wing. Cover her face; mine eyes dazzle; she died young. But the toads of the slums have ne'er a precious jewel in their heads, and the slum eye is too dull to be dazzled: it looks but drearily out at life or down at death, their ears dazed with the drone about the next world; they have but to be patient, for a better one is attached to the tail of death. They hear about the fine things stored up for all after death comes, provided those who hear do all the clergy advise, and take in everything they say inconstantinobly. The vision of marble hall, gold floors, pearly gates, the polished trumpets of the angels, fiercely blowing, would soon make us all, or most of us, sigh for the dew of the morning, the rose in the hedge and the song of a bird on a tree-branch. And these gaudy visions of vulgar pomp have kept us on the kee veeve for centuries, keeping us in a dream and preventing life from going ahead; the misery and ruin and sorrow born of ignorance and fear, gilded into a few tribulations that were to work out an exceeding weight of glory in a world to come.

Another thing Dr. Toynbee is very anxious about, and a crowd of others along with him, is what they call the respect due to individual human dignity. But what is this human dignity all of these thinkers, like all the rest of us (so they say), say is honeycombed with original sin, are so anxious about? And when we get to know what it is, how are we going to confer it, inject it, or preserve it, if it be already there, hidden away somewhere, like heaven within a soul; just how are we going to bring this nice condition of life into blossom within the life of every human individual? How are we even going to make it easy for every man to be decent? By religion, says Toynbee, and the crowd that jay-walk along with him. By religion! Religion is going to give man the power to resist a call to the wild. Does it? Did it, ever? When the European world knew only one hope, one faith, one baptism; when it was under the accepted ecclesiastical jurisdiction of one Bishop, called The Pope, it was a scene of robbery, rapine, murder, battle, and sudden death; so much so that many sheltered themselves under the cowl of a monk that a life might have a chance of living a little longer. All the wars in England, between these lords and those ones, were wars of Christians against Christians; the slaughter of the Irish, under the aegis of a Papal Bull, hadn't even Cromwell's excuse of destroying a danger to England's Protestantism, for these wars were waged by Christians against Christians; not Protestant Christian against Catholic Christian, but of Catholic against Catholic; and they were none the less terrible and bloody for that; just as an English Catholic king led an army to destroy a Catholic French army led by a French Catholic king. Prompted by a Catholic king, Catholic knights slew Thomas à Becket of Canterbury; murder and robbery with the clerics shutting eye and ear to almost all of it, except when it hurt themselves, even though every country at that time was pickled with churches, holy places of pilgrimage, monasteries, priories, and convents; when the air for miles up echoed with the chimes of church bells bellowing out the blessing of peace now, or the blast of war a day or so after; centuries through which bishops were often in battle dress, and the Pope slept with a sword by his side: and all thickly and chokingly enveloped in the religion that Dr. Toynbee now thinks is the world's one hope, the one way to persuade the wolf to feed with the lamb, and the lion to eat straw like the ox. Has he any idea how the Christian lords of the time treated their Christian peasantry? How these Christian peasants were praised when they stood at the flanks of the army of Crécy and Agincourt, famous long-bow men, shooting away, tumbling down the galloping French Christian knights and nobles in their gold and silver armour, and how they were taxed, their daughters deflowered, their property seized when one happened to die, how they were slaughtered if they murmured a word against the master when they came home? Who were the bastards, the rogues, the villains in the younger days of Richard II — the peasants behind Wat Tyler, or the nobles behind the King? What power had the civilising, the tender humanity, of Catholic belief in God, during the slaughter of Catholic men, women and children of Limoges by a Catholic prince? Was the dignity of the group, of the individual, exemplified, though buried, under these bloody heaps of slain souls? In all these wars, the peasant prisoners taken were no more than vermin, and would all have their throats cut, often as not, to get rid of them; for only those who could pay a ransom were preserved, bowed before, and nourished, till the ransom was paid, and they could hie home again to start the slaughter all over again, when the chance came and time was good; usually going to Mass before the battle to get the blessing of Jesus on what they were bent on doing. When the One Church split, like an exploding atom, into two wide divisions, one remaining good Catholic, the other calling itself a better Protestantism, the good work was started in earnest again of bringing souls through religion, so much admired by Dr. Toynbee, closer to God by way of the block, the fire, the religious wars (what a satirical name — a religious war!); reaching a peak in the

flourishing and busy daggers of St. Bartholomew's Eve.
Later on, during the first World War, one Church
after another forcing others to come into theirs, dagger
at throat, bayonet at back forcing them backward or
forward — a fine example of Dr. Toynbee's dictum of
religion bringing man dignity and shoving him closer
to God. After this war, in 1918, when the Catholic
Church became all-powerful in the new and bigger
and better Poland, they started off with a swing to get
lordship over the acquired province of Galicia, and to
teach the Catholics of the Byzantine Rite that a better
way to come closer to God was to be found in the Latin
Rite, and so, for the sake of their souls, they had better
come quick. The Catholic Ukrainians hesitated, and
the furious fun began, the slaughtering of those who
belonged to the same family of faith, submissive to the
control of the Pope, but using a different liturgy; just
for the reason that they weren't Poles, and their Rite
had a slight difference in the method of ceremonial,
and that the language used wasn't Latin, says
Donal Attwater, a Roman Catholic, said to be an
authority on the Eastern Rite:[1] 'The Civil War
was pursued with detestable bitterness and un-
scrupulosity on both sides; when one reads the out-
rages perpetrated by Catholic Poles in the churches,
monasteries, libraries, and so on of their fellow-Catholic
Ukrainians, one can hardly be surprised if certain
Ukrainian priests so far forgot their Christian duty as
to "preach in their sermons the extermination of the
Poles", as the Polish Government, truly or not, alleged.'
Surprised? Not a bit, brother: one knows well what
Christians can do to one another or to those who go

[1] *Studies,* a Catholic quarterly published in Dublin, vol. xxviii, no. 112
December 1939.

about with other thoughts than Christian; the sword of the Lord and Giddyun gets taken from its sheath, and the cry of 'Here goes for the love of God' teases the air. (Ever the hilt of a sword was used to affirm a holy vow.) The sign of the cross was on every instrument of war known to man. The Christian sword so often sheathed in the bowels of man, so often busy hacking heads off; and most terrible of all, their own dear Lord, Jesus, has been dragged around, and forced to see it all. That red sword of Moloch, masked as truth, has now been locked in its scabbard by the power and resolution within the courageous humanity of freethinker and radical; locked away for ever, let us hope. Had the Church the power it had in the days of auld lang syne, what would it not have done to Renan, to Lecky, to Ingersoll, and many another rationalist, who by argument, research, and scholarship helped to divest it of the power to imprison and to kill; or, later on, to Anatole France, to the Irish Joyce, and to the Irish Bernard Shaw? How would they have been brought closer to God by the religious? We don't know, but can't we guess! Stakes would have been driven down, big fires built in the Bois de Boulogne, in Stephen's Green, Dublin, or Tralalafalgar Square. With all their faults, pigeons are better than human bonfires, and these rationalistic pests would have been a core of fire in one or the other of them. Now, the Church can but murmur an automatic excommunication, and leave all miscreants to God, till Time wears all of them away. Her denunciations now have as much effect on the world as a tune from a juke-box. Inhumanism is the brightest evil-smelling flower the Church ever grew.

If we search the scriptures as Christians, Catholic

and Protestant, are advised to do, we see there (bar the first curse that first thrust man into forced labour, and turned man from the Garden of Eden into a concentration camp) that Jehovah promises, not sorrows, but prosperity and joy to those who worship and obey Him. The hardiest Christian expects God to deliver him, not into sorrow, but out of it. Do not let my child die — yet the death of a child might give a sorrow that, according to Toynbee, might do a heaven of good. Deliver me from this pain, one might pray, while, at the same time, waiting for the doctor to act as the mediator. How many during the last war, soldier, sailor, civilian, man or woman, prayed audibly or silently to be delivered from the wrath to come — not God's wrath, but Hitler's. This time was indeed a time of suffering, yet are the British people, for one nation, any the better for it? The British mother that still mourns for the loss of a child, a suffering that brings her a never-ending ache of loneliness, a constant pondering of what happened to the child. So the husband mourning a wife, a wife a husband: suffering that can do no good to body, soul, or spirit. What kind of suffering, then, is it that Dr. Toynbee thinks to be good for the nature of man? The sufferings within the infliction of disease? But we labour night and day, through Science, to cure it when it comes, and prevent it when it threatens. What then is the suffering that brightens man's soul with the gloss of a god? The pangs of mispris'd love, the insolence of office, the whips and scorns of time? A love lost can come on fairer ground, and give good fruit; man fights the insolence of office, and good manners have tripp'd along the way to high places; and time no longer carries such a heavy whip, and scorn gives way to sympathy; for man has willed it so, and man feels the better for the loss.

Poverty is the root of a lot of evil — disease, premature death, ignorance, malice, envy of others living a safer life; and when poverty goes, life will be broader, more homely and gracious, and many of the ills of the flesh will become forgotten. No longer can a nation become rich on the poverty of another. That dark day is over, and this step forward will take away many evils too. A sense of the community of life is vigorous now, almost everywhere, bringing a new feeling into heart, into home, into the nation's people; who now begin to realise that we are all of one family, however different we may look, however strange the language of another may seem to be. None of us anywhere will be unacquainted with grief, and many disappointments will come the way of every man, but each will be inevitable and none will come from causes that human ingenuity can prevent. The author, the artist, will grieve when what he tries to do is damned with poor praise, and the lover will imagine the world at an end when his love, or her love, is idly ignored or laughingly refused. But sorrow as sorrow will have gone, for we shall no longer believe that sorrow comes clad in a robe of light. To us L'Allegro is by far a more handsome and homely angel than Il Penseroso can ever be. Heaven became a goal of every earthly pilgrim simply because there no sorrow came. The vision lasted for centuries, but now we have realised that this nature of heaven must be nearer, at our doorstep, within our own achievement — nowhere else; by no other means. Does Toynbee mean the sufferings of those hungry and diseased ones in underdeveloped countries? Is it wise to leave them to suffer, for their own good, or to do what we can to help them to be healthy by feeding them well, and teaching them how to live in work and play so as to ensure that they will become able, vigorous, and handsome people? Doesn't the Christian Church herself pray to be delivered from plague, pestilence, and famine, asking God to keep them ever far away from us; if far from us Christians, why not far away from all peoples? Not only are we constantly asking God to save us from suffering, but we ourselves are hell-bent on escaping from it all in any and in every way we can. A cut hand, a bruised finger, suffered in the course of useful work, is enough for anyone, and even these are hurried by the recipient into healing as hard as a simple remedy can do it.

Putting Dr. Toynbee's buzz-fuzz of a philosophy into grander style are those who practise self-mortification to bring their souls at a quicker pace towards sanctity, like the monk of the monastery of Bonnie Prince Charlie, who never washed for years, bearing without audible murmuring the irritations of lice eating carnality out of him; who fell sick (and no wonder), and had to be whipped off to Torbay Hospital to get help from physicians there, arriving there in a state of prostration and dirt, giving the skilled, delicate-handed nurses the horrible task of scraping away the crawling orgy of lice that swarmed on his defiled body. An odd way, but not a unique way, of getting closer to God, this medley-minded idea of enduring suffering to promote sanctity, endangering the health, not only of the community with which this fool lived, but also of the spotlessly clean nurses who had to handle him. Phew! Disgusting and dangerous tomfoolery!

Let us destroy all the pain and suffering we can,

and bury it all deeper than the already dead who suffered too much before they left us.

Immanuel! God with us. Well, there we are; but where? Where now? Still said to be here and there, but growing shadier and shadier; fainter and fainter; half forgotten; receding with many other beliefs into a great distance from the mind of man. Passing even out of Christmas. Roman Catholics are plastering the hoardings with colored posters appealing to the passer-by to bring him back to Christmas again! So is the Vicar of St. Marychurch, Torquay (where I live myself), the Reverend P. T. Vokes Dudgeon (according to the *Herald Express*, Torquay, in its issue of 4th December 1959). He says: 'Bring Christ back into Christmas. Commerce has discovered that Christmas is good business, and surely that shows Christmas has made an impressive impact upon the world, but people are outrageously and happily ignorant of its significance. Please let us put Christ back into the commercial Christmas so that there, too, His redeeming power may be felt.' What a hope!

He goes on: 'Only God can convert the commercial world; and perhaps it may be the work of the Holy Spirit that we are urged to buy Christmas cards in August after all. The Holy Spirit may be behind the notion that Christmas is good business.'

Fancy that now. Infiltration. In the midst of the boyos making a good thing out of Christmas. Inspiring the red-robed, white-bearded lads in the commercial shops, cajoling the youngsters into clamoring for what the parents can ill afford to buy; the Holy Ghost busy giving a godly flavour to it all. Maybe, too, among the making of detergents, urging those who manufacture to make them whiter and whiter, dazzlier and dazzlier. A useful but rather comic-macabre expansion of Immanuel. Vulgar, too, unlike what one would expect from the tender and sensitive third person of the Trinity. To me, had I even a blind eye of faith, he would be seen in the clash and whirr of the machines, in the science laboratory among students of medicine and surgery, with nurses at the bedsides of the sick and injured, in colleges of agriculture, behind the electronic eye peering into the life of the cell, into the complex emotions of the human brain, in the song and in the story, among the paints and brushes of the artist, tensing the sturdy hand of the sculptor carving beauty out of stone, and with those who devise the public building and the domestic home.

No, no; not in the coo-coo of the Archbishop or the tinselled philosophy of a Toynbee, would I hear or find God, if I troubled to search; rather, friends, in Whitman's barbaric yawp sounding over the roofs of the world.

MERRICAL OF MIRACLES

THE greatest attacks on the Church have been unintentional; Darwin's, Galileo's, Frazer's: they have the Christian Faith by the throat, and I have often been accused by word of mouth, in printed page, in highways and byways, at different times, in different places, of attacking the Christian Church, or, alternatively, of molesting the Catholic Faith, neither of which have I yet done: press hard; though never would I deny the right of any mind to attack either, one at a time, or both together. On a number of occasions, I have questioned a complainer as to what is the Church, what is the Faith, and have always been defeated by a bubbly and indistinctive murrrrmur of baffled vibrations. Setting aside what is called The Faith, let us ask, or set out on a placard, a few questions as to what the 'Church' may be:

Is she the Knights of Columbanus, or The Legion of Mary, or the gathering of pilgrims by the waters of the Gave; or young men of the Christian Association gathered to spout about the Bible? Is she this Bishop, that Monsignor, yon Parish Priest, or yonder deacon peeping from behind a pillar? Is the Church all these *in toto*, or is she these in division, collectively or in *persona una*, several, or each for the time being as the bleat or blather; and is what each may bleat or blather of the substance and material that was, is, and ever will be, as eternally alive-O as Molly Malone's cockles picked from the Dublin seashore?

Let's have a cocktail while we think. In its issue

of 1st March 1957, the Catholic weekly, blessed by Pope past and present, *The Universe*, about whose *bona fides* there can be no doubt, within a column called 'Fancy as it Flies', has this to say and that to quote: 'To the late Emmanuel Mounier, whose death left such a gap in the ranks of French Catholic Intellectuals, we owe an antidote to that Cosy Feeling of which I often avail myself [you do, sweet child, and many more like you]. In an essay as bracing as a kick from a horse, Mounier sets it down that the leading characteristics of you, me, and the Catholic majority, are mediocrity [Irish critics *nota benedictus*], timorousness, stupidity, exhaustion of the instincts, and an abdication of the will; justifying Nietzsche's remark that the Ship of the Faith lies rotting in harbour when it should be sailing before the wind. In dubious taste, perhaps. No doubt many nice people pointed this out to Mounier.'

The Ship of the Faith, with the gunboat Protestant Faith lurching beside her, rotting within the Harbour Bar: SOS! Oh, SOS! What Mounier said about the French Catholic flagship, Dr. Walter McDonald said about the Irish Catholic cruiser. Here we have the whole caboosh of backward virtues — timidity, mediocrity, exhaustion of instinct, and a will that must crawl through a Bishop's ring before the soul is allowed to see what the mind thinks to be the light side of truth. An odd sight to watch abdication of will after will standing in a long queue waiting a turn to crawl through the Bishop's ring. Mounier and Mauriac can say what they think in agnostic France, because Radical, Republican, Socialist, and Communist, have shattered the fright once carried by an anathema, and have turned it into an idle wind which they respect not; Graham

Greene can write as he pleases in an agnostic and pagan England. The Bishop can't do anything about it; here, he has to go canny. He has deadlier critics to deal with than the cautious O'Casey.

The Ship of the Faith still tries to look good, sounds her siren on feast days, dresses over all with bravo-bunting in an increasingly anxious, often frantic, way, in threats or appeals from altar steps, pulpits, Sunday papers, radio talks, wordy wisdom peering from television screens; herding helpers into organised groups, like Salvation Armies, Church Armies, Legionaries of Mary, knights of this and that, plumed, caped, and sworded, high in ratline or on poop, with auxiliaries of Catholic Action rowing round in leaky boats watching to see how high the indifferent waters are rising above the Slimsoul Line: all feeling tired, all of them looking to onlookers as things hanging on to a life that is not; and passing into the lost kingdom of the ridiculous.

There is nothing left now but the Miracles, still numerous in the Land of Touch and Go. Stretchers crowding before the grotto. Row after row of them, those on them tossing or still; thinking to stretch towards life, but straying towards death that is hidden by a masque of hope. Mary save! Shall I be the one to be ransomed, even for a little while? Will it be me? Or the ones on either side or the girl behind me? Will my number come up in this sighing ecclesiastical gamble? Row upon row of them. A piling up of hopeless immortality; destined for Paradise, yet ready to stay with pain and a useless longing. Unite your suffering with the suffering of Christ on the cross. The leg-breaking of the two thieves. Silently joining together for a *deoch an dorais*, a last drink at the door of the end: *fin de partie*. Lifting the lid of the dust-bin

to have a last peep o' day at life. I want me pap.
They are near the end of life's fitful dither, and no
candle can light them, no crib can rock them, back
to life again.

There's money in this methodical madness. The
various touring companies charter aeroplanes to shift
the pilgrims to Lourdes; the clergy, often bishops,
organise parishes, districts, and dioceses, sometimes
numbering hundreds of travellers, and a good profit
is made from the credulity of those who hope that a
divine power may fling a cure, like a penny thrown to
kids, into the milling, praying mass of misery and pain.
Hundreds of Lourdes traders make a fine profit from
gaudily colored images, thousands of holy beads,
crudely colored holy pictures, and nicely labelled
bottles of holy water from the Lourdes rivereen; and,
of course, the holy Fathers who control the grotto
and imposing basilica, maybe take a rake-off from all
this mighty *miserere mei*. A priestly Petticoat Lane.
No, no; they do it all for nix.

In the midst of all this waste of energy, time, and
money, the hospitals everywhere still cry for help;
for a new operating theatre, a better laboratory, a
wider ward, more beds, a fuller staff. Calls are made
for money to carry on cancer research, to find the
cause of rheumatism, poliomyelitis, leukaemia. If this
scandalous waste of time, energy, and money, were
channelled into surgical and medical research, there
could be far fewer shrunken bodies, fewer hopeless
lives, travelling to where they find but the surety of
a petting paternoster and the comforting heat from a
Roman candle.

What, no miracles! No, none. So says Joseph
Acosts, writing in 1571. Acosts, we are told, was

Provincial of the Jesuit Order, its Visitor in Aragon, Superior at Valladolid, and finally, Rector of the University of Salamanca (where the Irish playwrights dig up most of their learned and cultured clerics). Acosta is said to have written only seven years after St. Francis Xavier's death. Explaining why the world's conversion wasn't so rapid as in the early days of the Apostles, he says that an especial cause 'lies in the missionaries themselves, because there is now no power of working miracles'. Acosta goes on to ask, 'Why should our age be so completely destitute of them?' and answers this question by saying, 'In Apostolic times illiterate men had to convert the learned, whereas in modern times the case is reversed, learned men being sent to convert the illiterate; so that in the early times miracles were necessary, but in our time they are not'.

Yet within passing years, legends and myth showered down wonders done by the Saint: he raised the dead, made the blind to see, the deaf to hear. Though it is said that he tells in his letters of the toilsome difficulty of learning to speak haltingly and feebly in the Japanese language, yet a legend says that not only could the Saint speak fluently and richly in the language, but that without trouble and hesitation, he was able to speak the dialects of many tribes gathered together in the one place and at the same time. Another miracle of this gentle Saint was the bringing fire down from heaven on a town which wouldn't listen, fire that burned the town to ashes. Heaven's atomic bomb. Man can do better now: he can turn a town to ashes without bother of prayer or invocation: press a blue button, and city goes for ever from the sight of man and God.

But miracles are popping up again in many places,

for religion needs cash; or, maybe, as Swift said, 'Religion seems to have grown an infant with age, and requires miracles to nurse it, as it had in its infancy'. So up they pop in this nook, in that corner, appearing as a vision over the moon behind the hill; or in the shade of the old apple tree. So the Immaculate Conception in a vision appears to a poor-minded lass at Lourdes, and a river springs up where there was but dry land; in Syracuse a statue of the Blessed Virgin weeps 'human tears' because an Italian woman's husband is a Communist (though the proof is equal that the Virgin weeps because the woman isn't a Communist herself); again, the Blessed Virgin is seen by kids (always kids) perched like a seagull on the roof of a church building in Knock, a village in poor wan Ireland; in an English church roses that refuse to fade (roses of Picardy?) and, brightest one of all, the blessed Sun dances at Fátima in Portugal! She did what she was never known to do before.

> As I came down the Highgate Hill,
> I met the sun's bravado.

But the boyo danced at Fátima. Poets have said everything under the sun about the sun, but I have never heard of one of them setting the sun into a dance. There he was in a jubilant dance, in a fine frenzy rolling about the sky, gay and flushed as a whore in flaming red taffeta. I'm sitting on top of the world! Odd thing that the Catholic Church should clap hands at the sun's dancing; oh, fie fie, lords and monsignors! Didn't ye know that the Church has all along frowned at the spurt and sport of the dance! All through the Middle Ages, they halted the hilarity of the dance where and when they could, though peasant and worker clung to it, finding in the dance a sacrament of rest and joy from their labours. Even Petrarch, lover of Laura, believed the dance to be a lascivious pastime and a sin; but the peasant and the worker danced and danced the sin away. Odd how some poets and writers shrank from the dance; Rousseau didn't like the jig, neither did Ruskin; and the poet Noyes, like Petrarch, saw hell open for dancing souls, setting down

> Fat wet bodies go waddling by,
> Girdled with satin, though God knows why;
> Gripped by satyrs in white and black,
> With a fat wet hand on a fat wet back.

Was this Joyce's god as a noise in the street? Noyes seemed to regard them as dogs' bodies rather than bodies made in the image of God. Whether they were these images or no, they could do a lot worse than dance; while they danced they were, at least, at charity with all men. Let the fairer mind and the gayer heart speak:

> Let Angiolini bare her breast of snow,
> Wave the white arm and point the pliant toe.

Bare her breast of snow! You see what the Bishops have to fear? This was the sort of thing that prevailed on the prelates in Maynooth assembled, time of Dr. McDonald, to issue a mandamus ordering ladies going to dances to lace bodices up to the chin, chain hems of dresses to the ankles, so that any wanton hand would have to stay on the outskirts; and, when actually dancing, to keep an arm's length from their partners so that there mightn't be any clustering calamity. Oh, daughters of caramel, take care! Yet dancing has its due in the scriptures. Christ himself tells us that when the prodigal son came back, his elder brother was in the field, and making for the house, he heard music and dancing; so Christ evidently didn't think dancing to be dangerous or deceitful; again, he said in an address, 'We have piped, and ye have not danced'; piping and dancing! Among the good things promised by God, through Jeremiah, to a restored Israel are, 'Thou shalt yet plant vines upon the slopes of Samaria; the planters shall plant, and shall eat them as common things. Thou shalt again be adorned with thy timbrels, and shalt go forth to the dances of them that make merry.' Oh, Jeremiah, Jeremiah! Dancing is a natural instinct in man, and there are few of us who haven't shaken a leg at one time or another somewhere in a dance of some kind; so why the hell shouldn't the blessed sun himself have a go, for his own pleasure, or for God's amusement, or in honour of the blessed Virgin Mary? So he did; at Fátima; only a short time ago, and Catholics there and Catholics here and Catholics everywhere saw the sun prancing about in the sky. No kidding. What kind of a dance was it; what did it look like? Accounts vary, it was seen to be done in a different way by differing eyes in different places. Such as? Well, a traveller standing on a peak in Darien said it was a tango; one on the roof of the Opera House in Vienna said it was a waltz; a Pole working a crane high in the sky, at Poznan, said it was a mazurka; an American who saw it from the roof of the Empire State Building said it was Jazz; a Gael up on the hill o' Tara, looking at the statue of St. Patrick, saw the statue suddenly point skywards with his crosier, gather his robes about him, and begin a jig, his mitre tilting to the back of his head, jaunting on the pedestal in the measure of a jig; and a woman sauntering in the Whispering Gallery up in the dome of St. Paul's, London, looked out over the city to where the sun shone, and swore an affidavit that she saw the sun doing the Lambeth Walk.

The sun danced and danced, at Fátima, over the hills and far away, and all the clerics shouted for joy. Dance, dance, dance, for the Lady! Pity the sun hadn't the moon as a partner. There was something lost there. What a lovely couple they would have made gliding through the sky! Footing it featly everywhere. On with the dance! Chase the glowing hours with flying feet!

Yet the sun is there in the sky because, it is said, God called it a day. The sun is subject, as all things are, to the irrevocable laws of nature; laws of light and heat, laws of push and pull. The great constable of our sky: keep moving there; keeping the planets and man on the go: no time for dancing.

That's just atheist materialism. You got all that from the Reds; I know. The sun did do a dance at Fátima. I seen it with me own two eyes and me looking from a window at the top of a round tower in Glendalough, with the whole wide waste of the skies expanding before me vision, gliding up, sliding down, lepping to the left, to the right, whirling round like one possessed. No, I wasn't drunk when I was looking — I was sober as a drudge. It staggered me. I felt dizzy. And dazzled. I could see, too, that that lascivious hussy, Venus, was high-flying with hope of a razzle when she saw sunny boy committing himself to a randy dance right where the boyo was in view of the shocked signs of the Zodiac, with the showy, naked hussy, Venus, urging him on and on, waving a welcome to him to come closer and do something more exciting still, and make a royal-rosy night of it; while

the angels near the fringe of heaven were cracking
their shoulder-joints trying to stretch their wings
around to hide their red-shamed faces from the sight
hilarious; all the time that one, Venus, beckoning
and decking her body about in a twist here and a curl
there, boostin' up, too, the passions of the lion, the
hunter, the poor twins, the ram, and the bull; leaving
the innocent virgin convulsed with conscientious envy
and malice at the seductive shines of Venus, hiding
herself for a swift flash, then out again in a swift flush
in an exposure that fluttered within conceivable range
of all the masculine signors of the Zodiac with illicit
longings, generated in a lower world; but the saucy
Venus turned aside from them to dimple her curved
proportions into tantalising the prancing sun, trying
to entice him into doing something hetheradittery,
while

Planets to left and planets to the right jollied and thundered
While all the world wondered.
Old men, afraid of a thrill they felt, piously pondered
Half a league down, half a league up, the sun lepped and
      cavorted;
While Protestants cold turned aside and loud-snorted,
Convinced against reason that someone had blundered;
But bishops cried out in sure frenzied enjoyment,
'You see now, you see now we're still in employment!'
And the soul of each raptur'd and half-dizzied gazer
Was entranc'd by the dance of the sunny amazer.
Poor Virgo cried out now, 'The position's alarming,
For that Venus is out to entice by her charming
This dancing gazebo to come forthwith and top her —
Will no decent body step up there, and stop her!
Oh, apostles and prophets, all saints and all martyrs,
She's loosing her zone and untying her garthers!
He's got her, she has him — they're mingling together,
In a flush and a flash, he'll be going to bed her;

The innocent sky's turning into a harem —
Is there nothing that's dead or left living to scare 'em!'
The scandalised sky-face gets darker and darker,
To hide the wild scene from the earth's nosey parker.

Whoremus

Oh, scholars, hurlers, saints, and martyrs,
Save us from legs, lipstick, and garters,
And from that thing so chic, so teeney,
Th' dread, eye-opening bikini,
Which on the beach sets souls aflutter,
And points out all it's meant to shutter!

And when we go in city buses,
Please save us from short-skirted hussies,
Who, seated, cross their knees until
The shortest skirt gets shorter still!
Oh, save us from th' Venus wile, her scarlet lips,
Plump thighs, bright eyes, white breasts, and curving hips,
The gown of nun, the bishop's skirt, is all
We need to save us from another fall;

And so to bed, to lie there calm and still,
Lapp'd up in safe desires, so sober, safe, and chill,
Amen, amen.
Oh, sober sleep, oh, quiet rest, oh, tranquil mind.

· · · · ·

Oh, Jane, Jane, me pretty Jane,
Stretch out an' close your eyes;
Lie steady till I get me legs
Fix'd firm across your thighs.
A priest has bless'd th' gorgeous thrill,
An' nature cries 'Oui, oui';
As I press down upon you, Jane,
An' you press up to me.

· · · · ·

Caw   Caw   Caw   Caw

A herald angel sings,
An' evenin's full of th' green crow's wings.

THE PEOPLE AND THE THEATRE[1]

THE people are the theatre. Nature sets the scene, and man plays his part through the changing scenes of seed-time and harvest, in the cold days when the frost comes and the keen winds blow. It is from the things manifested in the people's life — their love, joy, hatred, malice, envy, generosity, passion, courage, and fear — that the truest playwrights weave their sombre and gay patterns of action and dialogue. Every art is rooted in the life of the people — what they see, do, how they hear, all they touch and taste; how they live, love, and go to the grave. The question for all artists is this: Is the colour and form of what has been taken from their life done well or done badly?

Some timid ones of the theatre will say, 'This is a Bolshevist blathering', for the moment a mouth mentions the word 'people' the disinterested, clerical and lay, jump up to mark the brand of prejudice on the mouth's brow. A Bolshevist, but not just blathering, for he has good and amiable support for what he says; support written down by one of the 'lonely, majestical multitude', in 1904, when no one thought Bolshevism could ever be born. This strange champion of the 'people' is no less a figure than the poet Yeats; and his words should remind the august fellows going about in startling robes that they are no more and no less items of the people than the fellows working hard in hodden grey. Listen. 'The Irish upper classes put

[1] From *Theatre Today*, March 1946.

everything into a money measure. When anyone among them begins to write or paint they ask him "How much money have you made? Will it pay?" Or they say, "If you do this or that you will make more money". . . . All Irish writers have to choose whether they will write as the upper classes have done, not to express but to exploit this country; or join the intellectual movement which has raised the cry that was heard in Russia in the 'seventies, the cry "To the people!"'

My God, he even mentions the name of Russia! Yeats, Yeats, you had odd foreseeing visions at times. Edward Martyn, the quivering Catholic, didn't like this, and he argued in the press that the Irish actors should try to train themselves for the modern drama of society. The acting of plays of heroic life, or of plays like *Cathleen ni Houlihan*, with the speech of the country people did not seem to him a preparation. 'It is not,' said Yeats, 'but that is as it should be. Our movement is a return to the people like the Russian movement of the early 'seventies, and the drama of society would but magnify a condition of life which the countryman and the artisan could but copy to their hurt. The play that is to give them a natural pleasure should tell them either of their own life, or of that life of poetry where every man can see his own image. . . . Plays about drawing-rooms are written for the middle classes of great cities, for the classes who live in drawing-rooms; but if you would ennoble the man of the roads, you must write about the roads, or about the people of romance, or about great historical people . . . [There are critics here who look upon us as] foolish sectaries who have revolted against that orthodoxy of the commercial theatre which is even less

214

pliant than the orthodoxy of the Church, for there is nothing so passionate as a vested interest disguised as an intellectual conviction.'

There you have the greatest of Irish poets out against vested interests, commercially-souled critics, the money-hunger of the upper classes, and the chic curtained drawing-room of the middle ones. The young and ardent poet saw that all vigour in the art of the drama stemmed from the life of the people, or from the golden legends that brimmed over from the song and story, creating a golden stir in their sober and monotonous minds. The people, now, are coming out, slow but sure, from the twilight, and are taking on a far fuller control of their own lives. And as they move towards the control of the means providing what they eat, drink, and the wherewithal with which they clothe themselves, so will they enter into the life and laughter that is in music, in literature, and the drama. We shouldn't be frightened or scornful because many, maybe all, their first and second efforts turn out to be poor things; for the worst of them won't be as bad as the worst done to decorate the box-office with jubilee joy. They will be, at least, like the verses written by the poor Irish clerk or shop-boy, who wrote, Yeats says, 'for the glory of God and their country, so that there isn't one vulgar thought in the countless little ballad books that have been written from Callanan's day to this'. We must realise that good plays, much more great ones, will never be very plentiful, for good or great playwrights are far rarer than Hamlet's honest men. To help those who aim at fine art, we must pull into fuller prominence the hundreds already written by artists, half forgotten now save by the few who sit at home by the fire to sigh for the state of the theatre. We shouldn't, of course, stand beside Mr. Yeats's grandiloquent rejection of the middle classes and their drawing-rooms. That class in Ireland opposes many of his dearest, and, it must be said, fairest efforts; but it was a section of the same class that gave a fine support to all he did, and helped to give life and energy to the Abbey Theatre. He didn't like Ibsen, though, oddly enough, he never seems to have given much thought to a greater dramatist of the middle class — Strindberg. Tragedy may be screened as well by the velvet curtains of the middle class as it may be by the brocaded ones of the aristocrat, or the pathetic tattered muslin struggling to hide the tragedy of the worker, as Ibsen and Strindberg have shown; ay, and comedy, too, rich comedy well displayed in O'Neill's delightful *Ah, Wilderness!* If

> Love doth sing
> As sweetly in a beggar as a king,

then it sings, too, in the heart of a middle-class woman or man. And, anyway, many of the middle class are bidding farewell to their drawing-rooms and their imposing curtains of velvet. We must make the most of the best that has already been written for the theatre, so that we may see the art of the dramatist in action, and try to learn from it. The most of what is written for the theatre is bound to keep to a pretty common level; but we shouldn't let it sink down to an uncommonly low level — precisely what we have been doing, helped by the courageous timidity of the drama critics. The plain people get used to this low level so that when they hear an original mind speaking from the stage, they are surprised, annoyed, and, having been led astray by lesser playwrights, endure the novel play for a while, and then bid a hasty farewell to it.

Dramatic originality and poetic fancy will always be rare, but surely they shouldn't be quite so rare as they are in the present-day theatre; nor should the critics be allowed to frighten, or laugh, the people away from them. Why then are these two excellent qualities so often absent from the plays that strut the stage today?

First, of course, because of the difficulty of imbuing the plays we try to write with these fair qualities; secondly because of the money-making grip that tightens the very life out of the theatre of today; and thirdly because of the sensible cowardice of most of the critics, a fine number of whom don't seem to be able to tell a good play from a bad one.

The first reason is obvious to all who try to write a fair play; the second will be readily admitted by many; for the first and last question asked of the play (as Yeats has said aforetime), good or bad, is: 'Will it make money?' There remain the critics, who, instead of being stout and indubitable guides to where there are swans, invariably (as far as new work is concerned) lead the people to where there is naught but a gabble of geese.

During the war, in an issue of *The Critics' Circular*, we listened to the President saying: 'As an industry entertainment has been enjoying a terrific boom, managers have been embarrassed by the amount of money they have been taking [They have in my eye!]. In the face of these wartime conditions there might seem to be less need for the critic than usual. That would be a superficial and misleading view. Public discrimination, in the main, is less acute and more in need of guidance.' Is that the 'Reveille' or the 'Last

Post' the trumpets are blowing outside? Just imagine a critic or a man 'discriminating' among works of art! The English critics have given themselves a name — the modern Order of Discriminators. Further on, the President adds: 'Our quality is infinitely more important than our numbers'. Now the trumpets are playing 'Land of Hope and Glory'. In the same issue, we are told of Mr. Newman's resignation from the Circle, saying as he left that 'He felt that the Circle today did not, in his opinion, conform either in perception or practice to the Circle he joined twenty years ago'. It seems certain by what was said by the members discussing the resignation, that his departure was caused by the Circle allowing among them men whose minds were unable to fly higher than the rather low level of a gossip column. Looks as if the President's right royal statement should really have been: 'Our numbers are infinitely more important than our qualities'.

While certain about the quality of plays haloed by Time, the critics seldom, if ever, foresee a fine play on its first appearance, or seem able to judge between a miserable play and a sturdy one. The Circle seems to be a sheep-pen, dividing its members into two groups — one competent to give an opinion, but afraid to do so; the other, having no serious opinion to give, spouting them out by the hundred. And don't they take themselves seriously! Their monthly bulletin has at its top a menacing hand pointing to the 'Warning, Strictly Private, For Circulation to Members Only'. An everlasting secret session of the Critics' Circle. What are they afraid of? Is the job of a critic a hush-hush-hush one? One day or another, each will be going around with an armed guard. The irony of it is that while they are afraid to let themselves be heard, the motto charged in the Badge of the Circle, transfixed by a big quill pen, is *Audacter et Sincere*, which a friend tells me is Manx for 'Be bold', and evermore be bold, in keeping your opinion to yourself.

Listen to this: A council meeting was convened some time ago to consider a deep and daring question. According to a 'Strictly Private' circular, a critic of a big Sunday paper got tickets to go to a Priestley play: but the Editor of the Big Paper snatched them from him, and went himself with some friends. When he came back from the show, it is alleged, he gently ordered the critic to write a review of the play the critic hadn't seen, adding a rider that the critic was to quote a hymn of which a friend of the Editor was reminded during the passing of the play. The Editor, it was said, very kindly told the critic, who hadn't seen the play, that he could write his review on a review by another critic who had seen the play. The Big Paper's critic, like a man, refused to do this: but — less like a man — offered to write 'a colorless review about the general purpose of the play', stipulating that this review was to be unsigned. And all this, apparently, took place, not in the 'ideologically controlled theatre of the Soviet Union', but in happy-hearted, open-minded England. When the resentful Editor of the Big Paper ordered that the critic's articles on the Films should go unsigned too, the rebellious drama-film critic packed up and left the job. That's the *Audacter et Sincere* of the Critics' Circle in a nutshell. Apart from the difficulty of reviewing two such dissimilar arts — drama and film — at the same time, or thereabouts, what are we to think of a drama critic who sets out to review 'the general purpose' of a play?

And where does the playwright come in? What sort of unhappy-go-lucky criticism is this? Is it any wonder that *The Critics' Circular* is strictly private?

Criticism is a force in life; it brings change and often a new enchantment. Instead of having too many critics, we have too few; we have a crowd of opinioneers (opinioneers, opinioneers, I am one myself) who claim the title, God help us. A critic must be free to tell his full mind; he is above his paper, theatre, manager, and author. To him the play's the thing, and he who goes below this has not, within God's sight or man's reason, the right to the title of being a Drama Critic.

Whenever has a London critic, with clamor and encouragement, furnished the English stage with a new and first-class playwright, from at home or abroad? They have certainly, at times, labored to harness the word 'genius' to work of a second-class, or even lower, order. A good many of us remember the critics marching, with drum and colors, before *Journey's End*, while a well-known and warm man of the theatre hailed the author as 'the hope of the English theatre'. Critical bugle-calls, too, were sounded about the glory of the trashy *The Combined Maze*, and a critical drum-roll hailed a pathetic thing called *As Others See Us*. What the critics said shone like opal or ruby didn't even glisten like a hunk of quartz. In a recent article, Mr. Priestley has quietly and urbanely complained about these critics, saying: 'If they are timid and conventional, then there is a danger that the theatre, also, will be timid and conventional'. If! They are timid, and they have made the theatre as timid as themselves. All this is sad and annoying, and we can but hope that the incoming tide of the people will sweep away a lot of their swashing timidity of heart and voice.

The day of the old, supercilious, self-centred critics, wine-drinkers and chicken-eaters, is ending, to make way for the day of those who will love the theatre for its own sake, and not for the job.

It has often been said by some of the wine-drinkers and chicken-eaters that the proletariat aren't interested in the theatre; that while a few may have their hearts in the Highlands, the crowds pour out of their homes to dog-races and football matches, while the more re-fined spend their time with darts and dominoes. The electric hare isn't any great shakes, but the genuine one's a thrill, as I know, having beat one up in a turnip field with two fine poachers whose dogs were only a little less majestic than the hare; a first-class footballer is as much an artist as one who writes well or paints a picture in a royal fashion; and none of these things need destroy, or even weaken, a love for Shakespeare or Strindberg. As for the proletariat flocking to the music-halls, why, that's fine, too, for the 'Lambeth Walk', 'Boomps-a-Daisy' or 'The Blarney Groves' have a place in our lives as deep as the Parthenon, West-minster Abbey or Milton's *Paradise Lost*. But in the present-day theatre, a golden barrier keeps the people out. It is the Stalls that keep the theatre going today, and the Stalls will continue to keep the theatre going until the theatre is gone. It isn't reasonable to say that the people will keep away from anything new, classic, or experimental in the theatre, when conditions make it impossible to go. Can they go to Stratford-on-Avon? Might as well ask them to journey to the Shetlands. To Malvern? Might as well suggest Bayreuth or Oberammergau. It must be made as easy, or nearly so, to go to a theatre as to go to a pub.

And, oddly enough, it isn't always the plain people

that bring opposition to a strange and unfamiliar art. Educated personages (said to be educated, anyhow) have damned the strange and original by praising the commonplace and trivial. It was the critics who first hailed *Journey's End* as a great play (they'd hardly do so now); the people bought no pictures from Leighton, Tadema, or László; the people didn't reject with scorn and laughter the work of the first Impressionists; but the learned and aesthetic did, even George Moore against his own inner convictions. It was the great Gladstone who went down on his knees to kiss the hand of Marie Corelli; and we all know the way the wise and cultured ones treated James Joyce. The Leaders have let the people down.

And what is the highest tone the English theatre has reached during the past few years? Lest it be thought to be personal complaining, here is a quotation from Nathan's (the famous American critic) *Theatre Book of the Year 1944-45:* 'Review these British benefactions in the later season. In one, *Night Must Fall,* we were regaled with a pervert whose pleasure consisted in murdering females; in *Love from a Stranger* we were invited to attend the diseased intellect whose passion was marrying for the delight it provided him in strangling his successive wives; in both *Wise To-morrow* and *Love of Women,* on the other hand, we were bidden to relish the spectacle of Lesbian amour; *They Walk Alone* attempted to enchant us with a female pervert whose sensual gratification was achieved through letting the mortal blood out of any male corpus with which she came into contact; and *Murder Without Crime* sought to elevate us with not one but two male degenerates, one a sadist and the other a blighted neurotic who couldn't control his homicidal eccentricities; *Design for Living* offered us a pretty picture of impertinent effeminacy, and *Point Valaine* a male whose reaction to females was to spit in their faces.' Seven other examples of the same kind are given in the same chapter, but those I have set down are surely enough to go on with. The poorest proletarian play ever written is to be preferred to this sort of snaily conception of life.

When at last the people have rid the theatre of this slime, the people must depend on themselves. In an article advocating an intelligently assisted English opera, Ernest Newman said: 'Wherever opera has risen to the dignity of a great art, it has been because it flowered from a national idiosyncrasy'. So it was before with English drama, too, so it must be again. We can give no honor to Strindberg, Ibsen or Chekhov if we haven't already honored Shakespeare, Webster, Congreve, Goldsmith, and the rest of our bold and gracious dramatists. This 'idiosyncrasy' has its roots in the people; not in this or that party of the people, but in them all. This is the quartz from which the artist must furnish the polished gem. And everywhere, almost, the people are flowing towards the realisation of what an energetic people can do. Sooner or later, they will show what they can do in the English theatre; so let not our hearts be troubled, neither let them be afraid.

CULTURE, INC.

How we strive and struggle to keep Culture going and crowing! Agriculture (this word sounds more learned than Tillage), Horticulture (this word sounds more learned than Gardening), and so, to feel in the fashion, the modern man or woman Voltaire would urge you to cultivate your horticulture, and so we'd have bigger and better roses round the door. You see, *Ager* and *hortus* are Latin words, and give gardening and tillage a classical aroma or smell, linking them up and down with Homer, Plato, and the bould Virgil; so the gardener and the farmer's boy can wear the toga. It is supremely respectable and genteel, though gardening has a long lineage going back to the Hortus of Eden, and tillage to the time when Adam and Eve were flung out of the Hortus to be dumped into the wilderness of the thistle and the thorn. Then there are the cultures of this land and of that one; culture of this precious magazine and of that one; the culture of the Rolls-Royce car and that of the bubble-car tagging doggedly after it; the cult of the coterie, the cult of the personality, and even the cult of the cult itself, till we're moidered and murdered by this affluent society of cults and cultures: and yet, and yet, damned the one that knows what culture really was, or is, or ever will be. Meeting after meeting has assembled to spread its unction, its god, its frankincense, over the soul of man; critic after critic has told us all about it, its shape, its form, its function; yet no one knows; we all contend, fight, argue, denounce, disperse, then go home to bed, tired, and as confused as ever. There is no one can tell what culture is, no one, except me. I can tell you what it is by showing you all what it isn't, with the help of God!

I have read many books telling all men about literature, this author and that author, on drama, the novel, the poem, the painting; Wilenski, Berenson, Clive Bell, among others; lots of books about drama, Ernest Newman each week about music and song — all delightful and intensely interesting, but none of them ever able to give me that inner glow that play, symphony, novel, or picture, themselves gave me whenever I heard the music, watched the play, read the novel, or gazed at the painting. None of the reviews or books could give me the inner glow, but the inner glow already within gave me the sense and understanding to enjoy the books and the reviews. Always I came out by the same door as in I went.

Now, at home and abroad, there are two great efforts being made to coax and persuade the workers: one to bring them to God, the other to bring them to Art. Ha ha, the ruein' o' it! The High Ups go to church every Sunday morning to show the way to God, spiritual chicken on Sundays, but the workers go for the drink o' beer and a game of darts (and I say Well done, fellow-workers); art-lovers try to parade them, now and then, before a picture, or some compère flatters them with a certain guest artist singing a song by Verdi or Puccini — a glow within the flare of a Variety performance, mazing the dull ears of them who have the daring to listen to it, or dazzling the vision of them who never had eyes to see. Their eyes were closed, their ears were stuffed in the home, in the school, in the church, in the places where they worked to gain a living, and pushed down farther by the politicians sent to save them. With God, I have naught to do, nothing to say (about), for he can well take care of himself; but a lot has been said about this Culture, as incomprehensible as treatises published and sermons preached to explain the Trinity. Words as numerous as the sands of the sea have been said about the Trinity, and words as many as the stars in the Universe said about Culture, so, among the gigantic crowd of talkers, I'll be neither seen nor heard. Indeed, in the pack of the crowd, I'll but be talking to myself. One thing seems to be certain: culture cannot be injected into the mind, the way penicillin can be injected into the body. Right? So a people can't be thought of as a cultured crowd because they have a few museums, art galleries, and stone effigies straddling a few principal streets. Nor can they be thought of as cultured because of a few great scientists, writers, painters, or composers living among them. These guys don't belong to what Jim Larkin called 'the body politic'. They are outside of it, beyond it, and at a far distance. They haven't even anything to do with culture, or with those who breed them, though these may enjoy, and benefit from, their great creations, they cannot inherit from them. A people having them are no more cultured because of possession than the Jewish people were all holy when they had a saintly man sent from God whose name was John. At times, instead of being a stimulus, they seem to be a drug making the people drowsy, content to lie asleep under their feet and all around them, growling out 'High-brow' if anyone tries to poke them into a wakeful interest; shouting if one mocks them as a decadent community, 'We have Shakespeare! We have Constable! We have Rutherford!' Though few of them ever saw a live Constable, read a Shakespeare play, or listened to even a ten minutes' talk on Science over the wireless.

A people aren't cultured just because of a few, or a lot, of great men and women; museums, colleges, academies, though they may be a help, do not make a people delightful or great. Indeed, academies are often a menace: the Royal Academy of Arts in their annual exhibitions but give a satisfying chance for a parade of peacocks and parakeets hastening to sun themselves within the artificial sunlight of artificial art; never varying save when someone in a spasm of bravery shoves on a foreign show of great Italian, Dutch, or French paintings and sculpture; and Ireland's literary amazement of the Yeatsian years soon sickened and died after the Irish Academy of Letters had been signed, sealed, and settled among the Irish people; and all we get now from these great academicians assembled is a gala of snores. A nation will be judged by what the people are, not by what a few of them do. If the few great ones be the flowering and fruit of the many, well and good; then the many will share the greatness, and be one with the few; if the flowering of the few be that of a privileged section, then the people will remain as they are, the few will be but a part of a section, and that section will be but a colored dot within a mass of drabness.

How are we to hunt the flowering of the few away from the section towards the flowering of the many? How to begin, how to go on? Begin with the schools? The colleges, the universities? More galleries, more museums, more academies? Put the pressure on through these activities? Forcibly feed the many with the rich

pap of literature, art, and science? Well, a beginning
has already been made by shoving an odd symphony
into the Light Programme, an odd short talk on science
or literature, too, softly pinched out of the Third Programme, when those in authority think the listeners
will sit it out, a little bit here and a little bit there —
when they're not expecting it, taking them by surprise,
signing the programme off before they're aware it's
there; pricking the programme in to prick the people
on. Attaboys! Got them that time! (The one
activity I can recall at the moment that did bring
loveliness close to the many, that persuaded them to
shake hands with Beethoven, Mozart, and many great
creators, filling many ears with the melody of sad,
rousing, and always sweet noises, were what are popu-
larly called 'The Proms'). But these are but skir-
mishes; now, here and there, frontal pushes are being
made at one point of the compass by Kenneth Tynan,
and at another by John Berger, the one on ABC, the
other over Granada. This advent into the centre of
mass-men is reviewed by a critic in *The Times*, under
the title of 'Selling Millions the Idea of Culture'. As
the critic goes on, he writes: 'The point in common
between these two is that they are both run by young
socialist critics — John Berger and Kenneth Tynan —
writers of great influence whose judgements on drama
and graphic art are closely bound up with their political opinions. Both are doughty opponents of the idea
of art as a diversion for the happy few, and have made
resolute attempts to break down the walls and turn
the culture club into a civic park.' Well, they won't
break down the walls the way they're going; not on
your fanny. One can't knock down a wall by shoving
against it with finger and thumb. That both of these

gentlemen, Mr. Berger and Mr. Tynan, are well up in their particular professions, rich in talent, long experienced, the one with drama, the other with graphic art, there is no doubt; but to reach the hearts and minds of the workers is a matter of very different judgement, with an experience that must have been gained in the midst of the workers themselves: without these, their efforts will be laughed at, and ridiculed out of the way. They must first be at ease among a group of workers, and the workers must feel at home with them. One of the ways taken in this venture was for a young lady, Edna O'Brien, to take a couple of teenagers for a walk, squat them down on the grass within the railings of Kensington Gardens, and ask them to look at the Albert Memorial, and tell her what they thought of the minor colossus. The answers were brief and to the point: 'Junk . . . It's not for me . . . wouldn't fit in my mother's living-room.' Miss O'Brien sadly murmured, 'We didn't get very far with that, did we?' Far enough, lady, and fair enough, too, for the thing wouldn't fit even into the street where the teenagers lived; it wasn't for them (nor for me, neither); and many more minds, more eminent, would call the thing junk. Better to have set them down before Peter Pan, simpler, and no worse; for what is the Albert Memorial but a gigantic, empire and colonial Peter Pan? Better still to have led them for a walk through the Park, entering into a general chat, pointing out trees as they walked, to wonder what trees they were, to see if the teenagers knew — though maybe Miss O'Brien didn't know herself; or the plants in the flower-beds — what they were, their shapes, the families they derived from, and, maybe, with Miss O'Brien quoting some poem written around a few of them; the shape of the trees; the streets they passed through, the angles of houses, the skyline — there are so many things to be seen everywhere we go, if we keep our eyes open, even on the way to the Albert Memorial; for, if we fail to see what is outside of ourselves, how can we expect to see and admire an artist's vivid or odd impression of any of them? Poor Miss O'Brien, trying to give the teenagers a little bit of what they didn't fancy! It was an artistic mistake, too, to lead them to this thing upon which, for a long time now, art has turned her back, bahed away from this huge assembly of pretentious confusion. Better by far to have shown them St. Paul's or Westminster Abbey, bigger, indeed, but simpler; churches which the youngsters could understand — a place where people prayed; there she could say a few words about the building, and color it with a few sentences about the history in which both buildings are lapped, listening intently to whatever they may say, listening and answering as if out for a walk with two friends, meeting St. Paul's or Westminster as 'twere by accident. Many teenagers, because of their early environment, have come to a dangerous stage of mind-immobility, and their immediate and natural reception of something beyond them is one of derision, or they ignore it altogether. Here, seeds of culture fall on shallow soil, but one can never be sure, for God moves in a mysterious way, and there may be patches of deeper soil here and there, so we shouldn't be nervous before any derision; but studied attempts are no good—they just arouse silent or brazen laughter. Teenagers uninterested in any kind of art have a way to go back before they can step ahead, back to the day of leaving what was called a school, when they joy-

ously flung out of their minds for ever any mention
or thought of the drudgery of self-studentship. Fed
up with the crayfish literature of Billy Bunter's biography in Greyfriars School, they need no more; this
is glory enough, and they deride any invitation to enter
fresh woods and pastures new. Elderly persons are
past praying for, but we must not dismiss these in an
idle way, but admire, respect, even revere, them for
other good qualities. The kindliest and most generous
persons I have met have often been those who hadn't
an idea about what we call Culture, whose highest
hope was either the B.B.C.'s *Mrs. Dale's Diary* or *At
the Luscombes'*; all had what George Gissing said of
his housekeeper, in *The Private Papers of Henry Rye-
croft*, 'She had the intelligence of the heart', something
the finest Culture cannot give. Quiz and question,
Top-forms, boys against girls, county against county,
are ways and means to 'Culture', as the biography of
Billy Bunter in Greyfriars School is a way to literature;
or *Meeting Point* and *Christian Viewpoint* are ways to
the knowledge of an omnipotent God; or the singing
of old soldiers at an anniversary, singing 'It's a Long
Way to Tipperary', leads to a Mozart opera. The
one good thing, oral, for the very young and the not
so young, is the B.B.C. Children's Hour; very often
as good as the best of the other programmes, and often
even better; interesting and, at times, delightful, to
an educated grown-up. Not that old soldiers singing
old ballads are to be sneered at; God knows these old
ragged tunes and tottering words gave a strengthening
delusion to hardy and brave souls marching on a long,
long trail, and in terrible times; gave what no song
or melody from Mozart or Verdi could ever give.
Now, on the eve of the New Year of 1962, Eire is

going to flood the farms and firesides with rotten sights and sounds salved from the dustbins of England and the garbage cans of America, and call it all Culture! Blessed Mary Virgin, to whom the land is dedicated, will have to look and listen to it all; but will She clap her hands? Never mind, Lady among the lilies, no cause for alarm. Ireland's Culture Relations Committee and the Arts Council are on the watch by their camp-fire burning low.

Are we even civilised? Going farther and lower— are we educated? Oh, yes, we have had a thousand schools, numerous colleges, a fair sprinkling of universities for a long time, over many years, and what, in the name of God, have they done for us all? Excommunicated us from civilisation, made Aunt Sallies of the Muses. Let us leave the national schools alone in the outer darkness, for they have destroyed the keener senses of their pupils, leaving them only that of taste, to eat and to drink, without even the higher sense of being merry. There are the high schools, what was called in my days in Ireland the Intermediate System, which was thought to be what was called Secondary Education. I have known those of these who won gold medals, who held impressive rolls telling of passing with Honors (whatever they were); crammed tightly with bits and pieces that the mind vomited forth immediately after, and they became as slow, dull-eyed oxen, shying frightened away from everything outside of official words and classifying of forms, collar-and-tied robots; mumblers; no longer interested in the framed Intermediate School Testimonial hanging on the wall: one green bottle hanging on the wall; no public voice, just a silent vote on election day. Only now have they moved into life through industrial discontent; now in a resentful fight against a shilly-shally, catch-as-catch-can economy; out for a planned one to bring sense to industrial life, and so civilisation from which culture comes.

The Universities have been the Pale of the Privileged for centuries, and still are, particularly Oxford and Cambridge, and, bar London and Manchester, seem to hypnotise the other provincial universities with timidity; though now a better challenge will soon be flung before them by the creation of a good many more in different counties. The Dark Blues and the Light Blues have given the nation the blues long enough, and must lower their colors to the level of the Reds and Whites to make the nation of one hue in its effort towards knowledge and the facts of things. The scholarships for the clever children of the workers are a fraud, and a menace to those who win them. Needy at home, they remain needy in the university, and their speech and deportment betray them: Thou art from Galilee? Nay, thy speech bewrayeth thee! Then the glittering scholarship becomes dull cold lead before his eyes: he becomes a shrinker or a bitter, brooding lad. If he can, he joins others needy as he is, and they shrink in harness or they pool their bitterness together. This condition of things should be banished from life; there should be no Godfrey Peakes winning books, going in a castaway, coming out one too, none of them; plenty of Eliza Doolittles developing a retarded life into a full one. All who enter the gates should be equal in station, equal in upbringing, eating at the same table, drinking from the one fountain; Oxford's accent respected in Exeter's or Plymouth's university, as the Devon or Cornish dialects are respected in the halls and horizons of Oxford and Cambridge. University, young man? Bristol, sir. Bristol, right. Your university, young lady? Ipswich, sir. Ipswich, right. Yours, young man? Oxford. Oxford, right. Well, your diplomas and testimonials are all equal, but seeing there's three equal applicants, and but one post vacant, you three must abide by a draw from a hat. My secretary has put the names of your universities on slips of paper, mixed with a number of blanks; she twirls them round in the hat, and whatever university appears on the first slip drawn gets the job. Right? Okay. Off we go: blank; blank again; Ipswich. The job is yours, young lady; congratulations.

It is odd how, at times, an opposing or a different current of thought cuts straight into your own steady flow, disturbing it with its little sharps and trebles till the major flow pushes it aside, and goes on again in its even flow. Just as I was writing, an interview given by the well-known Sean O'Faolain to an *Irish Times* correspondent tells us all some weird things about American education. Mr. O'Faolain has been a lecturer in Princeton University for two years, and, in addition, has gone on a wide tour of the United States, lecturing in the smaller universities; so what he says about American education is sure to go farther than the fireplace. He doesn't like it, thinking that 'the Bachelor of Arts Degree has been debased to the value of a ticket to a job even as a door-to-door salesman' (so when an A.B. becomes a salesman, we see the death of an Arts Bachelor). 'They read only the books prescribed for their courses, and get no pleasure out of them.' He was frightened, apparently, when a class of twenty-five didn't know a thing about 'the Yellow Book period'. I wonder did they know

anything about the Book of Kells period; the Book of
Durrow period, the Book of the Old Dun Cow period;
or the period of the Book of Nicodaymus? What have
periods to do with Education as such? Education isn't
shut up, like an oracle in a school or university; one
can, if one be quick enough, shake hands with her
in a street or in a pub. Education is life, and life
is a continuous flow, always moving forwards and
as frequently lapping back again so that the mind
doesn't know which is which. This period business
is man-made to set a border round what is con-
sidered to be a possible or prudent amount to be put
upon students for study during a particular period.
These 'Courses', as they are called, are, as far as I
know, common to all universities, and in no way
peculiar to those of America; and if a student is to
fully cover the 'Course', he has damn little time to
read anything else beside or beyond it. One who
has come to love literature doesn't mind what period
hailed its advent; it belongs to any period and to all
time to her or him.

Another curious remark puffed out by Mr.
O'Faolain is that 'The American student of today is
a victim of his environment. He taboos emotional
pleasure and wants only facts in his university studies.'
How does Mr. O'Faolain know this? Surely, emotional
enjoyment of the arts is a surge within him or her
who feels it? It doesn't shine from a student's fore-
head like AE's Candle of Vision, or glow from the
student's face like a Roman candle, or bigger, better,
and more colorful neon lights on Broadway. It is a
living secret between the student reading and the
author. I met many students when I was in the
United States, and many, many more over the years

who came to see me here in Devon, and I must say I found all these eager young men and young women far from being unemotional, ready to pass from intellectual analysis to emotional enjoyment at the drop of a chat. It seems to me that the Americans equal the Russians any day in their amount of emotional output.

Mr. O'Faolain is distressed over the numbers of students in the universities. He says, 'In the larger universities there can be anything up to fifteen thousand students'. He calls these 'factories where it is impossible to establish a personal touch and the printed word has to suffice for examination time and for all time'. Surely, the 'personal touch' depends, not on the number of students, but the number of teachers? There could easily be a far better chance of a 'personal touch' in a university of fifteen thousand students than in one of a thousand. Besides, in a lecture, if the lecturer be a good one, the personality of the lecturer could flow through the personalities of all those listening to him or her; and then there is always the personal touch of one student upon another. There are many and great advantages, administrative and economical, in bigger universities; salaries to satisfy the best minds can be given; and also equipment can be provided, equipment which every college should have if it is to work effectively and well. If Mr. O'Faolain was concerned with this question, he would think of the most important part of education — the beginning; the primary schools; particularly as regards his own country where the 'personal touch' in these schools are the strap, the cane, the fist that could knock an epileptic unconscious, or pull half an ear off an unruly boy.

The oddest and most comic remark made by Mr.

O'Faolain was about a southern university: 'It was the Washington Lee University in Lexington, Virginia. The students here differed from the students of other universities in wearing collars and ties. They dressed formally, like gentlemen, like you and I do. Even at Princeton, students were apt to turn up in an odd assortment of garments in varying colors.' He doesn't like mass instruction, but, apparently, would clap hands if he saw the students marching by in massed battalions of collars and ties. Why not black bows and dinner-jackets or white bows and tails? It's hard to see why a collar and tie could make a student anyway look like a gentleman. Shaw once remarked that 'when a man came to die, the one thing to do was to die like a gentleman'; but I don't think he meant that when a man had to meet Death, he should meet him in a collar and a tie. Certainly, when the great man himself came to die, he didn't go dressed in a collar and a tie. More ironical than anything else is the fact that the huge mass of those who wore this badge of gentility, civil servants, government employees, professional men and women, since the dawn day of 1962, are moving away from the ideology of 'looking like gentlemen' towards comradeship with the smutty face and blackened hand of the work-bench and the production line. The condition of 'looking like gentlemen' pleases them no longer; and among the thousands who crowded the London Albert Hall, mixed with minor officials, were a number whose salaries topped the five-thousand-a-year mark.

In a review of a book about Freud recently written by Brigid Brophy, there is this passage: 'She [the author] is unconsciously analysing the unconscious underworld of all of us: our ambivalence [How reviewers cherish this damned word!], our will to hate and destroy ourselves and what we love, and to make war on the civilisations and cultures we ourselves have built.'

Our civilisation and culture! We don't destroy them, for we cannot destroy what we haven't got. We're on the way to civilisation and culture, but we're a long way off, with many a road-block before our march, with officials at each of them to make sure that no one goes by who hasn't a proper identity card, right class and appropriate beliefs. What do we think is indicative of our civilisation, examining the many clay figures in the national shop window? Our education? My God, our education! Read our daily papers, and most of the Sunday ones, after we have duly said the Lord's Prayer in a hurry; watch television for a whole day, the stately one, and the others who widen the mind, expand the soul, and tell us, yes us, what is good for the body, spending hundreds of millions yearly to ensure that we civilised and cultured people may make no mistake in getting the best that a little money can buy; buy, buy, blackbird! Listen to the radio; listen to the answerers on the 'Any Questions?' panel; listen to our politicians, and then, as a salve to the soul, listen to the salvoes of Jesu-jargon blather from bishop and priest and parson. Listen to the speeches made at a Lord Mayor's banq banket after the guests have dined on dishes of locusts and wild honey; then, listener, lie down and think how much wiser you have become after the bawl is over; think, and thank God for culture!

Is the Parliamentary system that took centuries to give us the collection, big posy of bright boys and girls, we have today an essence of our culture? The division of the Commons, headed by the Speaker, and the Lords and ladies, headed by the Lord Chancellor? This Parliament where nothing can be done without the Mace on the Table, or the comic custom of the Commons, headed by the Speaker, marching to the House of Lords to hear a King's or a Queen's speech; or the rule that when a man falls in for a father's peerage he isn't allowed to give it up, he must leave his common companions to sit among the gilded effigies. On occasions, when a member wishes to address the Speaker or the House, I understand he has to don a top-hat; but surely if he must wear a head-covering, why not be up-to-date, and wear a crash-helmet? Then there is the great hill of Hansards that have come from the bowels of the place, printed logos of British statesman, embracing those of Gladstone, Salisbury, Bannerman, Bonar Law, MacDonald, Baldwin, Chamberlain, Attlee, Churchill, who alone has left his people memorable phrases. But, then, Churchill is something of a poet, and maybe the poet Shelley was right when he said: 'Poets are the trumpets that sing to battle. Poets are the unacknowledged legislators of the world.' Are all these things Britain's civilisation, an evolution of absurdity? Part, maybe, of what is regarded as civilisation; but whatever it be, it has nothing to do with culture.

Is it then the Health Service? Even the Health Service (the best thing we can, so far, show to God) is hardly hopping along like Cassidy on the golden road to Samarkand. Its state can be judged by the Government's plan to build more than two hundred hospitals over the next fifteen years, at a cost of eight hundred million pounds — even a decimal system can't make eight hundred a unit less. They waited till the pound was worth but a ten-shilling damn. For years to come, doctor, surgeon, matron, nurse, cabined in utterly out-of-date buildings, will have to work and be efficient in the healing of sick and injured within a worm-eaten, worn-out and worrying environment; while research expert and worker have to go on persuading friends to stand at street corners, cap in hand, begging pennies so that research work may go on to find out the cause, discover the cure, for cancer, rheumatism, leukaemia, poliomyelitis, and other ruthless diseases. On almost every panel there are too many patients to mind, doctors are heavily overworked, and in hospitals nurse and sister have too much to do. In hospital myself, I saw a great commotion over a missing duster, with sister and nurses running around looking for it, for it appeared that the sister was responsible for every duster issued to her part of the hospital. I myself protested then, not because the damned duster was lost, but because sister and nurse, even the matron, had to waste time, and even be psychologically distressed, about such a tremendous trifle.

I wonder will each of these hospitals in the air be like unto the National Theatre, promised years and years ago, still to be found only in the land of Erewhon. Remember, citizens, we have more important things to do, and worst things must come first: that is the law and the profits. There is the Blue Steel to cost first twelve millions, now to cost sixty; and the other precious missiles, earth to earth, ashes to ashes — what am I saying! Land to land, earth to sky, air to air — the sweet young twins, triplets, and quadruplets of the magisterial Hydrogen Bomb; humanity's greater Lux Mundi that is to light every man, woman, and child going outa the world. These jewels of destruction do not bud from civilisation, and they slash away the baby mouth and burn out the frightened eyes of our infant culture.

However, we must allow poor humanity her due. She is ever on the side of life, and small praise to her for that, for she cannot help it, and she shares this with all sentient things. She is never so bad as some poets, novelists, and critics paint her. She never wishes the destruction of all, or of any, of the things she has achieved. In time of danger she gets anxious even about the bits and pieces she calls her culture; for that is what our culture is so far — bits and pieces scattered about picture gallery, museum, and private house; a few pictures, sculptured pieces, or pieces of bronze, a few buildings, mostly of past times, a few fine books, that a small number have written and a lesser number have enjoyed reading. In the heat of danger, poor humanity rushes to save what they've gotten, storing them in safer places till the danger goes by; and even when excited crowds gather in the West End of London, haste is made to blanket the statue of Eros away behind wood and winsey to keep him safe from Christian civilised hands, eager to make a few things look like a ruin that Cromwell knocked about a bit; and at times, these hands are white ones, well-groomed, belonging to members of what are called 'the ruling classes'; the very class that kept to themselves whatever bit of culture there happened to be in the land. During the writing of this chapter, E. H. Carr, Fellow of Trinity College, Cambridge, has been giving talks on the Third Programme, B.B.C., on 'What is History?', telling us a lot of what History is and is not, mentioning, and commenting upon, 'the prejudice of the old division between the humanities and science in which the humanities were supposed to represent the broad culture of the ruling class, science that of the technicians who served it.' (The artist, too, at this time, when he appeared before a few or many of the ruling class to entertain them with fiddle, trumpet, voice, or piano, was roped off from the elect of the gods. It wasn't a tarry rope, or a rough hempen one; no, it was a gorgeous crimson-corded one, but it kept the untouchable at a safe distance from Society's golden lads and lasses.) Then, the ruling class had neither a broad nor a narrow view of things in the quietude of Art and no experience within the rush of life. The paltry bits of Greek or Latin picked up at Harrow or Eton didn't give the youngsters of the rul- ing class even an idea of culture. The one common thing they shared with life, even with the outcasts crouched on the benches of the Thames Embankment, was the call of the body: they had to eat, drink, sleep, and cast out through the vent the waste rejected by the chemistry in the laboratory of the body.

It's comic to read of the toppers of the West speaking so pathetically about the 'Charter of Human Rights', declarations as authentic of truth as the pec- toral cross on a bishop's breast is of his unquestionable devotion to the teaching of Jesus. Here in England alone, with millions looking for a home; millions more living in dens, and glad of the shelter, thousands of young people afraid to marry, knowing that they have no hope of a home for many years to come; with over ten thousand families in London alone without a home, without even a den to go to, nothing in front of them but a wasteland of lofty office buildings already there or going up in style. Foxes have holes and the birds of the air have nests, but these have nowhere to lay their heads; over-crowded schools, over-crowded hospitals; sixty millions spent on Blue Steel and swarms of well-dressed beggars beseeching pennies to carry on research work — and we blather about the Charter of Human Rights!

Let us say we are personally honest and kind (as, by and large, we really are), webbed within a net of world dishonesty, fear, and ignorance; and sing dumb for the present about human rights; nor boast about our civilisation which doesn't exist; and our culture which is a ragbag of bits and pieces. Fact is, we shall not be truly civilised for many years to come; so for the sake of Human Rights, let's start again on the road to Samarkand.

How? Where to begin? Where d'ye think? Begin where life begins; when the babe taken from the womb should enter a clean and tidy home; not only tidy and clean, but airy and colorful; when its eyes have fashioned out to see things and to notice them, it should see a tree from a window, or, failing that, when blossom time is present, a bright flowering plant on table or window-sill — the civilisation and culture of its first environment. When the child has learned to read a bit by child-book or comic, it should be given a room of her (or his) own, one wall, as high as the young hand can reach, arranged so that the young hand can sketch there what it will; with its own table, and chair, a set of drawers wherein to keep colored pencils, crayons, and paper on which to draw the more precious pictures, and the treasures a child gathers from time to time — shells, colored stones, pine cones; things grown-ups regard as rubbish (the child should never know this), but which the child regards as the first great gifts the world has given her. Failing the room, the child should have a special corner of the biggest room, with table, chair, and all the other needful things. In this way, the child learns that she has her rights, her personal possessions, respected by the grown-ups around her; she learns too that others have rights too, and grows up to respect them, which is a firm and fine step in the development of civilisation within her nature; the colored pencils and even the crude colors of the comics adding a tincture of culture to the sense of a civil community. These developments can be added to delightfully by the programmes for the young over the radio during Children's Hour, and through the programme for schools, where are seeds that should spring up into a love for music in every form of rhythm and timing. When the new life leaves home for school, he or she should come into an intensified edition of the home in the way of reading, coloring, community play and work; the building itself being a bigger and more colorful place than home; and meet a modified edition of the cosiness, affection, and tolerance of his or her very own people. These are the vital activities where the good soil is, where home and school sow fertile, colorful seeds that will grow and bring forth fruit towards civilisation and culture, tenfold, fiftyfold, a hundredfold in days to come.

More and more houses; houses houses houses to be made into homes, homes; first, each home a fit world for the new-born infant; a stimulating and restful beginning for infant senses, giving the mysterious receptiveness of the developing mind its first and vital sensory and sensuous experience in the ways and manner of civilisation and of culture.

More and more schools, hundreds and hundreds
of them, now and quickly! Schools to carry on and
add to the perceptions formed within the home; buildings bright and airy, full of color, fair furnishing, with
spacious windows so that the air and sun can flow
through the rooms, and not have to force or push a
way through stony crannies; schools flush with teachers
so that they can form a friendly community with their
pupils, known to the youngsters as a friendly brother
is known, neither Sirs nor Madams, but Bill or Sally.
A building that has leaves of grass around it, with
flower-beds too, with trees in front, rear, or to the
sides, where the birds can come and go, sure of a safe
shelter, where they can sing the morning up and sing
the evening into the sleep of night. Mossy-minded
schoolmasters who send boys home because they wear
jeans and jerseys should be given a passport to retire-
ment, and they and all the Whack-O's should be
pickled, men and women, to be planted into a comic
museum as relics of a past scholastic barbarity. Harrow
and Eton should debag themselves of their fantastic
garments for the sensible and present-day jersey and
jeans and duffle-coat, to link up with the present and
popular wear of the life outside their hothouse walls.
Half of the pupils in these and in all other schools
should be girls, to learn with the boys, eat with them,
argue with them, do everything with them except
sleep together; and even if this should happen on
occasions, the world won't end. Much, much better
and highly natural to see boy and girl in bed together
than two boys there, or in other ways trying to satisfy
a sex urge among themselves. The skips from the
public schools and colleges should go, too, and middle-
aged women and young girls should take their places,

giving a whiff of civilisation and tidy grace, at least, to a dogged and dusty herd of boys and men. The educational authorities seem to regard women as a different race. They aren't, but the two, men and women, are complementary, the one to the other, and nature has shown it to be so. The segregation of girl from boy is as unnatural, as barbarous, and as ghastly, as that of white from black; and the sooner we abandon it the healthier we shall become, and show, in one way at least, that we are civilised.

None of these changes can come to us by any example from Buckingham Palace, the White House, or the Kremlin: they must come from a more animated outlook on life by the women themselves who have been too long satisfied with the kitchen and the corner. It is the women who have the spending of the incomes of these nations, but in England and the United States no one seems to think them fit to be bank managers; nor do women sit on the industrial boards; nor does any woman sit as judge in high court or low one;[1] nor, it seems, can they find even standing room where any Cabinet meets; though they are let risk their lives in the WAACS, the WRENS, during wartime; and, as doctor and nurse, take their lives in their hands in time of plague or pestilence; better by far than men as nurses, equal in skill and courage as surgeon and doctor, as has been proved in the Soviet Union, where all nurses are women and more than half of the doctors are women. Has there ever been a woman on the Board of the Royal Academy? Among the Commissioners of Inland Revenue? Is there e'er a woman Tax Inspector knocking about anywhere? So far there

[1] Correct when written. One has just been appointed a county court judge, thank God!

isn't a single woman to be on the New Economic Council in course of creation by the present British Government to keep the home fires burning, and the great film output, here and in the United States, still keeps on weaving the idea into viewers' minds that a woman's body is the one thing worth considering about her. D'ye call this colossal boycott and the picture-degradation civilisation? D'ye call it culture? D'ye think your parliaments, your bits and pieces in your galleries, an odd medieval cathedral here and there, powerful enough to make the balance fall your way?

There is, of course, the housewife to think of (many of them graduates fresh from college), who, when she finds herself with a baby in a town flat or a mortgaged house, within what is really a commodious cage, far away from the excitement of secondary school or college community life, however much of a mother she may be, however brave, feels lonely; and as the months pass she grows tired. From Botticelli to Picasso, Madonna and child look lovely, and lovely they are; but the background of the beauty lies in never-ending vigilance, hard going, and a good deal of drudgery, though thanks to Science, housework has been made much easier, and has lost most of its fright. The young mother soon finds out that her work-day is far longer than an eight-hour one, and, in time of illness, the night runs concurrent with the day. As well, a great deal of talent has to lie dormant, and so is lost to the general mind-and-hand build-up of the nation's productivity. Few of these young couples can afford a 'mother's help', and even an occasional baby-sitter is too costly. So in a State sensibly civilised, ways must be found to give the mother a fair do in rest and relaxation; a time when she can get away from all

housework and the care of children; there is hardly
anything more wearing and worrying than the care of
children during their gradual development towards an
independent life (as anyone can tell who has had a
hand in it, as I have had over many years). So civilisation should see, must see, that this great crowd of
young women, talented or just intelligent, get their
fair share of special holiday and general relaxation; as
well as more than a chance to use their talents for the
good of all. As for Culture, there is none; or rather,
nationally, the culture, even at its best, is but a bum
one. On the B.B.C. radio it is enshrined within the
Third Programme, and is often weird and absurd even
there, where a devoted few gather to hear the music
of Webern, while millions are content to rock 'n' roll
about in joy within the thunder-claps of 'Friday Night
is Music Night' on the Light Programme! To me the
most important programme is that of the Children's
Hour by which the very young are brought into close
touch with drama, music, and literature through the
story; and into touch with history too, while the
programme of 'For Schools' gives their first insight
into the strange forms and sound of other languages.
It is these youngsters, passing through good homes,
sensible and colorful schools, democratic universities,
who may grow into a generation which will remove
the awe from Webern and give grace and sweet
noises to the music of Friday Night's Music. So
thinking of what is recited over the radio and shown
on television today, there's hardly a reason for
the presentation of any lover's crown of myrtle
or any hero's crown of bays, for one thing after
another but adds ashes to ashes and dust to dust.
So many critics have said with different words, and

statements by powerful theatre people seem to confirm the requiem. One prominent figuro who is the owner of more than one playhouse is reported as giving this chance to hope; some laddo called Binkie Beaumont (relation of Fletcher's Beaumont?), 'he is faithful to audiences who want a well-made play with a star-studded cast. Money is no problem, and in London we have the best actors in the world. It's plays we want, good solid plays.' Pity he hasn't a Muldoon the Solid Man to write the solid plays for him. Another important thing, with all due respect to Binkie, money is the problem, for no West End manager would think twice about tossing a play, however good it might be, into oblivion if it didn't make a profit for him, were it even a play in the apostolic succession extending from Aeschylus to Eugene O'Neill, a much older apostolic succession — as Shaw has told us — than any Church known to men of yesterday and today. Another important figure in the theatre, Mr. Oscar Lewenstein, is reported to have said, 'Really there's no difference between backing plays and making sausages. Sometimes you hit on a recipe for making a good sausage. Unfortunately, today good plays seem rarer than good sausages. You see, it's an absurdly chancy business, although by normal standards the profits on a good commercial success are remarkable.' See? the money is no problem! The money doesn't matter. And these figuros of the theatre would try to convince us that they love the theatre. They may, just as the money-changers honored the Temple and all it stood for. Only today, 18th February 1962, Kenneth Tynan, writing about the theatre, mentioned some satire or other, built on the Ring Lardner style, but in England 'coarsened for public consumption'. Coarsened for public consumption! Where is our civilisation, where is our culture? There is a bit down in Stratford-on-Avon (I understand the Americans paid for this theatre), but all that appears there is not for public consumption; it is all for the few; none of it for the rough-and-ready boys. A sanctuary, a sanctuary! Keep the pagans out! Our own brilliant gesture (made seven or eight years ago) through the voices of Parliament, was a gift of a million pounds to build a National Theatre on the south bank of the Thames; an IOU not yet honored, its value fading in the tightened bowels of the Bank of England: the site is empty, the glamor gone; and police officers Skybolt and Blue Steel prevent all from trespassing.

How sad our Culture becomes when we gaze on a painting by Van Gogh or one by Gauguin, or some other artist, who in the days of their creative work hungered, getting little or nothing for their paintings, even failing acceptance when they tried to give any away, forcing the artists to leave many of the pictures lying desolate where they happened to be; but how our culture ran into rapture when, yesterday or today, these same paintings, in the market-place, fetched sums of money ranging from eighty thousand pounds to hundreds of thousands, and the rich and happy thieves in the Temple hurried off with their loot! Then the light that lighteth every man coming into the world dimmed down to that of the glow-worm's ineffectual fire when the matin showed herself to be near.

Sport, too, which, like science, literature, art, and music, is part of national culture, is ignored, except by a paying public and the Press tickling up the emotions of the people in extravagant ways for or against this team or that player; but as a national expression of culture, sport is neglected or completely ignored. As a nation, we do not even give our children places to play in, leaving it to the generosity of private persons to provide them; though government and nation rejoice when their athletes bring back gold, silver, and even bronze medals from the Olympic Games to be pinned on their banners of red, white, and blue. So it all comes down to the Home, down to the School. If the little ones have a colorful and affectionate home, a colorful and civilised school, by and large, when that generation grows up, we are bound to have a colorful and civilised people. But all impositions, all punishments must vanish from both home and school. For a start, all impositions, all punishments, should be banished from Christian schools as they are from the 'Atheist' schools of the Soviet Union. Recently (these comments are from the *Irish Times*, 20th February 1962) a number of eminent English educationalists visited the U.S.S.R.; they were Miss Reader Harris, Headmistress of Sherborne School for Girls, Dorset; Dr. Walter Hamilton, Headmaster of Rugby School; Mr. Arthur Foot, Headmaster of Ottershaw School, Surrey; and Miss Helen Roxburgh, Headmistress of the County High School for Girls, Winchester; with Mr. Mervyn Pritchard, Staff Inspector of Schools. Miss Harris said, 'We found the children were not regimented or repressed at all. The result was surprising; they were as good as gold.' The children were responsible for all the work in the school. The only place they did not clean was the kitchen. Therefore it was in their interest not to drop such things as paper as they would have to pick it up. 'Everywhere was very clean.' I wonder what Soviet

Union teachers would think of a Christian Catholic teacher who took a child of seven by the ear to wring it, and did it so skilfully that he wrenched half of the ear off; or of another Catholic teacher who attended to a boy of the same age having an epileptic brainstorm by knocking him unconscious by a lusty fist-blow straight from the shoulder — a fine fair knock-out! What would a Soviet teacher think of an English headmaster who used a cricket bat instead of a cane to punish his young pupils or of the 'chopping block' of England's precious college of Eton, at which the boys are birched, or of the stick said to be used at Dartmouth Naval College, England, to keep the younger cadets in order, a doctor standing by to see that the beating doesn't go further than the number of strokes given in the sentence, or to stop the beating if the boy shows signs of weakening under it. (Of course, the great body of teachers, men and women, aren't vicious indicates of humanity. By and large, they are an intelligent body of people, as kindly and as understanding as they can be under the outworn system they work in.)

In his play, *The Shewing-Up of Blanco Posnet*, Bernard Shaw makes his chief character, Blanco, say to the hypocritical gospel-spouting Elder Daniels, 'You can't cod God'. Our elderly Daniels can't cod God either with their outcries, shrill or mumbling, of 'Communism is anti-Christ, Communism comes from hell!' Make no mistake; none of you Christians is going to fly up to heaven, like Gerontius, on that clicheyed bawl, for its implication is just envious, savage nonsense. A police state for our children must be banished from home and from school.

Finally, let us look at the thing which threatens

ruin to the bit of civilisation we have; the thing which has no Christian mind, heart, or bowels; that makes our culture a pin-up show of paper chains and neon lights; an ugly thing, bearing a menacing grace — the damnable, death-bloated thermo-nuclear bomb! The Christians of the West tell us that its possession is the one thing that keeps the peace, but no one yet has seen upon it the imprint of the Prince of Peace. Of the three Western huggers of this terrible weapon, two are devout Roman Catholics, and one is an Anglican. We must assume that all three are partakers of Holy Communion, thereby partaking of the Nature of Christ, thereby coming close to him whom they call the Father of all living, since Jesus, as touching His Godhead, is one with His Father Almighty. Since Jesus, as touching His Manhood, is one with humanity, then if they rend humanity with the explosive power of this infernal bomb, they rend the peerless body of Jesus too. We rend humanity to blasted pieces before His eyes; before the eyes of Him who once said, 'Oh, Jerusalem, Jerusalem, how often would I have gathered thee to me as a hen gathereth her chickens under her wing, but ye would not!' Now we stand ready to destroy, not only Jerusalem, but a whole beautiful world of living peoples.

OUT, DAMNED SPOT

OPINIONS in plays are damned spots — so say the proud and the haughty. At any play venturing to give an opinion about certain aspects of social life, if this opinion has a jewel of rebuke for one thing, a jewel of praise for another, they hang their heads with shame, or point fingers of scorn at the playwright. They squirm in their seats and in their walk all the way home should they get a hint of a 'message' in a play, which is an opinion that unhappily cuts through an opinion of their own about what is art, what is literature. Opinions have nothing to do with either, only with life. One is with the kingdom of the stars, the other with the world of goosey-gander. Fair enough, for by and large life is made up of opinions; of gold, brass, lead, and dull cold clay. Each of us has within our bodies as many opinions as there are cells — opinions of friends, enemies, politics, religions, food, dress, morals, or the latest rise or fall of Charlie Chaplin. 'A playwright has nothing to do with opinions', said W. B. Yeats vehemently in my bothered ear once, failing to realise himself that this very declaration was one of the oddest opinions among the multitude showered down on the world of man. Every play, published or performed, is the expression of an opinion about something or other, things pleasant or unpleasant, things felt or seen, things foreshown; about the sun, moon, and stars; death, judgement, hell, and heaven. Opinions have made the world we know, in which we live, and have our being; yet elect and haughty ones say opinions have no place in a play. Didja ever hear the like!

The other day while the sun was shining in the heavens for all to see, a drama eclectrician uttered opinions enshrining a wish for an ideal theatre free from the necessity of attracting an audience where delicate cadences of creation wouldn't be soiled by passing through the stiff, questioning breath of a crowd. Apparently, then, the playwright is to keep his play unspotted from the world. The flowers of his thought are not for the crowd to pick. Is the word of a playwright fit only for the ears of the angels? The crowd may listen, but will not be allowed to hear. 'A play', he goes on, 'has nothing to do with an audience.' Here, we have an opinion from one who doesn't want them; a didactic remark: he is trying to teach us, or say, that an audience doesn't, or shouldn't, exist. But everyone outside of himself is an audience, and when he reads a play he's written, he plays audience to his own work in his own way. An audience, big or small, one must have for picture, poem, or play. Even God demands an audience of the nine Orders of heaven above, with an audience of man below — or so it is declared to be — then why should not a poor playwright have an audience for his play? Exile an audience out into the cold, and a playwright exiles himself out into the cold too.

And why? It would seem to me that this cry for isolation is born out of conceit for oneself, or out of what may be said of what we ourselves say in statue, picture, poem, or play. To me, the fear of what others may say brings an end to the artist. His own hand puts the cap of death on his own head. An artist who scorns opinions (he may well scorn many) by being afraid to face them, refuses to hear, is demanding in a curious way that all opinions should agree with his own; and, since that isn't possible, he is demanding the relief of basking in the uniformity of his own mind. Like it or not, we are plunged from birth into a wide tidal sweep of opinions, swimming with, or swimming against, currents flowing hither, swither, and thither, according to time, place, and circumstance.

In the haughty and proud and scornful rejection of opinions in a play, the hatred is invariably provoked only by an expression of belief in the inborn goodness of humanity and of any hope in its future; never against an impression or expression of despair in humanity's outcome. Orwell's *1984* invokes a *Te deum*, while a story showing off characters like the Cheeryble Brothers or Newman Noggs provokes a dismal *De profundis*. Some little time ago, the American drama critic, Richard Watts, Jun., wrote this down: 'There is a lot of nonsense written about plays with a social message. The theory seems to be that there is something a little dubious about them. Shaw is conclusive proof of how absurd such an idea is. He was the master of the so-called "propaganda" drama, and he was so triumphant a fighter that his radicalism of yesterday has become the accepted opinions of today; but though the "message" of most of his comedies is no longer timely, the plays based upon them are still far fresher than most contemporary "non-message" plays'. A damn sight fresher, if one asks anyone but the haughty and the proud.

Ay, and Shakespeare, too; although not deliberately 'propagandist', for that time had not yet come, except in a sectarian sense of the old Roman Catholic against the new Protestant mind, his plays twinkle

with messages, opinions, and even prejudices; even
the sonnets are decorated with opinions as merrily as
a Christmas tree. Lear is happy with opinions, and
Falstaff, too: Honor pricks me on. How if honor
pricks me off? Argument between one opinion and
another. *Troilus and Cressida* teems with opinions, and
a few messages hum away in it, too. Hadn't the bold
Prospero a fine time of it trying to teach everyone —
even Caliban? And Wolsey — 'When I am forgotten,
and lie in dull cold marble, say I taught thee.' Teaching! This bouncer, Shakespeare, even tried to make
England look at her history in his way. How are we
to think of La Pucelle? Inspired by God or by the
Devil? Which? A which, a which! The chat between an English king and a couple of his common
soldiers in the silence of the night. His testimony
against civil war in 'Enter a father who has killed his
son; enter a son that has killed his father'. But the
lads and lasses from Largymore say that Shakespeare
never was a teacher, never sent a message to a pal.
His queens, kings, princes, nobles, soldiers, peasants,
workers, clerics, and whores, babble opinions out of
them like a bubbling brook.

There are other great artists in the field too, writers
and artists of all lands. They not only speak opinions,
but they spout them. Russia has the sturdy, tenacious
Tolstoy, the laughing Gogol, the lanky lovable Gorki,
the singing Pushkin, the delicate, murmuring Chekhov,
the turbulent and must musical Mayakovsky; all in-
flamed to grasp this sorry scheme of things entire,
and mould it nearer to their hearts' desire. In America,
busy, bustling America, there were others, giants in their
own day, and giants in ours, too: Lincoln, statesman
and garlanded talker; Emerson turning his armchair

into a throne of thought and winding the world into a web of beautiful prose; Thoreau who could see God's face shining from a duckpond, a face of peace, or a face agitated within the whirl of a millrace; Whitman lounging around Parthenon or Acropolis, spitting out a scornful Bah! getting swiftly back to Manhattan, the new American Democracy, and the brotherhood of man (with W. B. Yeats one of the first to cry bravo!); Herman Melville who made a spiritual wonder of a whale, making the animal speak to all English-speaking people from the deeps of the ocean; and another great writer well known to Straker, Tanner's chaffeur, who said: 'The author who puts himself at the mercy of the public is obliged, instead of plotting it to his own taste, to shuffle about impossible situations, to snicker instead of to laugh, and to take his models from outside society, for fear of making a thousand enemies, not one of whom he dreamed existed when he was writing his sorry play.'

Opinions and messages flit about from every literary quarter; the dialectic of the right of king against the noble flooding the Chronicle Plays of Shakespeare; the dialectic of noble against noble, of merchant against both noble and king, leading to punctured hearts and slit throats in civil wars; dialectic of monarchy against republicanism as in the American Revolution, pale-faced Shakespeare chronicling the former standing aside lamenting the innocent and indifferent dead, showing us the soldier-proletariat, Williams, musingly murmuring, 'I am afeard there are few die well who die in battle': Shakespeare musing sadly over the savage and shabby futility of war. Shakespeare comic or serious, gentle or bitter, is often trying to send a message in the human heart. Others too: Keats in

thirteen lines (ominous number) of poetry, gives in
essence all that was given out later by Marx and Lenin;
Claudel, humorless, mass-wordy, bellows out propaganda for the Catholic Faith, and tries to bludgeon
Catholicism into every head he meets with a holy
satin slipper — if you can't butter it, batter it in;
Byron sent his comments out in poems to the world
at little and at large; Schiller vented many opinions
in his works. In a letter from Claus Helmut Drese,
dealing with the inauguration of the National Theatre,
Mannheim (bombed to pieces in the last war), he said,
'The Theatre's name is joined with that of Schiller's
genius whose revolutionary play, *Die Räuber*, was performed here in 1872 for the first time. Schiller was
nominated Honorary Citizen of the French Revolution, worked in Mannheim as a dramatic author and
drew up the famous programme which defines the
Theatre as "a moral institution" [Saints above, what
was the man thinking about!]. There exists, also, a
narrow contact between Wolfgang Amadeus Mozart
and the Mannheim Theatre.' Mozart, too! Mozart
the Freemason, not like the tiddley-wink ones here and
in Ireland, but live wires, powerful, too, spreading
radicalism and free-thought to a listening Europe; a
Magic Flute playing on the minds of people to wake
up and think and sing. Oh, Queen of Night!

But listen to this, listen to what a great poet once
said of the Nobility, possibly when he was in a testy
humor: 'You say a horse is noble because it is good
in itself, and the same you say of a falcon or a pearl;
But a man shall be called noble because his ancestors
were so. Not with words but with knives must we
answer such a beastly notion.' Well, well! Stout stuff!
and from a great poet; from the horse's mouth, Dante.

Dante andante no longer. There is no mind living that doesn't comment in one way or another on things around, especially in painting, in stone, in play and poem, in book, in speech; and all hearts unfold messages for others as they take messages in from all the social strivings and all the arts of life.

It is odd, and comic to me, that most, or a good many, present-day plays flood out messages of misery, of hopelessness, of the futility of life, and these sombre messages are hailed as profound meditations, incontrovertible, showing life buttoned up into everlasting woe. Critic and reviewer often bathe their poor parched souls in their puking revelations as Brutus and the conspirators bathed their hands in the blood of Caesar. Of course, we can no more reject sorrow and woe from life than we can reject the gay christening or the gayer wedding, the laugh and the song, and sorrow may itself have its own darkling beauty. Strindberg was often a sad dramatist, but his saddest play of all ends with the bursting forth of a lovely and gigantic chrysanthemum from the top of a dung-hill; and Socrates drinking his cup of hemlock still remains a brave and noble picture in the life of man.

So opinions and messages whirl about in every form of science, literature, and art; whirl about and collide, and new energy of thought and imagination is created, and Life gets a new message. Indeed, Life herself is continually sending new thoughts into the world to take the place of older ones. Every time a new intelligent infant is born, a new message is given to the world, else malice would be in the happy and brave declaration that 'Unto us a child is born'.

PURPLE DUST IN THEIR EYES

An eminent London drama critic, reviewing the play *Purple Dust* in the *Sunday Times* of 19th August 1962, says 'Sean O'Casey likes men and women. It is an uncomfortable combination for a dramatist who believes in revolution. How can one condemn to destruction, ruin, and spoliation, people in whom eccentricities are delightful?'

I don't feel in the least uncomfortable within the combination of revolutionist and a drama-maker. A dramatist is one thing, a revolutionist is quite another; one looking at life in the form of individuals, the other is part of the collective urge and forward thrust of man. In my mind I think, not of the revolution born in cannonpeal and riflefire, such as that which swept away colonialism in the United States, the one that swept away feudalism in France, or the last mighty revolutionary throe giving power to the Russian People to take over and control the wealth their labor produced, and use it for the general good of all. No: what is in my mind is the revolution brought about by Time and the slow-moving or swift-moving winds of change. The play, written in 1937–38, saw the disappearance of what was called the Empire, and so it happened, and with its departure from India, what was for long but a breeze became a fierce and destructive wind blowing over Asia, from Cochin China to the great expanse of land and people ruled over by the then invincible Chiang Kai-Shek, who failed to see or feel the tremendous changes the winds of thought

261

were bringing. The winds of change come, and no one feels them till they become strong enough to sweep things away, carrying men and women (however comic and enjoyable), bearing off their old customs, manners, and morals with them. So in the decline and fall of the British Empire (she seems to be in danger now of losing her Commonwealth) many picturesque things, some even lovely, fell with it, and are now but a little heap of purple dust. A few album mementoes survive, such as the Yeomen of the Guard and the cuirassed horseman standing under the archway of the Horse Guards centre, and the bearskin of the Household Regiments; quaint things now, and but part of an open-air museum. There are those who clutch at things that are departing, and try to hold them back. So do Stoke and Poges, digging up old bones, and trying to glue them together again.

They try to shelter from the winds of change but Time wears away the roof, and Time's river eventually sweeps the purple dust away. Fifty years ago one thought that Viceroys, Governors-General, with a host of lesser lights, would be always with us, but Time took them off while they yet lived; and even the mighty men of war, the generals, with the garden of colored ribbons on their chests, are passing into creeping, ghostly forms, for the true generals now are the scientists in the laboratory, or those standing by the launching pad. There were probably eccentrics among the generals, likeable, even lovable, characters among them, but revolutionary change didn't give a damn, but ruined, despoiled, and destroyed them. As a man the revolutionist playwright is much the same as the drama critic: he has to get better from an illness by sending for a doctor; his personal problems cannot be solved by a constant reading of the Communist Manifesto; so when he's writing a play, the dramatist is neither Tory nor Communist, but only a playwright, setting down his characters as he knew them, giving, if he can, an added depth, height, and lilt to the words he makes them speak.

Besides, these characters, these eccentrics, loved by the drama critic (loved by me, too, so long as I am independent of them, and amn't forced to live with them) are always a nuisance to those who live with them, at times a menace, despoiling and ruining the lives of others (as per Captain Boyle), hindering and thwarting sense and sensibility; so when Time and Change go too slow, life takes a hand herself, and shoves them out of her way.

The drama critic thinks that 'the prophecies of doom spring from an old national jealousy and dislike'. This is a mistake, I think, due to so many critics reading old hatreds and jealousies into every O'Casey remark, even into a farewell of 'so long', sensing every common saying with nonsense and deceit — the critic deceiving himself, then through his statements deceiving his readers. The critics now see a Freud in every bush and a Jung squatting on every doorstep. Better to leave subconscious as expression to those who have studied psychology and psychiatry most of their lives, and know something of what they write or talk about.

As for me, I abandoned the romantic cult of Nationalism sixty years ago, and saw the real Ireland when I read the cheap edition of Shaw's *John Bull's Other Island*; hating only poverty, hunger, and disease. For nowadays Jung and Freud seem to peer over every playwright, and appear as actors, as designer, director, even as stage manager, in many ways, almost all of them in fact. It looks as if this habit were becoming a fixation, not only within the nature of a playwright, but also within the nature of a critic too.

The critic says: 'At the end of the play, words scowl and mutter, and this would have been in order had not the playwright, in the course of the evening, so clearly fallen in love with the two characters to whose destruction they are addressed'. Quite so. The characters are foolish, inept, pompous; but they are comic, at times pathetic, and all through likeable, if not exactly lovable. But Time and Change do not care a damn for these lovable things, neither can the playwright care either. All that they are, and all they represent, must go; Time and Change will sweep them off, however hard they try to cling to the tinsel and brocade of a past life. A new age is not only knocking at the door, it has broken into the house, and taken it over. And in the course of the change, many a David will lose a Jonathan, many a Tennyson will lose a Hallam.

The other symbol in the play is of course the working class; they are realists, regarding the two gadabouts as fools, getting all they can out of them, before the two poor guys are borne off by the coming change of wind. All workers, including the Communists, give all the help they can to Nationalists in subject countries, though Communists look far ahead in thought and theory beyond all nationalist hopes; knowing that when national freedom is won, national unity tends to break up; new groups are formed, opinions differ, and the battle of the dialectics begins. Drama critics aren't interested in this kind of thought or action, indifferent, apparently, to the fact that these activities weave different strands of life round them-

selves, for better or for worse. Indeed, indifference
to most world affairs seems to afflict many of them
with blind eyes and deaf ears, inspired often by a
scornful shrug of the shoulders. They don't even turn
to glance at these faces peering in through the windows
of England, gawking at all that goes on inside, many
of them, indeed, within the English home taking a
part in trying to keep the house in order. I remember
once when James Agate was reviewing some Australian
play, he said among other things, that he didn't know
anything about Australia, and certainly didn't want to
know either; the remark striking me as an odd one
for a loyal Englishman to make about one of the more
important Members of the Commonwealth.

The eminent critic's review of *Purple Dust* was
bannered by the title of 'Doom without a Profit';
but there is no doom in a change except for those who
refuse, or who cannot accept, the change — those like
Stoke and Poges who tried to live in the past till the
present overthrew them. A change invariably brings
a profit, never a doom. The Irish peasants of the
play, less comic, less picturesque, less lovable maybe
(though I wouldn't agree to this), survive the winds
and the rising flood because they are more adaptable,
and so of the two contraries, the fitter to survive: life
— not O'Casey — chooses these and destroys the
others. It is true that while O'Killigain is a realist,
O'Dempsey is a romanticist, but as the play shows,
O'Killigain can understand, and further, the romanticism
of his friend, and O'Dempsey can understand, and aid,
the realism of O'Killigain. The change that came to
the farmer's field didn't bring doom to the farmer. I
can remember as a young man the handsome sight of
a team of horses pulling a plough, the ploughman

cheering on the animals while he drove a straight furrow from one end of a field to the other, the shrilling flock of birds boisterously picking up worm and grub from the tumbling rich soil on a hardy spring day; or, later, in the autumn, the sturdy row of mowers, advancing together, step by step, each in his own measured-out avenue, rhythmically swinging their scythes while the rich corn sank aside before them as they cut it down in a mass, beautiful movement of arm and instrument. Who sees that now? Millions of youngsters growing up today will never see a scythe in action, never hear the sharp, pleasant sound of hone-stone on a blade; never see the straining horses pull a plough, never see 'the ploughman homeward plod his weary way', for all have gone, and we have now the much more effective tractor and combine-harvester. The chimney-sweeper, mentioned by the drama critic in his review, is gone too; no more do we see the sooty-faced figure, black as a crow, a bundle of long, socketed rods on his shoulder, one of them topped by a circular brush, plodding a way through streets of city and town, crying out, shrill as a curlew, 'Swee . . . eep, swee . . . eep!' Electricity and gas have downed him, and he has been gathered to his fathers like the muffin man and the fish vendor, or the lavender lady crying her bunches of tiny mauve flowers that carried a melody of perfume into every home that bought one. No doom, but many profits came to the farmer when farming machinery invaded his fields; and no doom, but many profits came to the housewife when electricity and gas flowed into her home. I surmise that the drama critic takes these things for granted, for he probably never knew the spirit of evil irritation and dirt that lurked within the smoky kerosene lamp and the sputtery candle. Things outworn, drama critics and playwrights too, must, sooner or later, give ground to make way for the new, this being old in its time, must yield to the newer, and, again, the newer must shrink from the newest; and men or things that cannot pass from the old to the new, from the new to the newer, the newer to the newest, will be flung away, far away from the sight, mind, and sound of man. So Stoke and Poges, however comic and lovable, encumber the ground, and will inevitably be destroyed by those who are ready and eager to build better than the others knew. Often and often, we don't like this, but we've got to lump it.

Another eminent drama critic, Mr. Kenneth Tynan, in the *Observer* of 19th August 1962, dismisses the play, *Purple Dust*, as 'a tenuous [Why not thin?] one-joke jape'. This verdict, pronouncement, or dictum, is disappointing, for the labor used, the thought given, and the time spent in the creation of this 'one-joke jape' was far longer, deeper, and harder, than those energies in action would take Mr. Tynan to write a year's worth of his world drama reviews. However, time, labor, and thought do not prove the play to be more than what the critic thinks it to be; time alone can tell, so I record his decision in a more permanent form than that of a hurried and a brief-lived notice in a weekly newspaper. The critic makes some blimpish remarks: he says, 'What bores one about the English upper classes is not, as Mr. O'Casey insists, that they are ignorant of country life, but that they know it inside out and never stop talking about it'. O'Casey doesn't insist on any such thing: first, the Blimps aren't the 'upper classes', and if the critic thinks they are, he knows very little about them. Realistically, they

are of the many who do well in business or on the stock
market, and then come down to a country house
because they think it's the thing to do, and this is
made plain in the play. Mr. Tynan should know that
everyone who has a big title, who may fish, shoot, or
ride, isn't a member of the 'upper class', and never
can be one. He should know that aristocracy is a
closed shop; that no one is admitted without a genea-
logical passport; and that no member of this rigid
class would, for a moment, recognise himself in either
the comic frenzy of foolishness shown by Stoke on the
one hand, or by Poges on the other. I have never tried
to write about the 'upper classes', for I know too
little about them, but I do know something about
their apers. The upper classes were no fools, and in
spite of their gorgeous robes, their stars and garters,
their plumes and pennons, they were ruthless realists,
grabbing for themselves nine-tenths of the wealth the
workers produced, grabbing the best education the
times could give, denying any to the 'lower classes';
and so they developed a power within their families
that made them the governing class for many, many
centuries; but now things are altering, the working
class have whipped the pennons from them, have
seized part of the education, some of the wealth, so
that what was a power in the land is sinking down,
here and there, into little heaps of purple dust. (Tynan
puzzles me. In his review of *Red Roses*, he refers to
the character, Ayamonn Breydon, as an 'Orangeman',
though the play shows explicitly that, not only is he
no such thing, but is firmly against all their gaudy
bigotries. Yes. Tynan puzzles me.)

Mr. Tynan says that 'what bores us about the
English upper classes is not . . . that they are ignorant

of country life but that they know it inside out, and never stop talking about it.' Well, well! Though this is irrelevant, since I was not depicting the 'upper classes' in the figures of Stoke and Poges, the critic's remark tells us he knows as much about the country as he knows about the U. classes. It looks like he was thinking of those who gave a lot of time to fishing, hunting, and shooting, but these things don't make a country life, except an amusing or leisurely one for the few. Country life is a vastly bigger way of living than these three things, even were they carried on night, noon, and morning. The life of the country is the market town, the village, and the farm. Then there are the many things surrounding these — the roads, the birds and beasts, the bees and butterflies, the trees, the winds, the rain, snow, ice, and frost; parched lands and flooded lands; skies clear or cloudy; the landscape with its trees filigreed in a morning mist — as Corot so often saw them — and yet, and yet Mr. Tynan tells us with a yawn that talk of these things by 'the upper classes' bores him; 'bores us', he says, leaving us all to guess if he means all the others, or if he means only that this talk bores the critics. Artists and writers have revelled in all these things, but they bore Tynan. All of us at one time or another have talked about them; they are eternal matter, not only for talk, but for constant and anxious study, for they affect the life of every man, woman, and child, including — though he doesn't know it — the life of the critic himself. When things go contrary in the country, we all do badly; when things go smoothly there, we all do well. There are hundreds of scientists working in universities trying to solve the multitude of problems that outface the farmer in his never-ending work to produce the food of the nation; but Mr. Tynan says it is boring, and Mr. Tynan is an honorable man. I wonder why? Perhaps he knows the country only as a summer day's day-dream, unaware of the frosts of winter there, the fall-fall of life and leaf in the autumn, the sharpness in the hope of spring, and the push of all life among the kindly fruits of the earth when the sun is in his prime.

Frankly, from what the critic says about the 'upper classes' and the 'country', I'm afraid the critic doesn't quite know what he's talking about, though I'm sure he could tell a bee from a butterfly. But could he see the difference between an Aberdeen Angus, a Hereford, and a Devon Red? Does he really believe that the amusements of fishing, shooting, and hunting are the country? This is something like the belief of the many who see the country as a sea beach; that out of the cities all England is a wide and lengthy beach, a sight of warm sands and gentle wavelets, blue as the blue of a tourist poster. But there goes Mr. Tynan in swim-suit and sandals with stage hayseeds in his hair. Looks like he never peered over the gateway into Philip's farm, or even glanced at the brook bickering by to join the brimming river, itself on its way to join the sea. Some of the upper classes own large tracts of the country, and let out portions of it for others to till; but even so they do not deal directly with those who farm the land; they employ an agent, who deals with the tenant farmers, so that the agent knows more about the land, the country, than the upper-class landlord who owns it. I suggest to Mr. Tynan that he listens to *The Farmer*, broadcast every week by the B.B.C., and then during an idle hour or two of a winter's evening he should read Spenser's

The Shepheards Calendar, so that he might come to know a little more about the country before he mentions it in his critic's bulletin.

Then there is the airy dismissal of 'Ireland's past glories' as 'four-fifths incomprehensible'. Yet take one, 'The Sword of Light': there is the sword of the Lord and of Gideon; it was on the sword's hilt that the knights took their vows before they set sail to deliver the Holy Land from the infidel; there was Excalibur — this was the flash, I believe, that was worn on the jacket sleeve of those who were on General Eisenhower's staff during the last World War; and the Sword of the Spirit—enough to show the sword as a well-known symbol, but not, apparently, to Mr. Tynan. A number of the figures in the play are mentioned by Yeats in his poems, by Synge in his play about the Sons of Usna; by Lady Gregory in her *Gods and Fighting Men*, but maybe Mr. Tynan hasn't read any of these: he would know more if he had.

Why is it that this critic seems to dismiss a play that laughs and makes merry, or one that hangs out a banner on an outer wall? Is it that he sees nothing, regards nothing save what occurs on the farther side of the 'Straight-Edged Stage', the form of stage that he prefers to all others, according to his article. The round O could do a lot, but it couldn't put a world on the stage, and Shakespeare, as far as I know, never said it could; but though he didn't say the stage is all the world, he did say 'All the world's a stage'. A critic should know more about this world.

Mr. Tynan should occasionally squirm out of the round O, not only for his own advantage, but also for his own pleasure (as should other critics too), and saunter here or loaf there, in England and Ireland, giving a handshake over the Border to a Scot or two, not only when the sun shone, but also when the rain fell, the winds blew, and when frost lay thick upon valley, hill, and farm field; then he might know more about 'country life', finding out, as he would, that the farming population was a vast army, spending little or no time in shooting, fishing, or hunting. The land, the country, Mr. Tynan, employs three-quarters of a million persons, and of all these, though an odd farmer may join in an occasional hunt, the rest of them don't hunt, or shoot, or fish, preferring football any time to a rod and line. These, Mr. Tynan, are the 'country life' you obviously know nothing about; these are they who talk of country things, of everlasting things; talk that began when hunting, nomadic man halted to sow a first harvest and settle in one place; talk that goes on still, and will go on for ever; talk that bores no one, for it concerns the life, all life living in England, boring no one save only Mr. Kenneth Tynan.

Stoke and Poges were not pictured in the play as members of the 'upper classes', but as business men, or plutocrats who were aiming at being what they never could become; they were aping the 'upper classes', and Mr. Tynan should have known that the 'upper classes' never try to ape themselves, for they have been born into that condition of life, living it without needing to act what they naturally are. They might try to imitate the working class — 'pigging it', as one of them told me and he on his way for a holiday to one of the Hebridean Isles, but never so ridiculous as to aim at imitating themselves. Have you me, Mr. Tynan? As for 'the country', he will have to live longer, know more, before he can sit on a bank where the wild thyme grows, talking easily to Bill Brewer,

Jan Stewer, Peter Gurney, Peter Davy, Dan'l Whiddon,
'Arry Hawk, old uncle Tom Cobbley and all; or be
able honestly to whistle even a bar of *The Farmer's Boy*.

Is Sir Kenneth Tynan right about this play, *Purple
Dust*? Does he see clear, does he hear well, does he
understand it at all? It's not that he dislikes the play;
he simply despises it as 'a boring one-joke jape'. But
is he right? He thinks he is, so he lets out a piping
'Yes, Sean, Yes!' I call friendly drama knights to my
aid, who come cantering up, and let out a bellowing
cry of 'No, Ken, No!' I name them now: they are
Brooks Atkinson — for many years drama critic of
the *New York Times*; Richard Watts of the *New York
Evening Post*, backed by the shade of George Jean
Nathan of many a journal and magazine. All have
highly praised on papyrus and parchment the play
Tynan calls 'a boring one-joke jape'. Were all these
wrong and only Tynan right?

Just listen now, Mr. Tynan, to what comfortable
words George Jean Nathan hath said about this very
'one-joke jape'. Here we go: '*Purple Dust* is a
ringing moving melody, orchestrated with a resound-
ing slapstick'; recorded in the Random House edition
of *Five Great Irish Plays*. Another knightly defender
came trotting to my side only the other day; this
help came from John Gassner, Sterling Professor of
Dramatic Literature at Yale University, a writer of
many fine books about the drama of the western world.
In a letter to me from New York, dated 2nd September
1962, he writes about this very play, saying: 'I very
much hope that the Mermaid Theatre will do you
more justice with the remaining productions of the
O'Casey Festival. I was truly astonished that an
English cast should have spoken so poorly — so

indistinctly. Still, I found the play once more singularly funny [Does Tynan object to a play being funny?], tender, passionate, and poetic. It is no accident of the stage that the long poetic passages should have won spontaneous applause for the actor in the midst of slack acting that a tour in the provinces could have greatly improved.' Funny, tender, passionate, and poetic! J. C. Trewin, the Cornish drama critic, is of one mind with the four American critics. Each of these is as eminent a critic as Tynan; they have given a large share of their lives to the theatre; and each has a far longer experience of drama than has Kenneth Tynan; and they chorus 'Yes' when Tynan shouts 'No'. These have taken the ball from Tynan's toes, and left him kicking viciously at the air. It is natural, and I think fair, that I should gratefully accept the opinions of these five critics, and cast Tynan's into the waste-paper basket; but, instead, I have argued his opinions out, have tried to justify O'Casey's ways to the cause of drama, and, incidentally, have helped Kenneth Tynan to become immortal.

Of course it is quite possible that these five drama critics may be wrong, and Mr. Tynan be right; but since each of these five is as eminent a critic as he, and each has a longer and wider experience of the world's stage than he has so far; and since the playwright himself has a love for the drama equal at least to Tynan's, it seems to be very unlikely, and so a work of his deserves a kindlier regard than the insult of having this play dismissed as 'a one-joke jape'.

The London drama critics, with a few honourable exceptions (deviationists!), seem to have an edge on the Mermaid Theatre and on everything the theatre tries to do in the way of drama or play. When a new play is done there, they flock in and they pour out, the clumsy points in play or production burning the tips of their tongues, the good points in play and production hidden away in the darkest limbo of their minds.   The idea began in the persevering and buoyant mind of Bernard Miles, but it took a very, very long time to bring the idea to a practical pass; for he had to buy it brick by brick, plank by plank, and seat by seat before it stood where it stands now; and this great feat alone deserves, not a spiteful dislike of the great adventure, but praise and encouragement, for where there was no drama, there is drama now.

Of course, the productions at the Mermaid cannot be what they ought to be, for the theatre has a very lean purse.   The theatre at Stratford was already there for the gay producers, and few first-class actors would refuse the play there; the theatre has an artist snob value that excuses a reduced weekly wage.   The big commercial theatres can fling out ten-pound notes without blinking an eyelid; the one at Stratford and its subsidiary, the Aldwych, can dispense pound notes without heart-throbs; but the poor Mermaid has to count the pennies pulled out of a lean and hungry purse. Even the Royal Court Theatre does not seem to shiver when it hands out a pound note; but the Mermaid has always to be penny cautious.   Yet it has gone on now for three years and to my knowledge still flourishes, as results from my own plays show, facing out the almost unanimous objections of the London critics to the plays and the productions.

Mr. Tynan, dismissing the first play as 'a one-joke jape', the second one as sentimental nonsense, goes for the third play, *The Plough and the Stars*, because of its

275

long speeches. He quotes the late critic, James Agate, to prove his point, for this critic scorned speeches that were longer than a few lines, which for James Agate was a bellringer for Pinero whose plays are as dead now as the dodo; and Agate with his coadjutor critic, Archer, disliked the great Elizabethans (except Shakespeare whom they didn't dare despise). Probably Mr. Tynan shares Agate's dislike of these great dramatists, too, with their long speeches, and wouldn't say of one of them with Herrick,

> Candles I will give thee,
> And a new altar,
> And thy name, Saint Ben, shall be
> Writ in my psalter.

So Mr. Tynan's guesses are, at least, quite as good as Mr. Agate's. Tynan listens, but he doesn't seem to hear; he looks, but he doesn't seem to see; and the value of his review of *The Plough and the Stars* can be shown in his statement about the Easter Rising, when he says 'the brave were stupidly slaughtered while the cowards went out looting and came home gambling'. Now the looters gambled before they went looting, and to go looting was a brave thing to do, for the streets sang songs of menace from bullets flying about everywhere; and the play explicitly states and shows the courage of Bessie Burgess who risked her life for her neighbour, as did the bold Fluther, too; more, the sons, fathers, and husbands of thousands of these 'cowards', thousands of them, were fighting in Flanders, Mesopotamia, and on the death-swept Gallipoli peninsula. Mr. Tynan, too, should remember that the progenitors of these tenement people everywhere fought for, and created, the powerful Labour

Unions which made the Labour Movement possible, of which, I believe, Mr. Tynan is himself a member; and these great Unions still form the spearhead of Labour. I can tell him, too, that more civilians than combatants were killed and wounded in the general fighting of the famous week. Roses don't grow around tenement doors; pianos are rare in rooms; but brave people are there, and many have wider visions and more original chatter than others who come from dignified college or glossier high school.

THE END

PRINTED BY R. & R. CLARK, LTD., EDINBURGH